Lecture Notes in Computer Science

Edited by G. Goos and J. Hartmanis

Advisory Board: W. Brauer   D. Gries   J. St

A. Endres H. Weber (Eds.)

Software Development Environments and CASE Technology

European Symposium
Königswinter, June 17-19, 1991
Proceedings

Springer-Verlag

Berlin Heidelberg New York
London Paris Tokyo
Hong Kong Barcelona
Budapest

Series Editors

Gerhard Goos
GMD Forschungsstelle
Universität Karlsruhe
Vincenz-Priessnitz-Straße 1
W-7500 Karlsruhe, FRG

Juris Hartmanis
Department of Computer Science
Cornell University
Upson Hall
Ithaca, NY 14853, USA

Volume Editors

Albert Endres
IBM Laboratories
Schönaicher Str. 220, W-7030 Böblingen, FRG

Herbert Weber
Universität Dortmund, Fachbereich Informatik
Postfach 50 05 00, W-4600 Dortmund, FRG

CR Subject Classification (1991): D.2

ISBN 3-540-54194-2 Springer-Verlag Berlin Heidelberg New York
ISBN 0-387-54194-2 Springer-Verlag New York Berlin Heidelberg

© Springer-Verlag Berlin Heidelberg 1991
Printed in Germany

Printing and binding: Druckhaus Beltz, Hemsbach/Bergstr.
2145/3140-543210 - Printed on acid-free paper

Preface

The term *Software Development Environment* has been introduced in the 1980's to designate integrated sets of tools, techniques and processes that assist in the systematic development of software products. Software development environments are intended to support all phases of the software development cycle, namely requirements definition, design, implementation, test, and maintenance. Many environments provide explicit support for the different roles in a project, such as development, management and quality assurance.

While tools that support the implementation and test phases have quite a long tradition, powerful tools that also support the requirements definition and the design process have appeared only recently. Since these tools allow the employment of well-known software engineering methods, the term *Computer Aided Software Engineering* (CASE) has been coined. CASE tools typically make use of graphic manipulation facilities and rely on some form of development database to exchange various types of design objects between tools.

Facilitated by the availability of powerful workstations, implementations of these technologies are now within reach of every software developer. Their proper use and thoughtful introduction can take an organization a significant step forward towards higher development productivity and improved product quality. Inspite of this, we still observe a rather slow acceptance of these concepts in the industrial practice. This seems to be caused by a number of reasons:

- Many of the tools currently offered in the market place serve as stand-alone tools only and do not allow a true integration into development environments, nor do they support large team efforts.

- Sometimes, potential users of software engineering methods and software development environments are expecting a kind of magic or instantaneous solution to all their problems, the famous "silver bullet" (as Fred Brooks called it), and do not plan for the adjustment of available concepts to their environment.

- Other users fail because they underestimate the prerequisites on their part and the cost incurred for deploying software engineering methods and software development environments throughout their organization.

For this symposium a special attempt was made to bring together application development managers and top specialists involved in the selection and introduction of software development tools with leading developers of such tools and well-known authorities from the research community. The proceedings therefore contain first-hand information on practical experiences and requirements, development directions and strategies, and key research issues and results. All speakers were invited based on recommendations of an international programme committee. Although we seem to have achieved an almost balanced situation as far as the number of papers in each category is concerned, we did not expect to reach uniformity in comprehensiveness and style. If more time and more guidance were given to the authors, maybe more could have been done in this respect. But diversity exists, and cannot be ignored.

The symposium was organized by the special interest group (Fachgruppe) Software Engineering of the Gesellschaft für Informatik e.V.(GI), Bonn, the German informatics society, in cooperation with the Gesellschaft für Mathematik und Datenverarbeitung mbH (GMD), Birlinghoven, the leading German research institution in computer science, and the Steering Committee for the European Software Engineering Conferences (ESEC), a coordinating body sponsored by several European professional societies (such as AFCET, AICA, BCS, GI, ÖGI and SI) to foster joint activities in the field of software engineering.

We would like to acknowledge the help and advice of the members of the Organizing Committee and the cooperation and dedication of the authors and the other contributors and supporters. We hope that participants and readers will benefit from these efforts by putting them in a better position to make well-founded decisions in a critical area of today's information processing business.

Albert Endres, Symposium Chairman
Herbert Weber, Program Chairman

Contents

Development Directions and Strategies

Application Experience and Requirements

Research Issues and Results

Systems Engineering Environments of ATMOSPHERE

Henk Obbink

Philips Research Laboratories Eindhoven
P.O. Box 80.000
5600 JA Eindhoven
The Netherlands
(uucp:obbink@prl.philips.nl)
(fax:+31/-40-74-37-41)

1 Summary

The ATMOSPHERE project is partly funded by the Commission of the European Communities as an ESPRIT II Technology Integration Project (TIP). Its ambition is to make a major contribution to the progress of the state of the art of System Engineering in Europe. In order to do so, the project has adopted a very pragmatic approach which is reflected in the ATMOSPHERE acronym meaning: Advanced Tools and Methods for System Production in Heterogeneous, Extensible, Real Environments.

The Definition Phase of the ATMOSPHERE project was launched in February 1989. The studies carried out during this phase concluded that, rather than designing a general common Engineering System model, a few application domains should be selected and corresponding System Engineering environments supporting methods and tools appropriate to each domain should be constructed.

On the basis of these conclusions, a complete description of the project's technical work and organisation was produced and a four-year Development Phase was started in June 1990. The main partners in the Development Phase are BULL (F), CAP GEMINI INNOVATION (F), PHILIPS (NL), SFGL (F), SIEMENS (D), and SNI (ex NIXDORF) (D), with CAP GEMINI INNOVATION acting the Coordinating Partner.

The first part of the Development Phase effort (the so-called Toolset Phase), is about 250 person-years, is supported by 24 partners (main contractors, associate contractors and sub-contractors) in 10 European countries, including two EFTA countries.

The purpose of this paper is to give a general presentation of the ATMOSPHERE project. Section 2 defines the Mission and the Strategy of the project. In Section 3 the Technical Work breakdown is given. The concepts related to System Engineering and Integrated Environments are discussed in Section 4. Section 5 describes the work undertaken in ATMOSPHERE on Integration Technology. Environment Construction and Evaluation aspects for each of the five application-specific environments are presented in section 6. Section 7 is devoted to Technology Transfer and Standardisation issues. Finally, some concluding remarks are given in Section 8.

2 Mission and Strategy

As seen by the ATMOSPHERE partners, who include major IT supplying companies in Europe, the key issues affecting quality and productivity of software-intensive system development today and in the foreseeable future stem from problems such as increasingly complex systems, building blocks with incoherent life-styles (e.g. hardware and software), inaccurate requirements and design information, difficulty in managing changes, lack of integrated development tools, etc.

Symptoms of these problems are well known: Large backlogs of new developments, heavy maintenance, dissatisfied users, high costs.

ATMOSPHERE's mission is to contribute to the solution of these problems and thus to strengthen the position of European industry in the IT system development domain.

ATMOSPHERE's priority is therefore to lay the foundation for System Engineering through developing and experimenting with System Engineering Environments targetted for the development of Software-intensive IT Systems. To this end, ATMOSPHERE is to provide in the coming years:

- Knowledge and experience concerning general methodological aspects of the system engineering process.

- Advanced open toolsets, supporting state-of-practice and state-of-the-art life-cycle, management and quality assurance methods.

- System Engineering Environments, each adapted and targetted to a specific application domain and real users and each validating specific aspects of the above toolsets.

- Flexible Integration Technology, necessary to integrate the Toolsets into the Environments, which will be published for wider use.

- Transfer of technology to users of the constructed environments, mainly by carrying out industrial pilot applications.

- Tight feedback and feedforward between major players in this area (System Suppliers, Integration Technology Suppliers, Environment Suppliers and Tool Suppliers) to stimulate a fast advance and acceptance of the methods, toolsets and environments used.

3 Workbreakdown Structure and Coordination

3.1 Introduction

The definition phase of ATMOSPHERE produced a study of System Engineering taking the literature and the current state of practice within the members of the consortium into account.

A complementary study was carried out to define a rationale for the various methods and tools proposed for use within ATMOSPHERE their choice may be guided by specific requirements of the application domains, but is also influenced by usage, company policies and standardisation.

These studies give a sound basis for the construction of ATMOSPHERE system engineering environments supporting the methods appropriate for each application domain targetted.

In addition, the definition phase of ATMOSPHERE has concluded that there are, in principle and practice, two complementary approaches to environment integration.

3.2 Schedule

The development of ATMOSPHERE is organised in such a way that its starts from the current state of practice within the organisations of the partners for the automated support of the system engineering process in terms of system engineering tools and methods, as well as for integration approaches in order to progressively consolidate and standardise

- a common system engineering approach: process models and methods
- a set of complementary environment integration techniques.

The four-year development stage of the ATMOSPHERE project is divided into two phases of 24 months each:

- Toolset phase
- Environment phase

In these two phases two incremental versions of Application-domain-specific System Engineering Toolsets and Environments are planned to be constructed and validated by pilot applications.

In order to do so the project assigned itself very concrete goals of producing and validating application-domain-specific integrated system engineering environments, with two major milestones(M1 and M2), acting as synchronisation points within the ATMOSPHERE project:

- M1: INTRA process integration for Management Process support tools AND Lifecycle Process support tools AND Quality Process support tools achieved at (t0+18). Demonstration of achieved integration and consolidated results for V1 at (t0+24).
- M2: INTER process integration for Management Process support tools WITH lifecycle process support tools WITH Quality Assurance Process support tools (t0+42). Demonstration of achieved integration and consolidated results for V2 at (t0+48).

Where t0 is defined as June 1 1990.

The overall schedule for the ATMOSPHERE project is shown in Figure 1.

This paper describes the work planned for the first two years, upto milestone M1. The work described must, however, be interpreted in the four-year perspective. This means that on the one hand work on behalf of the second phase will take place during the first two years of the first phase and that on the other hand some of the integration efforts from the original second phase have to be brought forward to the first phase.

The first phase of two-year(Toolset-Phase) is again subdivided according to the schedule shown in Figure 2.

3.3 Work Package Structure

This section describes the work breakdown of the project and some of the underlying coordination mechanisms. The overall project structure is shown in Figure 3.

Four workpackages have been identified:

- **WP1** Management and Infrastructure
- **WP2** Environment Integration Technology

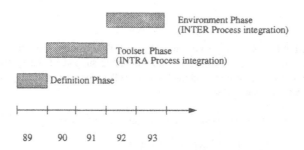

Figure 1: Schedule for ATMOSPHERE

- **WP3** Technology Transfer and Standardisation

- **WP4** Environment Construction Subprojects

Workpackages 1 to 3 will act as functional services in the project, taking responsibility for general/horizontal activities common to all the subprojects and guaranteeing the global coherency of the project.

Workpackage 2 in particular is the technical integration task force of the project. It aims to provide the technical basis on top of which integration will be performed. It will provide the subprojects carried out in Workpackage 4 with standard mechanisms, will promote the use of these mechanisms by the environment constructors and provide support when necessary, gather experience from the use of these mechanisms by the subprojects and provide feedback to them.

Workpackage 3 on Technology Transfer and Standardisation will ensure communication within the project, from the project to the outside world and from the outside world to the project. The second task of workpackage 3 is standardisation. In this mode it will work in relation with standardisation bodies, making the results of the project evolve from the explicit to the public and even standard status.

Workpackage 4 is organised as four subprojects. The four subprojects are complementary, as far as feasible, in their individual environment- and tool-integration approaches and respective application-domain orientation.

Within each of the subprojects of WP4, one or two application-domain-specific engineering environments will be constructed, (resulting in so-called **Constructed Environments**) validated and demonstrated by pilot applications. The environments to be used during the pilot applications are in general supersets of the constructed environments and are called **Pilot System Environments**. Emphasis is placed on environment construction and in-project technology transfer.

Each pilot system environment will provide a suitable coverage for the different activities of the life-cycle, management, and quality assurance processes for the application domain in question. Methods and toolsets will be integrated, re-engineered or developed as needs dictate so as to meet these requirements.

The experiences gained through the construction of the various environments will be fed back to Work-

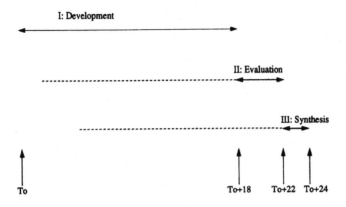

Figure 2: Master Schedule for ATMOSPHERE Toolset Phase

package 2 "Environment Integration Technology", which will allow the project to proceed towards a more standardised approach for the system engineering models, methods and integration techniques. This standardised approach will be introduced in turn in Workpackage 4 "Environment Construction Subprojects" and implemented in the different subprojects, so that the next versions (V2) of the environments as envisaged for the second phase could be based on more standardised models, methods and integration techniques.

Contacts with the external world and dissemination and standardisation of the experiences throughout ATMOSPHERE will realised through Workpackage 3 "Technology Transfer and Standardisation".

4 System Engineering Concepts and Environments

4.1 Introduction

In this section the main technical concepts of ATMOSPHERE are presented:

- System Engineering Models and Approach
- Method Integration and Process Modelling
- Toolset Integration
- Environment Integration

4.2 System Engineering Models and Approach

The development of large software-intensive information technology systems, as attempted more and more often, cannot be conducted via a simple "build and fix" approach. What is required is a determined

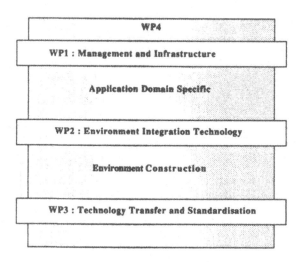

Figure 3: ATMOSPHERE Project Structure

and conscious use of a mature engineering discipline. Rather substantial progress, at least in theory if not in general practice, along these lines has been made in the engineering both of software and of VLSI systems. Management of the complexity of today's information technology systems increasingly demands a departure from traditionally compartmentalised engineering disciplines like software, VLSI, mechanical, etc. Rather, the implementation of a systems approach to engineering becomes an urgent necessity.

In order to arrive at a systematic treatment of System Engineering, it is mandatory to develop a model of System Engineering, which takes into account existing software, hardware, and system life-cycle models. The result is the ATMOSPHERE System Engineering Model ASEM (see Figure 4).

The ASEM is structured into the three main processes Life-Cycle, Quality and Management.

The use of the ASEM to perform System Engineering is elaborated as the System Engineering Approach. Besides explaining how to conduct the various processes of System Engineering, special consideration is given to development approaches that are particularly suited to the engineering of "quality products" (like incremental development and transformational development) and to development efforts that are essential to practical engineering (like maintenance, reverse engineering and reuse).

4.3   Method Integration and Process Modelling

The ATMOSPHERE notion of a method is based on the view that a method must at least include:

- a preferred notation;
- a defined number of steps to be carried out;
- some guidance in choosing and carrying out the steps.

Within System Engineering usage, there appear to be many mutually orthogonal dimensions of interpretation, including:

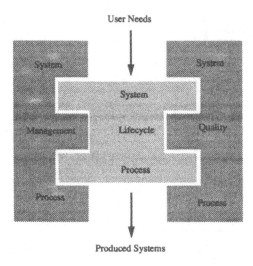

User Needs

Produced Systems

Figure 4: The ATMOSPHERE System Engineering Model

- the *granularity* of the method;

- its *linguistic content*;

- the *level of formality*;

- how prescriptive it is;

- whether it can be manipulated.

There were, however, a number of significant gaps identified in the integration of methods, which require work in the following areas:

- *INTRA-process integration:* The combination of methods, e.g., SDL and COLD, is felt to be of major relevance to industry.

- *INTER-process integration:* Configuration Management from the Management Process, and System Integration from the Life-Cycle Process may be based on a kind of Module Interconnection Language.

Work in the development phase of ATMOSPHERE will therefore concentrate on the issue of method-composition, both within a particular process and between processes.

ATMOSPHERE's work on process modelling is heavily routed in the experiences obtained in the Eureka EAST and ESF projects and concentrates on providing the necessary modelling and support facilities to enable the composition of methods.

4.4 Toolset Integration

Fully integrated systems environments for industrial use cannot be achieved in one big step. ATMO-SPHERE has therefore developed an incremental model for tool integration which is depicted below.

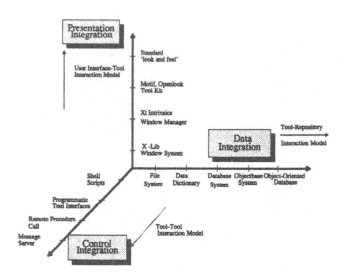

Figure 5: ATMOSPHERE Tool Integration Axes

This model clearly shows that in order to achieve integration for a particular set of Tools a number of smaller integration steps have to be taken along three more or less orthogonal axes. It only makes sense to make a step along one of the axes if the corresponding integration technology is available both in implemetation and specification.

The three axes are:

- Presentation Integration
- Control Integration
- Data Integration

Presentation integration is concerned with the appearance of the environment to the user: the major concern is with consistency between the representations used for output and the mechanisms used for input of similar concepts in different tools.

Control integration is concerned with smoothing the boundaries between the various tools that are used to support a process in terms of their invocation. This ranges from the ability to invoke tools through uniform mechanisms through to a level of control integration in which a tool may invoke or stimulate another tool to perform some process without it being apparent that more than one tool is invoked.

Data integration is concerned with minimising the effort required to enable data from one source to be used by all relevant consumers. The range here is from the knowledge that information of a particular type is available in a particular place through to a complete syntactic and semantic model of all data which is supported by the environment and used by all tools.

ATMOSPHERE Tool Model

The integration of the toolsets is done within an overall Environment Architecture and a standardised Tool Model shown in Figure 7 and Figure 6. These have been derived from the ECMA TC33 proposal and take international developments (e.g. CFI) into account. The ATMOSPHERE Tool Model requires explicitly identified Open Interfaces, to the data, control and presentation integration services (programmatic tool interfaces). These interfaces will have to be made public for tools to be integratable in other Environments.

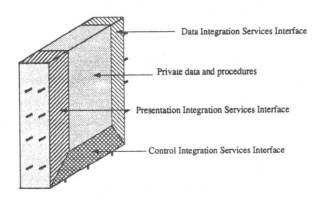

Figure 6: ATMOSPHERE Tool Model

4.5 Environments and Toolsets

Environments in ATMOSPHERE are considered to be composed out of sets of **Toolsets**. Toolsets in their turn are sets of **Tools**. The toolsets are hosted on an integration **Framework**. The definition phase work in the environment area concentrated on the framework driven approach.

As mentioned earlier in the development phase of the project, a number of environments will be built using not only a framework-driven approach, but also a toolset-driven approach.

Each toolset is actually a tool-sub-environment. They can be considered to be a domain within a complete environment. This view holds for both environment integration approaches. To achieve true integration of sub-environments it is required to develop a domain model or a conceptual schema for each of the integrated tool sub-environments.

Environment Architecture

During the definition phase, much effort was expended on the production of a reference model for system engineering environment frameworks. This addressed the conceptual and functional architecture of an environment.

ATMOSPHERE will continue the work of the definition phase, to enhance and consolidate the ATMO-SPHERE Environment Architecture Model (that has been derived from the ECMA TC33 proposal (see Figure 7) and takes international developments (e.g. CFI) into account) and provide environment constructors with an Environment Construction Guide, gathering the experience gained in the subprojects of WP4 and elsewhere. In addition, the model will then serve as a standard reference for the discussion

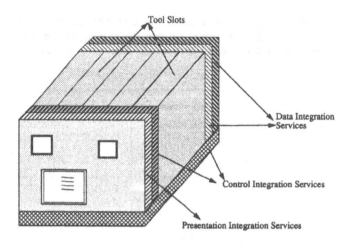

Figure 7: ECMA Environment Architecture Model

of ATMOSPHERE and other environments. One of its first applications will be in framework evaluation, where it will be used to draw up a standard set of criteria, against which existing frameworks and environments can be evaluated.

In the definition phase the emphasis was put on the data integration aspect, using an object management system as the central data integration service. Work in the development phase will have to extend the data integration work, (especially to include other data models than the basic ERA model which was used in the first year) and to include guidelines for control integration and presentation integration. Further work to be included is the definition of tool interfaces, both dynamically and statically. It is also felt that checklists of integration rules have to be identified. They would offer the tool writer clearer evaluation criteria for the level of integration achieved. The present tool writers guide must be extended to include the toolset-driven approach.

5 Environment Integration Technology

5.1 Environment Integration approach

Generally speaking, integration is required in a system engineering environment so that:

1. Toolsets can cooperate and operate in a coherent manner by sharing data, either from the data repository or by passing data between one another using some agreed interchange format;

2. Toolsets can be extended (openness), i.e. existing tools can be used to build more powerful toolsets;

3. Environments can be extended (openness), i.e., existing toolsets can be used to build more complete environments;

Although there is an enormous need for integration support for system engineering, it is also clear that full integration can only be achieved in an incremental and experimental way.

One objective of ATMOSPHERE is to demonstrate and apply integration technology through the construction and evaluation of a number of application-domain-specific system engineering environments employing the most promising integration approach which seems to be appropriate and feasible for the tools and/or toolsets to be integrated into the related environment. The only restrictions to be taken into account by these different integration approaches refer to X11 and OSF/MOTIF for the user interface. The different integration approaches employed by the different workpackage 4 subprojects are roughly fall into two main categories, **Framework-Driven** and **Toolset-Driven**, which, however, do not always mutually exclude one another in single subprojects.

- **Framework-Driven**

   Environment construction consists of (re-)engineering and consequently of integration of pre-selected toolsets determined by the mechanisms provided by a pre-selected high-level tool interface (frameworks, suchas e.g. PCTE in its role as public tool interface, NMP-CADLAB, VGI, and TeleUse). Toolsets in such environments share basic facilities like an Object Management System and User Interface Management System. The toolsets to be integrated have to fit into a particular predefined Environment Architecture.

- **Toolset-Driven**

   Environment construction consists of the integration of pre-selected toolsets available on platforms (e.g. PCTE in its role as operating system, UNIX, VMS, etc). The integrated tools don't necessary share a single Object Management System or User Interface Management System. The toolsets to be integrated don't have to fit into a particular pre-defined Environment Architecture, because the cooperation of the tools is more communication-oriented than data-oriented. It is even possible that environments of the first kind are components of environments of the second kind.

Again it has to be stated at this point, that by means of the "integration" activities of this workpackage the different integration efforts should achieve a certain commonality in order to ensure portability/interoperability of tools, toolsets and frameworks horizontally to all the vertical environment construction sub-projects. This may mean, for example, for the integration of tools and/or toolsets that they are possibly integrated according to a common integration schema.

5.2 Levels of Integration and Aggregation

In many cases it is difficult to say where integration starts and where it stops and what type of integration is meant.

In order to structure this complex situation ATMOSPHERE has identified two domains of integration in the context of System Engineering. The first domain addresses integration of the hierarchical concepts: Process, Method, Activity, Action. The second domain addresses integration of technological artefacts: Environments, Toolsets, Tools and Services (Procedures). Within each domain four corresponding levels are identified, which are explained for the technological domain in the next paragraph.

In Figure 8 this is illustrated with their mutual correspondence.

ATMOSPHERE distinguishes the following four levels of aggregation/integration for the technological artefacts:

1. **Tool level:** Tools provide automated support for an activity within a particular Life-cycle, Management, or Quality method. In many cases the tool supports an individual.

2. **Toolset level:** Toolsets provide automated support for a particular Life-cycle, Management, or Quality-method as a whole. The toolset is often used by a team.

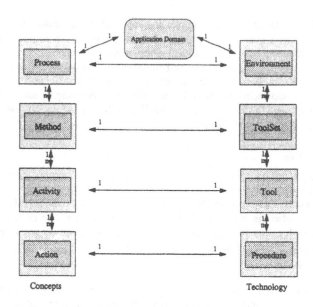

Figure 8: ATMOSPHERE Aggregation Levels

3. **Environment level:** Sets of integrated Toolsets provide automated support for particular set of methods, which arae required in a particular application domain, by a particular organisation. In many cases environments support a whole system development project, which consists of a team of teams.

4. **Factory level:** Sets of cooperating Environments. This higher level addresses the integration and interoperability of environments, which would in general support sets of projects (possibly at different locations).

At all levels the need for interoperability between related components of different frameworks might arise. The bulk of the work in ATMOSPHERE deals with integration at level 2 and some at level 3.

ATMOSPHERE at present does not explicitly address level 4 in its WP4. The environment integration and framework tasks in WP2, however, have to take this level into account as an important issue.

So the discussion and the scope of the project is limited to the integration of various toolsets which together form Application-Domain-Specific System Engineering Environments.

6 Environment Construction and Evaluation

6.1 Functionalities of a System Engineering Environment

The environment construction workpackage is planned and organised as to start from the current state of practice within the partner's organisations for system engineering tools, methods as well as for environment integration approaches in a particular application domain.

It is divided into four subprojects, each addressing the following three goals:

- the construction of an Application-domain-specific System Engineering Environment (ASEE),

- the application of a particular integration approach, and

- the evaluation of the resulting methods, toolsets and environments in industrial pilot projects.

Each of the ASEE's is targetted to implement automated support for an application-domain-specific instance of the ATMOSPHERE System Engineering Model (ASEM). The ASEM directly maps on a Functional Model of a System Engineering Environment which is shown in Figure 9.

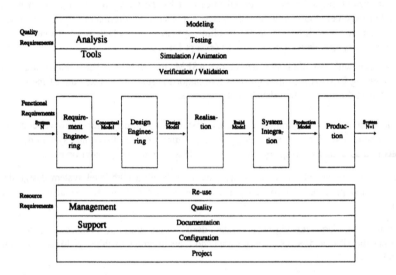

Figure 9: The ATMOSPHERE Functional Model of a System Engineering Environment

The ATMOSPHERE Functional Model of a System Engineering Environment depicts the different functionalities taken into consideration within the ATMOSPHERE project with respect to an overall System Engineering Process. For the environments constructed in the subprojects of Workpackage 4, these functionalities are provided by corresponding Toolsets.

As presented in Figure 9, ATMOSPHERE distinguishes three types of toolsets:

- analysis and evaluation toolsets which correspond with the quality part of the ASEM,

- life-cycle toolsets which correspond with the life-cycle part of the ASEM, and

- management toolsets which correspond with the management part of the ASEM.

As the different life-cycle functionalities concern the different levels of system abstraction to be addressed during the system development process, these functionalities are depicted as a sequence delineating the logical ordering of those abstraction levels. Due to the fact that the management and the analysis respectively evaluation functionalities represent concepts rather independent of system abstraction levels, the corresponding boxes are consequently included in Figure 9 as accompanying and covering the complete sequence of life-cycle functionalities.

In Figure 9, we see that the environment effectively transforms an application-domain-specific system of version N into a system of version N+1. The model therefore inherently supports incremental development and evolution. Whether version N of the system is already based on information technology does not matter. The system supplier who has to produce system version N+1 has to do this of course within the specified

1. quality requirements,

2. functional requirements, and

3. resource requirements

belonging to the corresponding concrete system development.

These separate though related concerns are taken care of by the respective main components (analysis, lifecycle, and management toolsets) within the system engineering environment. The first two components are mainly requirements with respect to the resulting system as a product, while resource requirements mainly refer to the system development process (except for reuse).

In correspondence with the life-cycle part of the ASEM, the ATMOSPHERE Functional Model of a System Engineering Environment distinguishes five major toolsets which take care of the main transformations conducted during a system development process:

1. *Requirements Engineering* transforms the user/external requirements for a new version (N+1) of an existing system version (N) into a user- and application-oriented functional system description and results in a so-called **Conceptual Model** of the new system and its environment.

2. *Design Engineering* transforms this conceptual model into a high-level system design description (which is independent of a particular realisation technology) and results in a so-called **Design Model.**

3. *Realisation* transforms this high-level system design description into a realisation description which describes the HW- and/or SW- components and their interrelationships, yielding a so-called **Build Model.**

4. Integration transforms this realisation description into a production description the so-called **Production Model** .

5. *Production* generates from this Production Model a number of instances and variants of system version N+1.

ATMOSPHERE's Application-domains-specific System Engineering Environments don't cover the production part. It is, however, necessary, in order to have worthy validation of ATMOSPHERE technology to interface with industrial production systems. This interfacing will be done in industrial pilot projects.

6.2   Application Orientation and Integration Approach

The four subprojects are, as much as feasible, complementary in their respective application domain orientation, integration approaches, and target organisation:

1. Aerospace Systems and Distributed Information Processing Systems with a framework-driven integration approach, led by Bull;

2. Digital Computer Network Systems with a framework-driven integration approach, led by SNI;

3. Communication Systems with a toolset-driven integration approach, led by Philips;

4. Process Control Systems with a combined framework-driven and toolset-driven integration approach, led by Siemens.

With respect to the three axes of the ATMOSPHERE Tool-Integration Model, the following holds:

Data integration in the subprojects is complementary, and respectively:

1. based on PCTE;
2. based on NMP-CADLAB;
3. based on a Common Data Interchange Format and ultimately on PCTE;
4. based on a Common Data Interchange Format and VGI.

Presentation integration is foreseen by means of OSF/MOTIF in most of the subprojects.

Control integration is still a matter of investigation in all the subprojects.

Within each of the subprojects, one or two application-domain-specific system engineering environments will be designed, constructed, validated and demonstrated by pilot applications. Each environment will provide suitable support for the life-cycle, management, and quality assurance methods for the application domain in question. Methods and toolsets will be integrated, re-engineered or developed as needs dictate so as to meet these requirements.

6.3 Structure of Workpackage 4

The vertical subprojects of Workpackage 4 are shown in their overall project context in Figure 10.

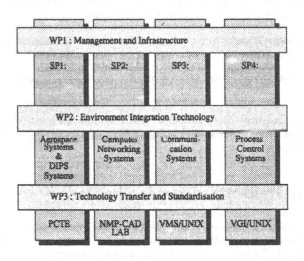

Figure 10: ATMOSPHERE Project Structure

The general structure in terms of tasks and results for each of the subprojects is depicted in Figure 11.

Each of the subprojects is divided into 5 tasks, each of them delivering a number of major results which will be internally employed in the subproject itself or in one of the tasks of WP2 and/or WP3:

- **Task 1: Method - Toolset Construction** delivers enhanced Toolsets, Method Descriptions, and a Toolset Construction Guide to be used in Tasks 2, 3 of WP4 and Tasks 2, 4 of WP2.

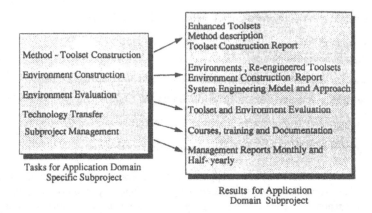

Figure 11: General structure of an Application Domain Environment Subproject

- **Task 2: Environment Construction** delivers Environment(s) re-engineered Toolsets, Environment Construction Guide(s), and an Application-domain-specific System Engineering Model and Approach to be used in Task 3 of WP4 and Tasks 3 and 1 of WP2.

- **Task 3: Environment Evaluation** delivers Evaluation Reports for the Toolsets and Environment to be used in Tasks 3, 4 of WP2 and Tasks 1 and 2 of WP4.

- **Task 4: Technology Transfer** delivers Courses, Training and Documentation to be used in WP3 and in Task 3 of of WP4.

- **Task 5: Subproject Management** Delivers Monthly and Half-yearly progress and QA reports to be used in WP1.

The Environments resulting from Task 2 are called Constructed Environments and are in general subsets from the corresponding environments applied in Task 3 and Task 4. The latter environments are called Pilot System Environments.

7 Technology Transfer and Standardisation

Technology transfer and standardisation form the subject of the Workpackage 3. It is the role of the External Relations Manager to co-ordinate the activities of the workpackage. The External Relations Manager is assisted by the Technology Transfer Team, a team consisting of representatives from all the main partners. Thus in total there is an even contribution of all partners to the work, ensuring that information transfer can be achieved to maximum effect.

The overall objective of this workpackage is to establish ATMOSPHERE in the European and international system engineering community. This relates both to the project itself as a major ESPRIT initiative in the domain of system engineering, and to the visibility and viability of ATMOSPHERE results, in terms of the constructed environments, their tools and associated integration technology.

Beyond this, it is clear that effective technology transfer, ultimately should result in the creation or adoption of engineering standards. ATMOSPHERE, through its strong commitment to standards, is both to submit and to push proposed standards in important areas of system engineering technology as well as monitor closely all relevant standards bodies for the adoption of new or existing standards.

In order to achieve these objectives, the workpackage is divided into two major tasks: one for technology transfer and one for standardisation.

8 Conclusions

The ATMOSPHERE partners, including major European Information Technology industry companies, see the ability to master the engineering of increasingly complex systems as a strategic issue for their business in the coming years.

They decided to launch and to support the ATMOSPHERE project because they believe it gives themselves and the European industry in general a unique opportunity to gain a world leading position in this domain.

On one hand, they reckon further investigation and experimentation need to be conducted in the project on such areas as Process and Method Integration in which research work still needs to be pursued.

On the other hand, however, the very pragmatic approach consisting in constructing and evaluating a limited number of application-domain-specific environments was preferred to the creation of a single monolithic general purpose - and perhaps somewhat illusionary - System Engineering Environment. This choice clearly reflects the will of the ATMOSPHERE partners to have the project producing practical and tangible results and to exploit them.

9 Acknowledgements

I gratefully acknowledge the contributions made by various members of the ATMOSPHERE consortium in review, criticism and encouragement provided to the author throughout the development of this paper. Furthermore I want to thank the support of the Commission of European Countries and in particular D. Callahan.

References

[1] Alley, W., TOOL BOX - A design Philosophy, Peat Marwick Mitchell and Co., London, Leicester, 1987.

[2] Long, Fred, Software Engineering Environments, Proceedings on International Workshop on Environments, Chinon, France, September 1989, Springer LNCS 487.

[3] Habermann, A.N., System Development Environments, Carnegie- Mellon University Pittsburgh.

[4] Thomas, G. Boudier, F. Gallo, R. Minot, M.I., *An Overview of PCTE and PCTE+* Proceedings of the Third ACM Symposium on Software Development Environments, Boston, November 1988.

[5] Ryan, J.A. Redmond, K.T., *Prospects for a method-driven Software Development Environment,* Software Development, vol. 29, no. 8, p. 421, Dept. of Computer Science, Trinity College, October 1987.

[6] Humphrey, Watts S., Managing the Software Process, Addison-Wesley 1989.

[7] Pyster, B.W. Boehm, M.H. Penedo, E.D. Stuckle, R.D. Williams, A.B., *A Software Development Environment for Improving Productivity,* IEEE Computer, p. 30, TRW, Digital Sound, June 1984.

[8] Sage, Andrew P., Concise Encyclopedia of Information Processing in Systems and Organizations, Pergamon 1989.

BUILDING IPSE'S BY COMBINING HETEROGENEOUS CASE TOOLS

Peter Göhner
Gesellschaft für Prozeßrechnerprogrammierung mbH
Kolpingring 18a, D-8028 Oberhaching

Abstract:

Today's computer systems consist of increasingly complex software and hardware components. The development of these systems can only be managed by integrated software tools for the different application areas and for the different project participants. This paper illustrates the main advantages of using an integrated project support environment built by heterogeneous tools to support efficently the development of complex systems from the initial requirements specification through system design and documentation to long-term maintenance. It outlines the requirements for such an IPSE and discusses the EPOS System as an example which satisfies these requirements.

Introduction

CASE - some years ago a term only for insiders - is now an important catchword for selling software tools. The range of CASE includes today tools, which reach from user friendly editors to integrated project support environments (IPSE).

CASE tools have been created in recent years to support work-intensive activities, to reduce human failure and to manage the enormous amount of information involved with the development of complex software/hardware systems.

The first generation of these CASE tools consisted of independent tools from different sources, each supporting only one part of the development process. The main difficulties in using these randomly connected tools in a project were the overlapping application areas and the absence of a predefined, well-structured project model.

To avoid overlapping application areas, the second generation consisted of tool boxes containing different tools in some kind of order. Each tool used its own information system and its own user interface. The transformation between the different information systems had to be done manually, making it very difficult to guarantee the consistency of information over the whole project life cycle. The variety of user interfaces was yet another handicap in using tool boxes.

The third generation of CASE tools, more aptly called tool systems, combined adapted tools and used a solid database and one user interface. Applications of such tool systems have shown that the aims of reducing development costs, improving quality, coping with project complexity, and implementing efficient project control are not sufficiently served by using three different tool systems: one to support software development, another to develop the hardware, and a third to support project management.

Therefore the fourth generation of development tools must be integrated tool
systems which support technical development, project control, configuration
management and quality assurance (IPSE's).

Requirements for an IPSE

The requirements for such an integrated project support environment can be sum-
marized as follows:

1. all information stored in a consistent data base

An unconditional prerequisite for all project work is consistent information for all
project participants. If there is any doubt in the consistency of computer produced
documentation the information is worthless. To realize consistent information there
are two approaches:

- o There is one tool in the centre with frontend and backend components

- o There are different tools on the same level with different tool
  specific information which is semantically connected.

2. support over the products's life cycle

The development of technical and commercial systems consists of four phases:

- o requirements engineering
- o system design
- o implementation
- o operations and maintenance

Although these phases are very different in nature, they are to high degree
interrelated. Between successive phases there are transitions in both directions.
The main transition is in the top-down direction because the results of the earlier
phases are the starting point of the following phases. But all projects contain
iterations which make it necessary to go back and redesign former levels. It is
therefore indispensable to have computer-aided transitions among the different
phases and computer-checkable relations between them.

3. support of all project participants

In an industrial software development project there are a lot of different kinds of
project participants: customer, analyst, project manager, software developer,
hardware developer, quality assurance, user, ... Some of them are only interested
in results produced by evaluation components, others need assistance in the
acquisition of information. To automatize the development of complex software
systems it is necessary to support these project participants.

4. specialized tools for the acquisition of information (phase, application and design method dependent)

Software/hardware system are complex structures which require different types of
elements. For the development, implementation and understanding of such systems, it
is necessary to know:

- o the sequence of functions
- o the module structure
- o parallel activities and the corresponding triggering events
- o the dataflow

o the data structure
o the structure of the hardware system

Various types of development methods can be derived from these different viewpoints. Depending on which of the above are dominant, the following methods can be distinguished:

o function-oriented
o module-oriented
o event/process-oriented
o dataflow-oriented
o data structure-oriented and
o hardware-oriented development methods

Which of these design methods is the best? The published results of numerous investigations show that there is no one "best" method. Each method has its specific advantages and disadvantages, which depend upon the respective problem as well as on the respective development phase. Therefore it is good practice to select the design method according to the problem at hand, and if necessary, to change the method during the design process, or to use different design methods in different subsystems.

An efficient and widely applicable development support system must integrate the different design methods in a method base. So the developer may select the method most appropriate for a specific task.

5. specialized tools for the evaluation of information (phase, application and design method dependent)

For the development of complex systems the following evaluation components are important

o documentation system
o analysis system
o management support system
o test work bench
o code generation system
o simulation/prototyping system
o quality assurance system

These evaluation components must be integrated in the IPSE.

6. open for the integration of other tools

The components of an IPSE are not fixed over a long period of time. Some tools must be replaced by new ones. Others open new application areas. Therefore it is necessary to integrate new tools in an easy way.

7. semantic integration of the tools

To have a close connection between different tools of an IPSE the tools must be integrated semantically, i.e. if there are relations in the information described or used in one tool, which are similiar or equivalent to the information described or used in another tool these relations must be checked automatically or mapped to store it only once.

8. modern user interface

To minimize the acceptance problems for such complex development systems the user interface must be excellent, that means it must be based on modern concepts as OSF/Motif or WINDOWS 3.0.

9. support for the usage of existing programs

In the development of new software systems more and more parts of old program systems in use today must be adapted and integrated. Therefore it is necessary in an IPSE to support reverse engineering activities.

The aim of a complete reverse engineering is to create a consistent system specification for existing software, making its structure more transparent and enabling, if necessary, this software to be converted into another programming language.

10. support for development, project management, quality assurance and configuration management

Although project management and development tasks are different in nature, there are significant reciprocal relations between them. The development team reports on the current state of design progress, including problems and estimates to complete, and proposes change requests. The project's management group plans, monitors and controls the project using development information to release work packages, to fix deadlines and to give cost limitations.

In addition to the interdependence between project management and technical development, there are also strong connections between project management and configuration management and between technical development, configuration management and quality assurance. For this reason it is necessary to have an integrated quality assurance tool which works directly on both the technical and management data base. If a separate configuration management tool is used, information must be repeatedly and redundantly stored, making it very difficult to ensure that developers use the right version corresponding to a baseline fixed by management.

Heterogeneous versus homogeneous tools in building IPSE's

There are two different alternatives in building IPSE's. One way is the a posteriori integration of industrial available tools coming from different developers building a heterogeneous IPSE. The other way is the development of integrated tools by one company building a homogeneous IPSE.

The degree of automation is higher for a homogeneous IPSE where the tools are closer together and share the same information. Figure 1 shows the structure of a homogeneous IPSE.

In a heterogeneous IPSE there is one dominant tool which is responsible for the project data base. The integration to the other tools, frontend and backend tools, is realized in form of temporary files which build the link between the tool specific information and the project data base. Figure 2 shows the structure of a heterogenous IPSE.

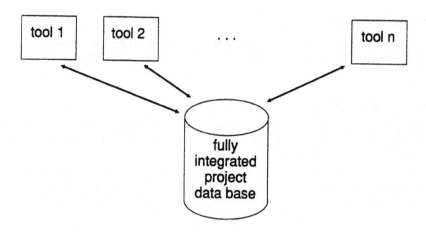

Figure 1:   Structure of a homogeneous IPSE

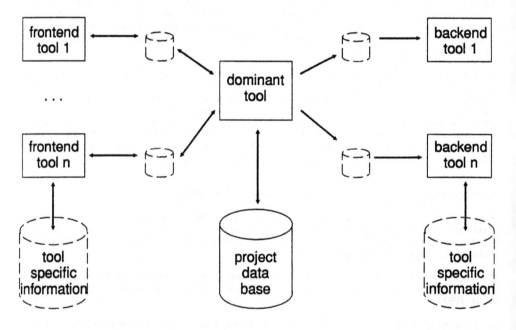

Figure 2:   Structure of a heteregeneous IPSE

The main difficulty for a homogeneous IPSE is the effort necessary to develop a priori integrated tools. In the last years it has been shown that there exists a 5-5-5 rule for the development of complex tools, that means

-    5 years for research and the first prototype

- 5 years for the development of a product

- 5 years for commercial success

Even if for less complex tools the necessary time can be reduced it is very time consuming to achieve the features of existing tools available for industrial applications today.

Therefore the only way to use the benefits of an IPSE today is the integration of heterogeneous tools where the realization of the transformation from one tool to another is less time consuming.

Fundamentals of EPOS

Objectives

EPOS (Engineering and Project Management-Oriented Specification System) is a software tool system designed for computer support of development and project management activities. Its aim is to dispense experts (technologists, system analysts, project managers, software developers, programmers), engaged in software/-hardware projects, from tedious routine work, enabling them to spend more time on development activities. Table 1 shows the various objectives of the EPOS System in detail:

1.	Homogeneous computer support in *all* phases of a project
2.	*Integrated* computer support for development, project management, product management and quality assurance
3.	Computer support for *various development methods*
4.	Computer support with *graphic representation* and *graphic user interface*
5.	Computer support for *software and hardware development*
6.	Extensive static and dynamic *checks* including a horizontal and a vertical *prototyping*
7.	Automatic, up-to-date *generation of documentation*, according to documentation standards
8.	Automatic *code generation* and *code feedback* (tracing)
9.	Computer support for service and maintenance as well as for *reverse engineering*
10.	*Accessability* for other tools, possibility of integration into an IPSE

Table 1: The objectives of the CASE Tool System EPOS

Structure and components

Figure 3 gives a summary of the structure and the essential elements of the EPOS system:

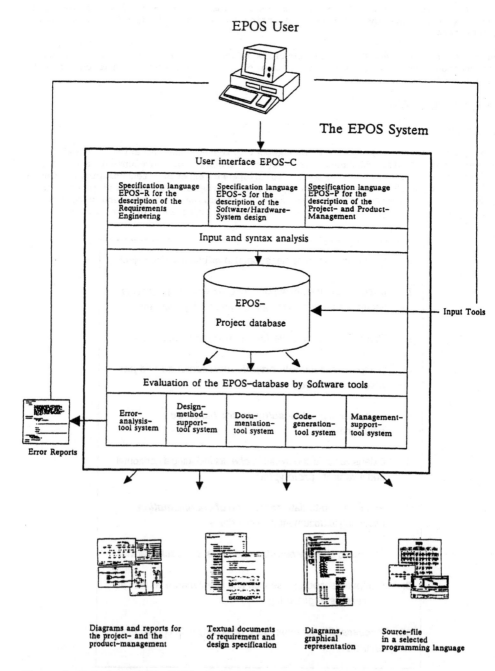

Figure 3: Overview of the EPOS system and its components

EPOS comprehends

o   three specification languages named EPOS-R (for requirements specification), EPOS-S (for system specification) and EPOS-P (for project management specification).

o   functions for the input of the data described by the specification languages.

o   an EPOS project database, for storage of all data described by the specification languages.

o   several software components for the evaluation of the EPOS project database and for the output of results for the EPOS user: the error analysis tool system for performing static and dynamic analyses and for the output of error reports, the design method support tool system for providing systematic guidance and assistance in the design method chosen by the user, the documentation tool system for automatic documentation generation, the code generation tool system for automatic program code generation in the programming language selected (including a code feedback) and the management support tool system for computer support during project planning, project realization and product administration.

The basic concepts of EPOS

The activities of a technical project can be divided into four different fields, as illustrated in figure 4:

o   development activities, starting with requirements engineering (definition of the demands and establishment of a suitable technical problem-solving concept), followed by the design of a software/hardware system and its realization, including, among other things, programs in a certain programming language and testing and setting the whole system into operation.

o   project management activities, i.e. the project planning with the scheduling and the determination of results to be achieved (the "deliverables"), the assignment of work packages to project members, the project monitoring, including deadline and cost controlling, decisions about admissible changes etc.

o   configuration management activities. These activities include the management of all interim and final results of the project development

o   quality assurance activities, i.e. the control of the quality of the development activities and the final results.

These activity fields are, however, not independent of one another, as there are mutual effects and relations. For this reason, the basic concept of EPOS is based on an integrated computer support, which reflects these references in the form of relations between the different specification languages.

Figure 5 illustrates an example of these relations: the processing of selected parts of the problems to be solved in requirements specification is laid down in project structure plan work packages (relations between requirements specifications and project structure). Similarly, the resulting parts of system design are also set out in work packages (relations between design specification and project structure). At the same time the system design has relations to the corresponding source files.

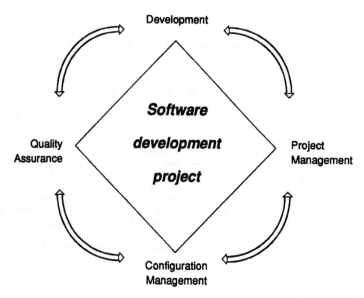

Figure 4: Engineering activity fields of a project.

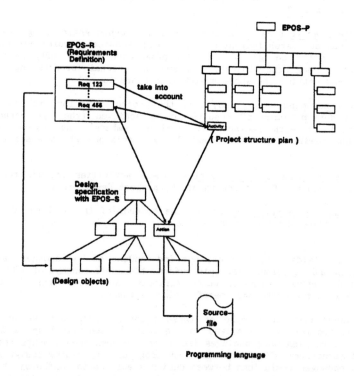

Figure 5: Interdependencies between development and management activities through relations between the objects of the programming languages EPOS-R, EPOS-P and EPOS-S.

EPOS in the centre of a heterogeneous IPSE

The EPOS System has been used in industry, governmental agencies, research institutes and universities since 1980. By September 1990, more than 1000 EPOS installations with more than 5000 EPOS work places have been delivered by GPP.

Demands made on EPOS in these installations are far-ranging: it has been successfully used to develop

o   small assembler programs for mass-produced items,

o   extensive technical systems implemented by different firms with differing computers using various programming languages,

o   complex safety-critical real time systems,

o   commercial programmes

o   pure software systems and

o   distributed hardware/software systems

Examples of application areas in which EPOS has been used today are:

o   avionics control and navigation systems

o   various technical applications

o   motor vehicle systems

o   transmission systems

o   development of hardware-oriented software

o   commercial software for a building society

o   simulation and rapid prototyping in real time applications.

During this time EPOS was integrated according to customer needs with a lot of different tools specialized for distinct applications.

Figure 6 gives an overview of the integration of EPOS with frontend and backend tools.

The global idea of this integration is to store the complete information produced by frontend tools in the EPOS project data base and to give a subpart of this information to the backend tools.

Table 2 lists the different tools, their application area and the developer/distributor.

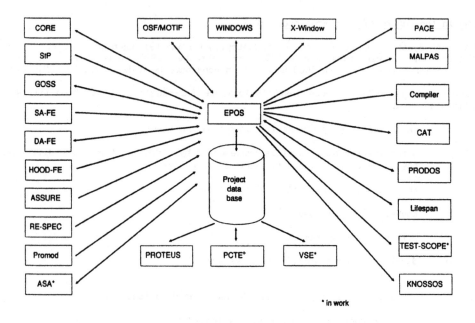

Figure 6: Integration of EPOS with frontend and backend tools

Tool	Developer/Distributor	Application Area
CORE	BAe	Requirement analysis of realtime systems
StP	IDE/GSE	Graphical support for SA, SA/RT, ER, OOD
GOSS	Langhagel	Graphical support for SA, SA/RT
SA-FE	GPP	Graphical support for SA
Promod	GEI	Graphical support for SA, SA/RT, ER
DA-FE	GPP	User defined generation of EPOS-S specifications
HOOD-FE	GPP	Graphical support for HOOD
ASSURE	Langhagel	Graphical support of PERT-Diagrams
RE-SPEC	GPP	Respecification of source files
PACE	Dähler / GPP	Simulation and animation of realtime systems
MALPAS	RTP / GPP	Formal analysis and verification
Compiler		FORTRAN, Pascal, C, COBOL, Ada
CAT	MBB	Hardware design
PRODOS	University Karlsruhe	Support of SPS-Systems
Lifespan	YARD / GPP	Configuration management
TEST SCOPE	SCOPE	Test environment
KNOSSOS	GPP	Development of knowledge based systems
VSE	GPP	Formal verification by proof systems
PROTEUS	GPP	Prototyping

Summary

As computers grow even more powerful and sophisticated, it becomes increasingly necessary for system designers and project managers to have computer support for the development of software and hardware systems. As projects grow in complexity and life-cycle duration, separate support tools for individual project stages are no longer sufficient to meet development and maintenance needs. Only a comprehensive, integrated support system can provide the assistance required by development, management and maintenance personnel to manage the sheer bulk of information involved.

It has become evident that for real industrial applications the integration of existing tools to a heterogeneous IPSE is today the only way to succeed. IPSE's builded by homogeneous tools are not available yet and will not reach in the next years the performance and the practicability of heterogeneous IPSE's.

EPOS used in a lot of different complex projects is one of the most advanced CASE tool systems today. EPOS represents with the integrated frontend and backend tools the completest IPSE available for use in real industrial projects. The EPOS-IPSE will be supplemented by new tools for specific applications in the near future to go on the way to the automation of the development process for complex software systems.

Literature

/ScFk86/   Schuler, T., Frank R.S. and Kratschmer W.:
           Successes and failures using EPOS as a software production tool. Proc.
           IFAC/IFIP Workshop "Experience with the management of software projects",
           Heidelberg
           Oxford: Pergamon Press 1986, pp. 125-130.

/Lemp86/   Lempp, P.:
           Development and Project Management Support with the Software Engineering
           Environment EPOS.
           Int. Conf. Software Eng. Environments (I. Sommerville, Ed.), Lancaster,
           Great Britain
           London: Peter Peregrinus 1986

/Goe86/   Goehner P.:
           Integrated Computer Support for Software-Hardware-System Development.
           Preprints, NAECON 1986, Dayton, Ohio.

/ToGR86/   Torick R., Goehner P. and Rainer, A.:
           EPOS Development Imperatives to Life Cycle Maintainability.
           Proc. Nat'l Conf. Softw. Reusability and Maintainability, Tyson Corner,
           VA Sept. 1986

/Laub87/   Lauber, R.:
           Automated Software Production. A1AA/NASA
           International Symposium on Space Systems in the Space Station Area,
           Washington D.C., June 22-23, 1987

/Laub87b/ Lauber, R.:
           Integrated Computer Support for Software-Hardware-Systems Development.
           10th IFAC World Congress, Munich, Germany. Pergamon Press 1987.

/LeLa88/   Lempp P. and Lauber, R.:
           What Productivity Increase to Expect from a CASE Environment: Results of
           a User Survey.
           27th Ann. Tech. Symp. of the Washington, D.C., Chapter of the ACM
           "Productivity, Prospects and Payoffs", June 8, 1988 Washington, D.C.

/LeTo88/   Lempp P. and Torick R.J.:
            Software Reverse Enginering: An Approach to Recapturing Reliable
            Software.
            4th Ann. Joint Conf. on Soft. Quality and Productivity, Crystal City,
            VA, March 1-3, 1988.

/LeZe88/   Lempp P. and Zeh A.:
            Interfacing a Development Support Environment to a MAPSE Through Ada
            Code Generation and Code Feedback: A STEP Towards an APSE.
            NAECON '88, May 23-27, 1988, Dayton, Ohio

/Laub89a/   Lauber, R.:
            Integrated Project Support Environments. Encyclopedia of Computer
            Science and Technology (Kent A. and S.G. Williams, Eds.), Vol. 20
            Supplement 5.
            Marcel Dekker, New York 1989 pp. 262-286

/Laub89b/   Lauber, R.:
            Forecasting Real-Time Behavior During Software Design using a CASE
            Environment.
            The Journal of Real-Time Systems 1, 61-76 (1989) Kluwer Academic Publ.,
            Boston.

On the Functional and Architectural Integration of CASE Systems

Günter Merbeth
Softlab GmbH Munich
Zamdorfer Str. 120, D-8000 Munich 80

1 Integration Aspects and the historical Development of CASE Tools

"Integration" is one of the most often used terms in the field of CASE tools and systems. One reason for this is that the same term is used to describe many different topics. Most of the topics, however, did not originate out of the intense discussions concerning CASE in the recent past, but instead have been known and debated for the past twenty years in the context of software development tools. Figure 1 shows the most important stages in the historical development of CASE tools. These stages will hereafter be described, and the most important aspects of integration relevant to each phase examined.

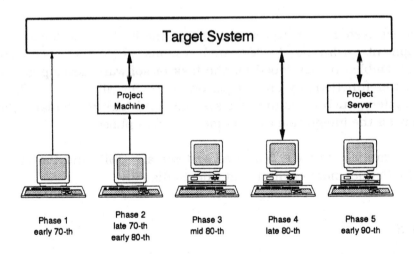

Figure 1: Historical Development of CASE systems

Phase 1:

With the appearance of time-sharing systems at the start of the seventies the interactive use of computers for software development became possible for the first time. In such an architecture, developers work at terminals with tools running on the time-sharing target system. A typical example for such a system is IBM's TSO.

Integration aspects:

- all developers of a project team are able to work on-line on the same data and can communicate electronically with one another.

- library systems, which are used to manage source and object code, and copy-books, coordinate teamwork and make it possible to automate consistency checking over multiple elements.

- data dictionaries, when used by all software developers, ensure the consistency of the software system being produced.

Phase 2:

The target system is, however, not always the best choice for a software development environment. Dedicated systems which have been specifically assembled or developed for the task of software development often offer better functionality and/or performance. Specific tools in the dedicated system, such as editors, file systems, and "electronic mail", provide support for the integration aspects mentioned in phase 1.

Typical examples of such dedicated systems are UNIX and the Maestro I software development environment from Softlab.

Phase 3:

The appearance of powerful PC's with graphics capabilities allowed the implementation of computer support for application system analysis and design techniques which had, in many cases, been developed on paper in the seventies. Well-known examples for such PC-based tools are Excelerator from Index Technology and IEW (Information Engineering Workbench) from KnowledgeWare.

As a result of these CASE systems (the term CASE came into vogue with the introduction of these products), a new integration issue came to the fore, because traditional file systems were inadequate for the data storage of these graphical tools. Editors for entity-relationship diagrams, data-flow diagrams, tree diagrams, and so on, require for their data storage a data dictionary or an entity-relationship-attribute-based database (see /HMF 91/). Tool integration was achieved through the use of a common database. However, another aspect of integration which had already been achieved in phases 1 and 2 (support for teamwork) is currently still lacking with these PC-based CASE tools. This shortfall is, however, to some extent ameliorated by the fact that such front-end tools are only used for the early phases of software development.

Phase 4:

Aside from the lack of support for teamwork, the PC-based single-user front-end tools often have a further serious problem: they lack connections to other tools, and in particular to the so-called back-end tools such as code generators. CASE systems which have such connections are classified here as phase 4 systems. This integration aspect has turned out to be so important that a separate market niche has developed to respond to the users needs. An example for a product in this niche is "Exchange" from the English firm "Software One". It transfers and transforms data between different CASE tools via an internal universal data model.

Phase 5:

Phase 5 systems are those which unify the architectural concepts of phases 2 and 3. User interface software and most tools run locally on PC's or workstations, whereas data integration, data management, and team support functions such as communication, run on a project server. A tight integration with target environments is of course also necessary. Such an architecture is called a workstation/server architecture and will be referred to frequently in the following sections. An system implementating this architecture already exists: Maestro II from Softlab.

2 Integration Issues

The various aspects of integration have been discussed above in the context of the development stages of CASE tools. The specific issues involved are summarised in figure 2.

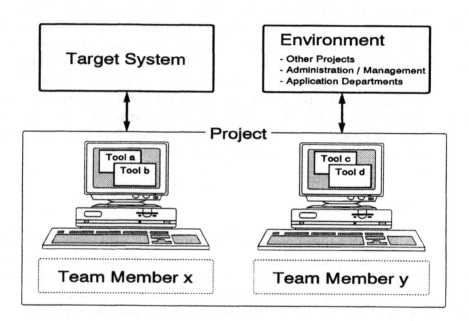

Figure 2: Integration issues in CASE systems

Figure 2 describes the following situation:

- Multiple developers work on their PC's or workstations.
- Each developer uses different tools.
- Multiple developers work together on a project.
- In the project, an application is developed for a specific target environment.
- The development is carried out in a commercial or governmental setting.

On the basis of this situation, we can distinguish the following integration issues:

(1) All tools must be based upon a common user model. Syntactically, this means that they must all work underneath a common user-interface, since this is practically speaking the only way that a common look-and-feel can be achieved. It should be noted, however, that a common user-model is more than just common syntax, it also implies common semantics for the use of the different tools.

(2) All tools must be integrated via access to common data. Alongside teamwork support this is the most important issue in integration, since the interoperability of the tools can be guaranteed through the use of common data.

(3) The individual activities must be unified via a process model. The tools for each activity are embedded in the process model and tool use is steered via the process model.

(4) Teamwork must be supported via the integration of the data of all members of the team. This implies that the data storage for all tools must be multi-user-capable. This is the case not only for the file system, but also for the databases used by the various CASE tools.

(5) Integration with the target system must be assured by the following mechanisms:
- data exchange between development and target sytems
- support for testing and debbugging on the target system
- support for use of target system tools.

(6) Integration into the development environment must be supported via links to and consultation of:
- other projects
- administration and management
- users.

Only issues (1), (2), and (4) will be discussed in depth in this paper, (1) and (2) in chapter 3, (4) in chapter 4 as part of the discussion of team-support.

3 Interoperability of Tools

The development of software is a process composed of many different activities. The individual activities are supported by tools. From the perspective of integration there are two components of these tools which are particularly important: user interface and data storage.

The user interface issue has become a particularly important one since the advent of modern graphical user interfaces and windowing systems. With Windows for DOS, Presentation Manager for OS/2, and OSF/Motif for UNIX, a set of interfaces is available today which will without doubt generally and also specifically for CASE tools become standards. The issue of a common user interface can thus be regarded as syntactically solved in the medium term, even if today many tools still have their own user interfaces. As was mentioned above, the other aspect of a common user model, common semantics for tool use, is also of great importance. We will however in this paper concentrate upon the issue of tool integration via data storage.

At least with modern CASE tools, data is rarely stored directly in the file system. Instead Entity/Relationship or object-oriented databases are used. Thus in the following sections it will be assumed that the tools work with databases.

As has already been mentioned, the individual activities, and thus also the tools, are not isolated, but rather interdependent and based upon each other in ways which are formalised in the process model. Typically, the outputs of one tool are inputs of the next. This situation is exemplified by the following scenario:

(1) In the Analysis phase, data-flow diagrams (DFD's) are used. The tool used is a data-flow diagram editor. Assume that a store containing a data element is present in the DFD. The editor requires the definition of the data element, and stores this definition together with other information in the database of the DFD editor.

(2) In a later phase the masks for the application system are designed using a layout design editor. If data entry for the data element mentioned above is carried out in a mask, then the layout design tool will require, in

addition to mask-specific information such as the position of the input field, the definition of the data element in order to define the length and display attributes of the input field. Thus the definition of the data element must also be stored in the database of the layout design tool.

(3) If a separate generator is used to generate source code for the mask, then this generator will also require access to the definition of the data element. This is because the generator will produce the necessary input-/output operations for the field. The generator will also require all other information concerning the mask and a place to store the generated program code.

The example demonstrates that identical data will often be needed by different tools. A possible solution to the integration problem sketched above might be the transport of data from the database of one tool to that of the next. However, since the different tools will often require the data to be structured differently, it is often the case that the data must be transformed as well as transferred. Figure 3 shows the consequences of such a solution when five different tools are involved. The simplest form is a chain, as is the case in figure 3 for tool 1 to tool 3. In this case we speak of tool-chains, or the chain model for tool integration.

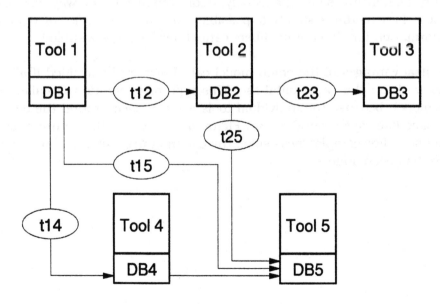

Figure 3: Chain Model for the Integration of Tools

Tool-chains can in special cases be quite sensible and successful, however as a general solution for the problem of data integration with CASE tools they are unacceptable. The reasons for this are:

- The number of transformations rises rapidly with the number of interoperable tools.

- If a new tool needs to be integrated, then in general a whole series of new transformers must be written.

- Tools are often not used in a strict sequence, but instead in cycles and at random. Frequent data transformations and transfers hinder the user, even if the tools and transformers are built to allow it. Tool-chains are at most in the case of traditional waterfall process models imaginable. Together with modern process models such as the spiral model of B. Boehm (see /BOE 88/) this approach fails completely.

- Data are held and edited redundantly in the various tool databases, a method which commonly leads to inconsistencies. Clearing up these inconsistencies requires additional effort.

- Since in a large project the various software developers will be working with different tools simultaneously, data exchange in the way described above is sometimes simply impossible, and the availability of required information for all team-members cannot always be guaranteed.

The disadvantages of the chain model can, however, be avoided if all the tools work on the same database. This type of integration is called the star model, because the individual tools are arranged around the central database like rays around a star. Figure 4 is a schematic picture of such a tool star. For completeness sake, the common user interface mentioned above has been added.

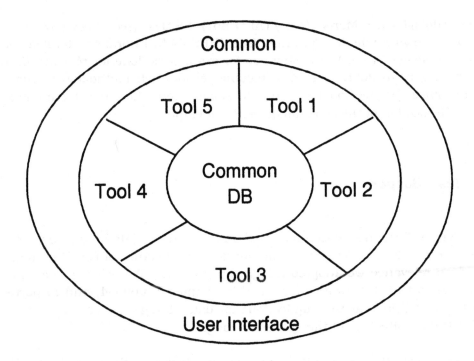

Figure 4: Star Model for the Integration of Tools

The use of a common database for all tools is, however, not enough to achieve full tool integration. This can be made clear by reexamining the example described above with the DFD-editor and the layout design tool. There we saw that both editors use the definition of the data element. However, the editors can use the same definition only when they both work with the same format. If the two tools assume different data structures, then little is gained by storing the data in a common database. The tools must therefore agree upon the form of the representation of information in the database.

In general, one can say that tool integration over a common database is only successful when all tools use the same common data model. To distinguish this model from the data models of the applications being built, the term metamodel is used. In IBM's AD/Cycle initiative, the metamodel is referred to as the "Information Model".

A metamodel is the most important part of a methodology package, in which tools are bundled together in such a way that they consistently and completely support a specific development methodology. Examples for methodologies are Merise (see /TARD 85/), SSADM (see /SSADM/), and Softlab's own methodology, SEtec (see /HES 84/). In order to implement methodologies in a CASE system, as for example is done for Maestro II, it is necessary to define a special metamodel for each methodology. However, since the methodologies use to some extent the same techniques, the intersection of these metamodels is not empty.

4 Team Support

In chapter 3 the discussion focussed on the issue of data storage as it relates to tool integration. Since the physical architecture of CASE systems had no relevance we adopted a logical perspective. We will now examine the support for teamwork mentioned in chapter 2, point 4, and in particular we will look at the implications for data storage. We can ignore the physical architecture of the system no longer.

A number of different architectures are conceivable as the basis for CASE systems. However, because of the heavy load on the processor caused by graphical user interfaces and modern CASE tools, the workstation/server architecture has become most common. Due to the necessity for teamwork in software development, these workstations are most often linked together and with the target system(s) via a LAN (Local Area Network). The primary question which must therefore be answered is: on which machine(s) should the CASE database run in such an architecture?

On the basis of the requirements discussed above, a distributed database running on all workstations would be the correct answer to this question. However, distributed database technology is currently not yet mature enough to allow of practical use. On the other hand, the tool integration aspects discussed in chapter 3 require that the database be accessible from all workstations and all tools. There is only one alternative given current technology: a central database running on a server. The type of the server machine is for our purposes irrelevant: it could be identical with the target machine. A dedicated server has, however, certain advantages, above all in that the same CASE environment can be used to develop software for multiple platforms.

Figure 5 shows the architecture implied by the discussions above. In addition to workstations, servers, and the LAN, the possibilities for links to target systems are also shown.

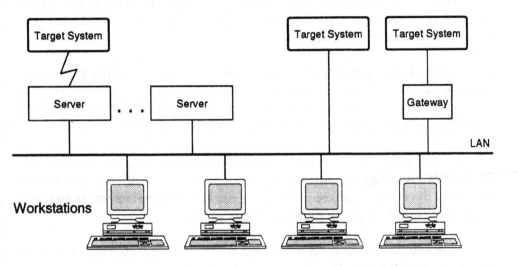

Figure 5: Typical physical Architecture of CASE Systems

From the perspective of the way in which the tools work with the central server database, there still remain a couple of alternatives:

- Workstation tools work directly on the central database.

- The tools use local databases on the workstations. The local databases are then synchronised with the central server database.

The use of a local database on the workstations has a number of pros and cons. The pros are:

(1) Access time for the database is dependent only upon the load on the workstation, and not upon net traffic or load on the server.

(2) The workstation can for a while be used independently of the server. This is particularly useful when the net or the server go down, but is also important for on-site discussions and demonstrations with users, or for the on-site testing of real-time software which is built into immovable machinery.

Arrayed opposite the advantages are, however, a number of serious disadvantages. The most important are:

(1) The identification of the data required by the tool is generally not easy. This can then lead to the situation that, either too much data is (b)locked in the central database, or data must be loaded onto the workstation as it is needed (a time consuming activity).

(2) Teamwork support is limited. This is in part because of the first disadvantage mentioned above, because checked-out data cannot be accessed for update by other users. In part though it stems from the fact that there is a delay before updated data becomes available to other users.

(3) Global consistency checking is only possible on the central database. Since this can only be carried out upon integration of the workstation data into the central database, conflicts are not detected early enough and must be cleaned up (often inefficiently) ex post facto.

These disadvantages can be avoided if the tools work directly on-line on the central database. That this unavoidably leads to a common meta-model was shown in chapter 3. A single common database thus serves both to increase tool integration and team support.

5 Summary

Integration is a central and variously used term in discussions about CASE. This paper has examined the following aspects of integration: tool integration above common data storage, tool integration via a common user interface, and teamwork support (user integration) with a multi-user database. The last aspect in particular will in the future be the subject of much analysis, research and many developments, since most currently available CASE systems are especially weak in this area. At the same time, the expected developments and standardisation efforts in the field of object-oriented databases will further stimulate activity, since the object-oriented approach is clearly most appropriate for the CASE and server databases discussed here.

References

/BOE 88/   Boehm, B.W.: A spiral model for software development and enhancement. Computer, May 1988, pp. 61-72

/HES 84/   Hesse, W.: S/E/TEC: Software-Produktionsumgebung von Softlab, in: Balzert, H. (Ed.): Moderne Software-Entwicklungssysteme und -werkzeuge, BI-Reihe Informatik, BD. 44 (1984)

/HMF 91/   Hesse W., Merbeth, G., Frölich, R.: Softwaretechnik: Grundlagen, Projektführung und Produktverwaltung. Erscheint 1991 als Band 5.3 des Handbuches für Informatik, Oldenburg.

/SSADM/   SSADM Reference Manual, Vers. 3, CCTA, London.

/TARD 85/   Tardieu, H. et al.: La Methode MERISE. Les Editions D'Organisation. Paris, 1985

DEVELOPMENT OF A METHOD DRIVEN CAS^{2}E TOOL

Jonah Z. Lavi , Michael Winokur
Israel Aircraft Industries
Ben Gurion Airport, Israel

ABSTRACT

The development of the current complex embedded computer systems and their software requires very advanced methods and computer based tools. The development of such tools requires coherent supporting methods. It is very difficult to develop generic tools suporting different methods. IAI - Israel Aircraft Industries, developed ECSAM, a method for the analysis of such systems and provided financial support fot the initial development phases of Statemate, a tool designed to support the method.

This paper briefly describes the ECSAM method and some aspects of Statemate. It describes the historical highlights of the development of the method and the tool and discusses the problems associated with their dissemination and the lessons learned.

- **Index Terms** - : Design, CASE, Computer Based Systems Engineering, Dynamic, ECSAM, Embedded Computer Systems, Executable specifications, Multi-systems, Reactive Systems, Event Driven Systems, Requirements, Software, Specification, Statemate, Statecharts, Systems.

INTRODUCTION

Modern embedded computer systems are very complex. Many of them are hierarchical multilevel systems that contain many computers in each level. Others are composed of many loosely coupled "subsystems" . Each of these "subsystems" may be complex and large by itself and implemented as a multilevel multicomputer system. A typical example is a modern integrated avionics system, which is composed of many subsystems, e.g. the navigation, radar and electronic warfare systems, each of which is itself a multicomputer system. Systems of this type are classified as "multisystems" (WHIT87). Most of them respond dynamically to random external signals and sequences of external events. Their dynamic behavior also depends on the operational history of the systems and on very complex logic conditions (WHIT85). Such systems cannot be developed without adequate methods and CAS^{2}E (Computer Aided Systems and Software

Engineering) tools. IAI recognized these factors eleven years ago. Further, it realized that the development of methods and tools should begin with the most important life cycle phase, the software requirements phase, since it is impossible to successfully progress with any of the other life cycle phases unless a well prepared requirements specification is available. At that time IAI decided to use SADT (ROSS85) as an analysis method and purchased PSL/PSA (TEIC77) as a generic tool supporting the analysis. We soon learned that SADT was insufficient for the analysis and specification of dynamic embedded systems and that PSL/PSA could not support our analysis method. We had to augment the method to suit the class of problems described above. To support the enchanced IAI requirements analysis method we decided, in 1985, to provide AD-CAD, a tool builder,(later bought by i-Logix) with partial financing for the development of STATEMATE (HARE88),an advanced CAS^{2}E tool. The development of the method and tool has been progressing by rapid prototyping approaches and by their applying them to real projects. AD-CAD could not afford to build a tool customized to suit IAI's unique analysis method because of commercial factors. This has caused many delays and problems in providing the enhancements needed to make the tool fully support ECSAM's current needs.

This paper briefly describes briefly the ECSAM model of complex embedded computer systems and their software which forms the basis for the ECSAM analysis method developed at IAI using STATEMATE as the supporting tool. It proceeds with a discussion of the highlights of their development and their dissemination process in the company. It also briefly describes required enhancements and the lessons learned in the development of a method driven tool.

THE ECSAM MODEL AND THE SUPPORT OF STATEMATE

The development history of ECSAM and Statemate can be explained more easily if we first briefly describe the model underlying the ECSAM analysis method, called the "ECSAM model". ECSAM, an Embedded Computer Systems and Software Analysis Method has been developed by IAI since 1981. (LAVI91, WINO90, LAVI89, LAV882, LAVI86, LAVI84). ECSAM is a comprehensive method incorporating many of the ideas which were presented in the systems engineering and software engineering literature, augmented by numerous original ideas developed at IAI. The method also addresses the issues of multisystems and multilevel systems. ECSAM is suitable for the analysis of entire embedded computer systems as well as for the analysis of software systems and modules.

Applying ECSAM the system is analyzed using four complementary views (Figure 1): three functional views and an architectural view. The three functional views, which comprise the ECSAM model, are; the logic module view, the operating modes view and the process view. The system's capabilities, signal and data flows, derived during the analysis of the ECSAM model, are mapped to the fourth view which describes the system's architecture. The system specifications and the top level design are derived from the ECSAM model and its mapping to the architectural view.

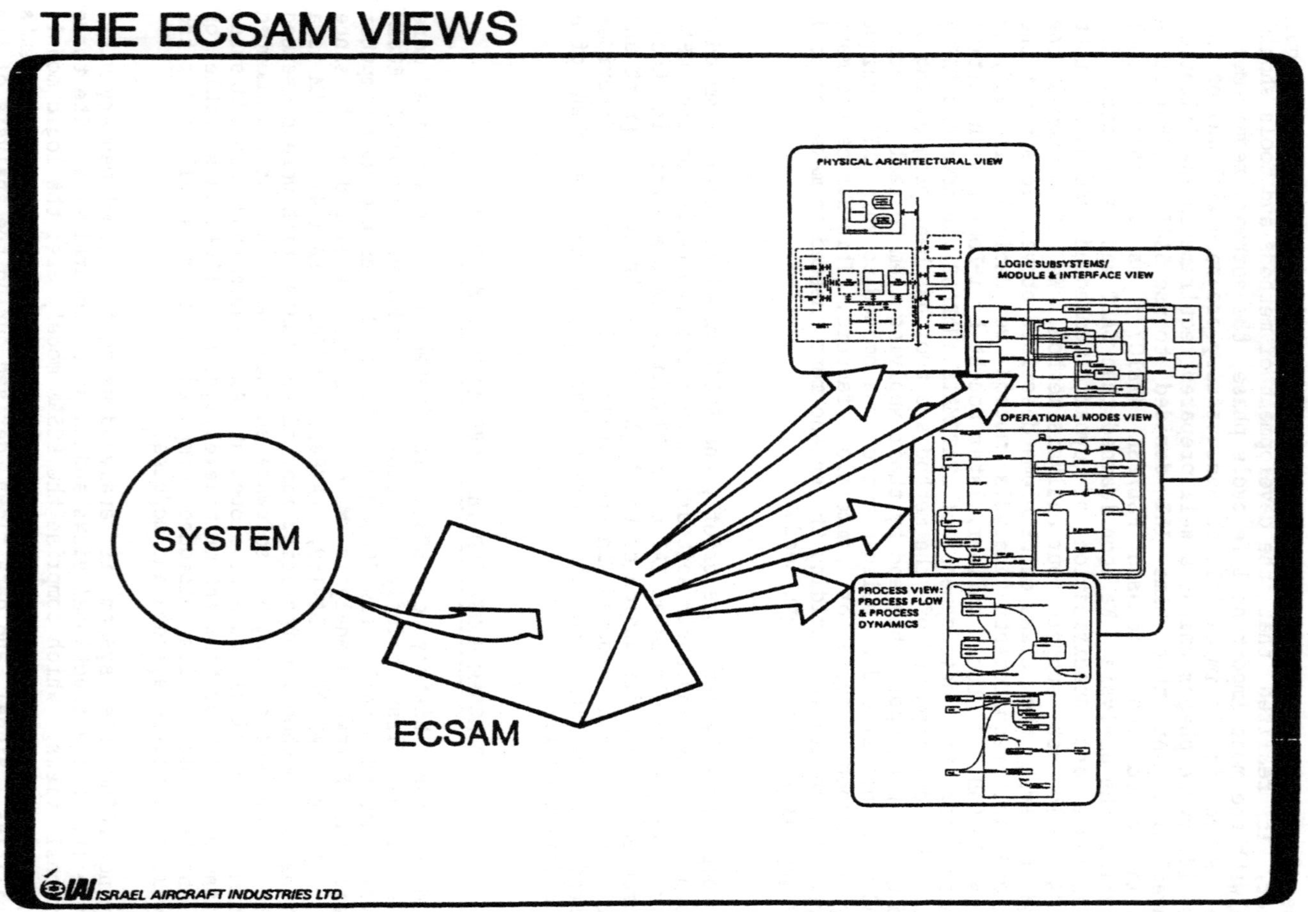
THE ECSAM VIEWS
SYSTEM
ECSAM
PHYSICAL ARCHITECTURAL VIEW
LOGIC SUBSYSTEMS/
MODULE & INTERFACE VIEW
OPERATIONAL MODES VIEW
PROCESS VIEW:
PROCESS FLOW
& PROCESS
DYNAMICS
ISRAEL AIRCRAFT INDUSTRIES LTD.

Figure 1

Graphic techniques are used in the representation of the various views.
Experience has shown that these representations are comprehensible and
provide the basis for an effective exchange of ideas. Their use also
allows easy and fast modification of the specifications during early
phases of project development, as charts can be changed more easily than
long textual documents.

The three functional views, which comprise the ECSAM model, are;

> - **The Logic Module View** describes the partitioning of the
> system into its functional subsystems, the information that flows
> between the system's external environment and the internal
> subsystems, as well as the flow of information between the
> subsystems. This view also describes the functional capabilities
> (activities) performed by each of the subsystems.

> - **The Operating Modes View** describes the main operating modes
> of the system and the transitions between them.

> - **The Dynamic Process View** describes the behavioral processes
> that occur in the system at its various modes in response to
> external or internal events.

The three functional views of the ECSAM model are interrelated. Their
relations can be explained using the ECSAM generic model of embedded
compuer systems (LAVI84, LAV882).

The system capabilities, signal and data flows derived during the
analysis of the ECSAM model are mapped to the ECSAM fourth view, the
architectural view which describes the actual layout of the physical
system, its hardware and software constituents, and signal and data
channels interconnecting them. The use of the ECSAM model allows the
development of reuseable generic specifications of models of specific
system families, e.g. radars electronic warfare and RPV systems. These
generic specifications can be mapped to different physical architectures
meeting different customer needs. This allows us to reduce significantly
the systems development time.

STATEMATE - The Supporting Tool

Systems specifications developed using the ECSAM method are very complex,
due to the complexity of the systems describe above. They can be be
documented and analyzed only if supported by computer based tools.
STATEMATE (HARE88) the tool developed by AD-CAD, supports ECSAM.
Statemate incorporates three graphical editors which support the analysis
and requirements specifcation of the three ECSAM functional views.
Statemate does not currently support the architectural view and its
relationships with the three functional views. The tool is based on
formal semantics which allow testing and simulation of the system's
static and dynamic behaviors (HARE87).

Development History Highlights

The approach we adopted in the process of developing method driven CAS^{2}E tools is described below. We typically formulate a CAS^{2}E development problem in an area which we currently perceive as being the most important. We try to search for an existing available method or try to develop it ourselves. Strong emphasis is placed on the development of graphical presentation techniques. We then try the method experimentally on small real projects or on some of their smaller subsystems. Once we dicover that the basic method works effectively we try to buy or build initial prototype tools which are also l evaluated on small projects. Concurrrently with that phase we try to teach the methods. We also search for existing or new tools which are again tested on real projects since it is difficult to invent meaningful "toy" problems for their evaluation. The testing and evaluation is done with the support of coaches from the central organization which developed the method. Once the techniques and the tool seem to provide adequate results we start an intensive dissemenation process through courses (LAV882) and on the job coaching. Working closely with the projects teams we get ideas and requirements for the developement of additional enhancemnets in the area of methods and tools, which in turn initiate new development cycles.

The actual development history of ECSAM and Statemate is described briefly in the following paragraphs. As mentioned previously we realized in 1980 the need for a specifications method and tool. Following an intensive survey we adopted at that time the SADT method and purchased PSL/PSA a generic tool to support the analysis process. SADT and PSL/PSA were adequate for the analysis of what we regard today as the logic module view.

In 1983, we recognized the difficulty of analyzing multicomputer systems using only the SADT method. We recognized that the systems we are developing are multicomputer hierarchical systems. Their structure can be represented by the generic model of embedded computer sustems and their software (Figure 2) which we formulated in 1983 (LAVI84). According to the model each system is decomposed into a group of subsysytems controlled by a conceptual logic controller. Major elements of this controller are described by state transition diagrams. We realized that conventional state transition diagrams are difficult to use. At that time we started a joint research project with pilots specifying the LAVI A/C avionics and with Prof. Harel trying to devlop better graphical method for the drawing of state transition diagrams. This resulted in the development of the Statechart concepts and their formal semantics (HARE87) The latter allow the presentation of state hierarchies and cuncurrency. The Statechart graphic technique was actually used on the real project while it was being developed and it was found very useful by all the people involved with the specification of the LAVI avionics. It was used at that time mainly for the anlysis of the Lavi avionics process dynamics. Later we mainly used it for the analysis of the operational modes view and currently it is being used for the analysis of this view as well as for the analysis of the dynamic process view. At that time, we tried to generate an advanced tool using a meta tool developed by the ISDOS project, the builder of PSL/PSA. That did not work. Consequently,

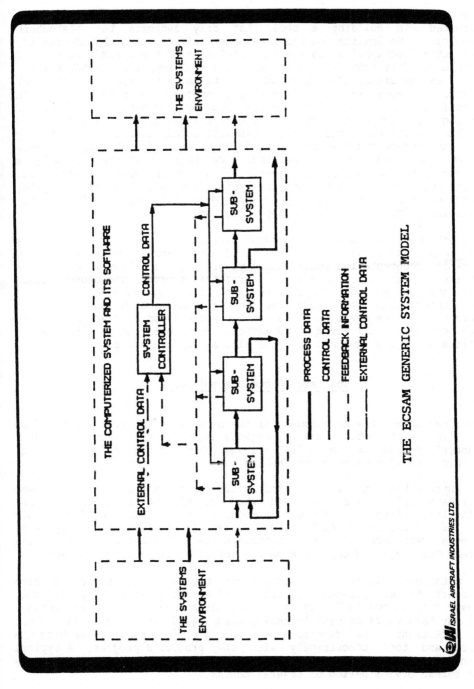

THE ECSAM GENERIC SYSTEM MODEL

Figure 2

we started to negotiate a development contract with AD-CAD. They were interested in building a tool that only supports the Statechart technology. We insisted on the development of a tool which supports the three ECSAM functional views and the simulation of the dynamic aspects of the model. Convincing AD-CAD to develop a tool supporting ECSAM was not easy. As we proceeded with ECSAM and with the introduction of the tool on real projects, we realized that many aspects have to be augmented in the tool to support the ECSAM analysis. Some of them have been augmented, allowing us today to support the three functional views. The urgent need for the architectural view and its benefits became clearer while working with the method and the tool on real projects. Unfortunately this view is not supported yet by the tool. We require that the tool will be provided with an additional graphic editor for the architectural view. We are again in a rapid prototyping cycle learning the necessary mapping methods on real projects and trying a prototype tool which will hopefully evolve into a fully functional supporting tool.

We briefly discussed some of the major milestone of these projects. There were many additional ones associated for example with supporting automatic documentation tools, which we are not describing in detail due to time and space constaints. The presented approach has proven itself again and again. Our experience shows that one cannot buy effective tools unless they are supported by or based on a coherent method understood by the developers and one can not develop good advanced tools based on generic all encompasing methods. Such tools end up like washing machines which are supposed to serve also as kitchen mixers.

Tool and Method Dissemination

As was mentioned, the development of the method and the tool was based on work done with real ongoing projects within IAI. Working on "toy projects" proves to be ineffective and reconstucting or "redeveloping" past projects is even more ineffective.

The introduction of methods and tools calls for special people who understand their importance and who are willing to face all the difficulties involved in their introduction to the first project. This type of people are crucial to the success of the dissemination process. We were very lucky to find such individuals within IAI who were willing to take the risks and apply the method and the tool to large projects.

The methodological support is of extreme importance. It is easy to teach engineers to manipulate the buttons of the tool. It is very difficult however to change their way of thinking using new and advanced methods. That may take years of very intensive coaching. Courses are necessary but not sufficient. We developed an on going project seminar teaching the method and tool concurrently with the project's progres. A typical seminar consists of three to four sessions each one three to four days long spread over a period of several months.

Introducing such advanced tools without the proper methodological support and coaching is very ineffective. We describe many such examples, one of which is documented in the literature (KASK90).

An important help in the dissemination of such methods and tools are well structured and graphical reports describing the analysis results in an easy to use manner. We developed templates for many such reports which are currently our best selling agents.

CONCLUSIONS

Our approach to the development of tools based on a coherent method has proven itself for several years. As a company developing systems we are not in the business of developing such tools ourselves. We naturally have to find independent tool vendors interested in the development of tools supportin our methods. This causes problems since tool vendors typically can not write the necessary methods textbooks required to support the sale of the tool in the open market. Further, for commercial reasons, they are interested in the development of tools which support a wide range of methods. On the other hand, as engineers in the industry, we try to develop and to disseminate methods and tools and can not find the time to write these text books. This is one of the major problems in the development approach which causes delays in the wide-spread dissemination and marketing of advanced tools necessary for the development of embedded computer systems and their software. We can not demand from commercial tool vendors to fully support a unique method. However, as in our case, if the tool supports most of our requirements we can successfuly apply it in a wide range of projects.

REFERENCES

HARE87   Harel, D., "Statecharts: A Visual Formalism for Complex Systems", Science of Computer Programming 8 (1987) pp. 231-274, North-Holland.

HARE88   Harel, D., et al "STATEMATE: A Working Environment for the Development of Complex Reactive Systems", IEEE Transactions on Software Engineering, Vol. 16, No. 4, April 1990, pp.403-414.

KASK90   Kaskowitz, R., Kuehl, C.S., "Lessons Learned From Selecting and Implementing Advanced Enginering Methods and Tools in an Integrated Computerized Environment", Procceding of the Computer Based Systems Engineering Workshop organized by the Israel Chapter of the IEEE Computer Society. Neveh Ilan, Israel, May 1990.

LAVI84   Lavi, J.Z., "A Systems Engineering Approach to Software Engineering", IEEE Proc. Software Process Workshop, Egham, UK, Feb. 1984, pp. 49-57.

LAVI86   Lavi, J.Z., Kessler, E., "An Embedded Computer Systems Analysis Method, "in Proceedings of the Israel First Conference on Computer Systems and Software Engineering" Tel Aviv, June 1986.

LAV881   Lavi, J.Z., Winokur, M., "Embedded Computer Systems Requirements Analysis & Specification - An Industrial Course", in "Software Engineering Education - Proceedings of the SEI 1988 Conference", Lecture Notes in Computer Science, Vol. 327' Springer Verlag, 1988.

LAV882   Lavi, J.Z., Winokur, M., Dagan A., Rokach, R., "Multi Level Analysis of Complex Embedded Computer Systems" in Proceedings of Third Israel Conference on Computer Systems and Software Engineering" IEEE Computer Society Press order Number 884, June 1988.

LAVI89   Lavi, J.Z., Winokur, M., "ECSAM - A Method for the Analysis of Complex Embedded Computer Systems & their Software", Proceedings of the Fifth Structured Techniques Association Conference, Chicago, III., May 1989.

LAVI91   Lavi, J.Z., Winokur, M., Kudish, J., Gallant, R., "Embedded Computer Systems Specification and Design, The ECSAM Approach", IAI report, June 1991.

ROSS85   Ross, D. T., "Applications and Extensions of SADT", Computer, Vol 18, No, 4, April 1985, PP. 25-35.

TEIC77   Teichroew, D., Hershey, E.A. III, "PSL/PSA: A Computer Aided Technique for Structured Documentation and Analysis of Information Proceesing Systems", IEEE Transaction on Software Enginering, January 1977, pp. 41-48.

WHIT85   White, S. M., Lavi, J, Z., "Embedded Computer System Requirements Workshop", Computer, Vol. 19, No. 4, April 1985

WHIT87   White, S., "A Pragmatic Formal Method for Computer System Definition", Ph.D. Dissertation, Polytechnique University, New York, N.Y., June 1987.

WINO90   Winokur,M., Lavi, J.Z., Lavi, I., Oz, R., "Requirements Analysis and Specifications of Embedded Computer Systems using ECSAM - a Case Study", Proceedings of the IEEE CompEuro Conference, May 1990, Tel-Aviv, Israel, pp. 80-89.

VSF and its Relationship to Open Systems and Standard Repositories

John N. Pocock

Systematica Ltd

3-7 St Stephens Rd

BOURNEMOUTH BH2 6JL

UK

Synopsis

In an environment of continually evolving technology the need for automated development environments to be "open" is increasingly significant. This need imposes requirements both on the architecture of such an environment and on the individual tools which it will comprise. The Virtual Software Factory (VSF) is a meta-CASE tool-set, enabling the rapid development and evolution of commercial quality CASE tools. The facilities provided by the tool-set are designed to enhance the applicability of VSF solutions for Open Systems environment. VSF-based tools can be configured to interface with any of the emergent standard Repository systems, and with other complementary tools without significant impact on the tools themselves; individual tools may support multiple external meta-models, and multiple inter-tool communication environments. In this paper we discuss the nature of the requirement for an Open System approach to CASE tools, and the relative roles of standard Repositories and specialist "point" tools in such an environment. The structure of a VSF-based CASE tool for an Open Systems environment is outlined in order to demonstrate how the VSF facilities are used on support of an Open Systems approach.

1.   The Virtual Software Factory

Recent years have seen the emergence of so-called "meta-CASE" technologies, whereby the construction of Computer-Aided Software Engineering (CASE) tools may be facilitated. The usual approach followed is to simplify the implementation of the perceived components of a CASE tool by reuse of standard components: a DBMS or Data Dictionary, a configurable graphics editor, a syntax-editor generator, a user interface generator, and so forth. A contrasting approach is that exemplified by the Virtual Software Factory (VSF) in which the technology provides a unified formal definition of the Method to be supported, and a kernel environment for the execution of such a specification, in the form of a CASE tool supporting that Method.

A VSF Method definition comprises essentially two parts

a.   A Semantic Model of the Method

This model defines, formally, the concepts embodied in the Method (i.e the abstractions that it employs), their inter-dependencies, and the semantic integrity rules that define meaningful and consistent designs expressed using those abstractions.

```
define: System = unstructured;
define: Function = unstructured;
define: Datastore = unstructured;

define: ParentObject = union(System,Function);
define: ChildObject = union(Function,Datastore);

define: Decomposition = <ChildObject —> ParentObject>;

define: DataSourceOrSink = union(Function,Datastore);

define: DataFlow = product(DataSourceOrSink,DataSourceOrSink);

define: UncleOnDFD = product(DataSourceOrSink,ParentObject);
```

Figure 1   Cantor Set definitions for Hierarchical Dataflow model

VSF provides a language, called Cantor, for the definition of semantic models. In Cantor the model is defined by considering the instantaneous design as a collection of sets. Sets may be defined to be an identified collection of named elements, or be defined in terms of other sets using Cartesian Product, Union, and Intersection operations, or by inference, as subsets of other sets, using a fully quantified predicate logic. Figure 1 shows the set definitions for a simplified hierarchical Dataflow model.

Mechanisms provided in the language for defining integrity are

- The imposition of *Constraints* on the evolution of a design. By this mechanism integrity is (incrementally) ensured by predicating valid changes to the design on the source state (i.e the set members identified therein). In Figure 2 are shown the basic constraints needed for balancing of Dataflows (but not of data structures associated with those flows).

- The definition of *invariant conditions* on the state of the design. By this means the instantaneous state of a design may be checked for integrity, and for completeness,

```
constrain: UncleOnDFD =>
        /*     This Function does not interact with this Parent */
        (    {      DataFlow(??1,??2) },
             {      DataFlow(??2,??1) } );

constrain: DataFlow =>
        (    /*     only allowed between children of a the parent
                    function/system ...*/
             {      Decomposition(??1,?parent),
                    Decomposition(??2,?parent)
             /* ...      or between children of the parent Function
                         if there is a data flow in the same
                         direction between the sibling and the
                         parent function */
             {      UncleOnDFD(??1,?parent),
                    Decomposition(??2,?parent),
                    DataFlow(??1,?parent) },
             {      Decomposition(??1,?parent),
                    UncleOnDFD(??2,?parent),
                    DataFlow(?parent,??2) } );
```

Figure 2   Constraints for Dataflow Balancing

and inconsistencies reported.

- The imposition of *Consequences* on the evolution of a design. By this means a change to the design may propagate other changes, thus enabling the (incremental) maintenance of the integrity of parallel, dependent, semantic structures.

The same predicate logic as is used for inference, is also used for the definition of Constraints, invariants, and Consequences. The choice of mechanism used for the realisation of any particular Method rule (inference vs explicit propagation by consequences, incremental validation via Constraints vs static invariants) may be chosen according to the intended operational characteristics of resulting CASE tool.

b.   A Syntactic definition of Textual and Graphical presentation

For a given collection of abstract concepts, there will be a variety of forms of presentation, both textual and graphical, corresponding to the views of the design defined by the method. Any individual "fact" or collection of "facts" in the design may appear in any appropriate form (or in several simultaneously), and may be modified by modification of any or all of the appropriate views. To support this concept, VSF provides a Viewpoint Definition Language, with sublanguages for the definition of textual and graphical views.

Graphical and Textual abstract object types may be defined, with attributes defining their visual properties, the editing operations available on them, and the meaning to be attached to each instance of the type. Meaning is defined by associating "facts" from a design conforming to the semantic model with the objects, and defining the changes to the design implied by each textual and graphical operations. In the VSF model, the facts which attribute meaning to each textual or graphical object, and the meaning of each operation, are determined from the context in which the object exists and/or the operation is performed, thus enabling context-sensitive syntax structures to be modelled.

A method defined in this form may then be animated by the VSF execution kernel, referred to as the Analyst Workbench (AWB). This kernel provides the ability to display and edit any of the graphical or textual forms defined by the model. Any number of textual or graphical representations of the design may be visible in multiple windows at any one time. Each view is dynamically generated from the underlying design and thus any change to a textual or graphical viewpoint which impacts another (textual or graphical) view is automatically propagated to that view (whether it is visible or not)[1], and navigation of the design may be achieved by a "hypertext" style mechanism allowing any (textual or graphical) representation of an object to be used as an index for making any other view of the same object, or of any related object, visible. As a result a formal definition of a method, in terms of semantic rules and textual and graphical notations, automatically produces a CASE tool supporting the method through

- a multi-window GUI
- incremental design validation (scoped over a complete design, not just individual diagrams/documents)
- "hypertext" design navigation

which provide significant productivity benefits for users of the method.

In order to minimise the effort required to develop and validate such tools, VSF provides a rapid prototyping environment, referred to as the Methods Workbench (MWB) which enables the interactive modification of both the semantic and syntactic models of a running AWB.

It is important to notice that VSF is specifically aimed at the production of compliant solutions to the problem of effective and productive design using a specified method. In a "real world" development environment many kinds of activity other than those appropriately described or supported using this kind of technology will be taking place, and the use of tools to support all of these activities must be integrated within an overall management approach, which may be subject to greater or lesser degrees of automation. In the design of a CASE tool, the impact of the user environment must be considered, since the utility of the tool in practice will be primarily determined by how well it integrates into this wider scenario. In order to understand these issues, and the facilities provided by VSF for integration of a generated CASE tool with other, complementary, facilities, the nature of this overall project environment requires analysis.

---

[1] Layout information associated with graphical views is preserved, and changes in content resulting from changes in other view are merged with existing layout (which may be modified as required by the user).

2.   The Project Environment

A development project may be characterised as a highly complex, distributed process, comprising a large number of highly inter-dependent parallel activities. This complexity, of course, is the motivation behind the desire to use technology, exemplified by computer-based tools, to simplify the management and performance of the process. There are three general directions from which the provision of automated support for the development process may be approached, which we summarise thus

- the *process* view

    Whereby support is provided for the definition and management of the activities which comprise the development, and the resources needed to perform those activities. This is typically the domain of Project Management tools, and of the emergent "framework" technologies such as the Atherton Backplane, and SUN Microsystems' Network Support Architecture (NSE).

- the *product* view

    Whereby support is provided for the generation and validation of "deliverable" products of activities comprising the development (Specifications, Source Code etc). This is the area in which both "lower CASE" (compilers, debuggers, source code analysis etc) and "upper CASE" (requirements and design support) tools are primarily targeted.

- the *construction* view

    Whereby support is provided for the coordination of the products generated by parallel, inter-dependent activities. This is typically the domain of Configuration Management, Change Control and Integration tools.

Each of these areas imposes a different set of requirements on computer support, and has a different degree of automation in different user organisations. Because of the complexity of the overall complexity of the total problem, technology for the support of these areas is continuously, and to a large extent independently, evolving. This leads, then, very naturally to the need for what have come to be called "Open Systems" solutions to the problems of computer support.

3. The Nature of Open Systems

The requirement for Open Systems derives from the complexity of the overall development process, and independent evolution of computer based support technologies for different domains. That is to say that "openness" must be defined in terms of ability to support incremental change in the support environment, in other words the ability to replace individual components, or add new components, to an environment comprising both computer based tools and management procedures, without impacting other components. This requirement for evolutionary capability impacts both the architecture that needs to be put in place for a development support environment, and the facilities which need to be provided by the individual tools which will comprise that environment.

First of all, then, the development environment itself must be "open". This means that its architecture must be such as to facilitate the introduction of new capabilities (i.e new tools or collections of tools). The ease with which a new tool may be introduced into an existing environment is determined by the impact that its operation will have on the operation of other, existing, tools, and, to a lesser extent, by the similarity of the User Interface that it offers to the "look and feel" provided by other, existing, tools.

In order to minimise the impact of one component tool on another, an open environment must provide common inter-tool communication mechanisms, and common access mechanisms for shared information. If the environment provides only these mechanisms, however, then there remains much scope for interference; there also needs to be some measure of common understanding between interacting tools of the "meaning" attached to communicated or shared information by its originator(s). Any tool in the environment which needs to access information which may have been generated or changed by another tool must know exactly where and how this information may be accessed. This then implies that an essential component of an open environment will be a common model of the structure and semantics of information which is to be shared by multiple tools. This leads naturally to the concept of a standard "repository" system as a vehicle for supporting openness by enforcing such a common information model. We shall discuss the role and necessary functionality of such a system below.

Secondly, even given an open environment architecture, the tools which support the various activities within a development process must themselves be "open". We have already identified that the environment must be resilient to the introduction of new tools; it is equally true that the tools themselves should be resilient to changes in the environment architecture. This must include changes to the common information model, and changes to the communications and access mechanisms provided.

In addition to these "logical" requirements on point tools, there are commercial imperatives on the suppliers which will tend to drive in the same direction. Firstly the market for the tool will be severely restricted by being specifically tailored to one environment architecture, leading to a need to be resilient to differing architectures. Secondly the optimisation of information structures for specific functionality is, in a world of standardised User Interfaces, the major source of added value available to a tool vendor, leading to a need to be resilient to differing information models in use outside of the tool.

4.   Open Environment Architectures

From the above discussion we may identify, at a conceptual level at least, the components which should make up an "open systems" development environment, and the characteristic functionality which they should exhibit.

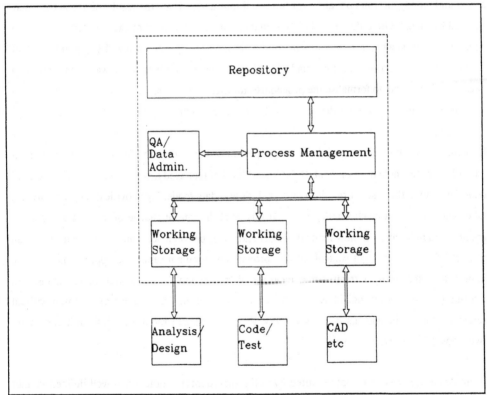

Figure 3   Logical Architecture for an Opens Systems environment

Figure 3 represents, in a simplified form the architecture discussed below. At the heart of the environment we identify a *Repository*. This component essentially localises the realisation of the requirements derived from the *construction* view of the environment. The role of the repository is to provide a stable base of shared information used, generated and modified by multiple parallel activities.

If we examine carefully the ways in which activities interact the characteristics which a repository system needs to have become clear. In order to make it possible to effectively manage the development of complex systems, a "divide and conquer" approach is normally taken. The total task is sub-divided hierarchically into less complex sub-tasks until a level of complexity that can be handled by a small number of people (typically less than 5) is achieved. In the nature of such a process, in which different parts or aspects of a design are being developed in parallel, the likelihood of conflicts arising between the assumptions made and the results produced by individual activities is high, and tight controls need to be exercised over the rights granted to individuals to access and modify information, and over the conditions under which the results of one activity may be used by others. Good design techniques enable the decomposition of the problem to result in components in which the potential for conflict is reduced by minimising the dependencies of decisions in one area on decisions made in others, however conflicts will always arise, and it is necessary, in general, to formalise the procedures for their resolution. Such resolution will normally involve considerations beyond the scope of the individual conflicting products.

If the problem is fully decomposed into single person activities then this allows tight management control over the whole development. If the lowest level of managed activity is performed by a small team (as is often the case for requirements analysis and data modelling activities) the same process takes place, but on a much smaller scale. At this level the rate of change of information is much greater, and there are generally many more dependencies between decisions. In order for the team to work effectively the tight controls of the "project" environment cannot be applied, but there is, nonetheless, the need to retain some measure of "protection" between individuals: changes to information used by an individual, for which he is not responsible, cannot be imposed without reference to that individuals ongoing activity, and conflicts still require analysis and agreement (with possible rework on all sides).

From this it becomes clear that the integrity of the shared information, whilst well-defined, cannot be enforced but must be maintained by procedures which cannot be wholly automated, involving as they do qualitative assessment of conflicting human decisions. Since many activities will involve the modification of existing products, part of the integrity of the shared model involves the knowledge of which collections of components are required to be consistent, and which may be allowed to be inconsistent (for example, when two components are both changed, it may be necessary for the original versions, and the revised versions, to be consistent with each other, but the revised version of one and the original version of the other may quite validly be inconsistent).

Thus we may characterise the "Repository" (which may, of course, be implemented as a collection of actual environment components)

- The Repository provides storage and access for persistent, potentially shared, design components, represented according to some common information model.

- The Repository should provide mechanisms for verifying (but not enforcing) the semantic integrity of well-defined collections of design components.

- The Repository is responsible for maintaining multiple versions of shared components, and the dependencies between them.

- The Repository is responsible for providing authorization and security mechanisms to control the access to, and modification of, shared information.

In conjunction with the Repository we may identify a function, variously called *Quality Assurance*, *Data Administration*, or *Integration*, responsible for performing or coordinating conflict resolution on proposed Repository changes. Whilst amenable to tool support, this is, as discussed above, an inherently non-automated function.

In this architecture the requirements of the *process* view are localised in a *Process Management* function, responsible for the allocation of resources to development activities and the authorization of access to and modification of the Repository. In small team environments, as discussed above, this is wholly informal, but will be more formalised, and may even be partially automated in larger, more complex developments.

The information in the Repository is generated and changed as a result of the decision processes undertaken during various development activities. Each update is typically a composite of changes to many shared components, which are only meaningful (in the sense of maintaining the semantic integrity of the model) when taken together. This collection of changes is the end result of a complex decision process, which may have led down many blind alleys, with much backtracking and many iterations. The individual decision steps are of no interest, only the resulting end state, when it comes to "publishing" the resulting decisions. We can view the management of the Repository as being transaction oriented, in the conventional DBMS sense. The decision processes that generate the update are supported by individual tools or families of tools, which are optimised to the particular task in hand. These toolsets, then, provide support for the *product* view of the environment.

Within a Repository transaction (that is, during the decision process which leads to an approved update) the supporting tool or tools require their own *working storage* areas. In these they may store and manipulate temporary information generated for support of the tool activity, and will store copies of those components of the shared information base (the Repository data) to which they require access. This use of copies of Repository information and the (at least logical) separation of the working storage from the Repository storage is essential

- to maintain the openness of the tools

  Allowing the Repository architecture and the overall environment architecture to evolve with minimal impact on the tools, and enabling the tools to be suitable for multiple environments.

- to allow optimisation of tool functionality

  The Repository architecture must be optimised for secure access to dependent information groups, and must support multiple versions of those groups. The specialised functions of individual tools may require, or may be better supported by, different storage architectures (semantic networks, attribute grammars etc) - certainly, for example, it is unlikely that the Repository architecture would be considered suitable for a compiler database.

- to isolate parallel activities

  The highly iterative nature of the individual design activities results in highly unstable information. If this instability is reflected in the transaction streams of the repository then firstly this instability may propagate through the development, with information changing at a rate greater than those using it can effectively assimilate, and secondly the Repository itself will be subject to unnecessarily (and possibly excessively) high transaction rates.

Typically the design activity (of generating a Repository update) will be supported by a family of cooperating tools, providing different aspects of the decision support. Clearly, the same requirements for tool openness apply for the individual component tools within such a family as apply in the overall environment.

5.   VSF Tools in the Open Systems Environment

We have described, above, the VSF approach to providing CASE tools that are capable of supporting essentially arbitrary specification techniques. The ability to achieve this, however, is not sufficient. If we characterise the CASE domain, relative to the above discussions, as providing decision support for analysis and design activities, there are many desirable facilities which VSF itself does not provide. In an Open Systems environment this is to be expected - individual vendors should not be expected to become expert in all areas, but overall objectives should be achieved through cooperation. VSF is specifically targeted towards supporting the evolution of semantically consistent design components, that is to ensure that any repository update is internally self-consistent, and has an appropriate level of completeness for the task in hand. Typical complementary functionality include dynamic analysis and simulation, and the so-called "lower CASE" technologies (compilation, debugging, source code analysis etc).

In order to make VSF-based tools "open" in the sense identified above, the "internal" configurability of VSF is extended to enable all of its interfaces to complementary tools also to be configurable. A diagram summarising this is shown in Figure 4.

a.   Data Integration

Within VSF there is no fundamental concept of a "composite" object, all information is managed at its most detailed semantic level; thus, for example, the existence of an "object", the existence of a value, and any association between them, are separately managed "facts". This level of detail is rarely, if ever appropriate for a Repository, where the stored information is generally grouped by dependencies, so that the values of "attributes" are deemed not to be meaningful apart from the "object(s)" with which they are associated, and a coarse-grained structure which can readily be version managed and accessed as a unit is stored.

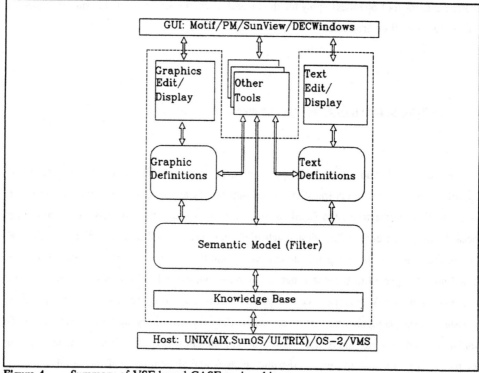

Figure 4   Summary of VSF-based CASE tool architecture

Within VSF such composite structures can be created as viewpoints of a design by means of the Viewpoint Definition Language. Any transformation of the concepts used within VSF to Repository structures may be achieved through inference or by means of the consequence mechanism, and for any Repository which has a textual syntax for representing updates a textual presentation of the view in that form may be generated. Such a view may be exported from VSF, either in the defined textual syntax or in a VSF-defined ASCII representation which may be directly re-loaded by VSF. In either case any associated graphical layout information may also be exported.

In a similar manner, where a complementary tool provides a well-defined input syntax, or import format, information required by that tool may generated in the necessary format from within VSF

Any transformation of the VSF model into a complementary model (used by a Repository or complementary tool) is reversible, and thus it is possible, in a similar manner, for objects extracted from a repository or information generated by a complementary tool to be imported into VSF[2]. A key requirement when accepting information generated from outside of VSF is that the integrity of the design should be maintained. For this reason the VSF import mechanisms provide full scope for consistency checking between imported components, to ensure that the import will result in a meaningful and consistent overall design (within the scope of that activity).

b.   Functional Integration

In addition to providing for data integration with other tools (including Repositories) VSF is able to take advantage of whatever standard communication and data access mechanisms provided by the environment.

- all of the export and import functions of VSF may have associated command scripts which are executed, as appropriate before or after the export or import is performed. These scripts, written in the host environment script language, are able to manipulate and/or analyse the VSF inputs/outputs and the context of their invocation, and perform any appropriate processing.

- any graphical or textual object type may have associated a number of *External Tool* scripts. These scripts, comprising host environment commands, interleaved with commands which perform functions within VSF (extraction of design data, update of the design), are able to manage sophisticated interactions between VSF and complementary tools, by enabling them to act as cooperating coroutines within the environment.

These mechanisms allow transparent access from within VSF to update or retrieve information in a repository, and allow VSF tools to transparently pass information to and receive information from complementary tools, in order to incorporate their results into the evolving design and/or use their results in support of design decisions.

---

[2]   Depending on the repository access mechanisms, it is sometimes necessary to post-process the Repository outputs prior to import.

6.   Conclusions

The objective of this discussion has been to show how CASE tools derived from VSF support the use of standard repository systems, and enhance an overall Open Systems approach to development environments.

We have seen that the sophisticated Conceptual Modelling facilities of VSF, and the separation of presentation from semantics allows integration with the meta-models used by other tools, and especially the standard Repository meta-models. In particular it means that a CASE tool may be designed and implemented in VSF without knowledge of the external meta-models with which it may potentially be required to integrate. Furthermore, such a tool may be built to incorporate data integration with a variety of different external models, allowing the same tool to be used in many environments; addition of new external models is straightforward and rapid, using the interactive prototyping capabilities of the VSF MWB.

In addition we have seen that access to standard Repositories and cooperation with complementary tools, once data integration has been achieved, may be provided transparently, without modification to the CASE tool itself, and may also be changed without modification to the tool.

An effective Open Systems approach to the development environment, in theory, allows an evolutionary approach to the adoption of automated support, and facilitates the exploitation of new technologies and ideas as they are developed. For this to be achieved CASE tools (indeed all of the component tools in the environment) must also be capable of supporting such evolution. The key to this lies in true separation of concerns and a clear identification of the roles and responsibilities of different components of the total environment. The practical use of VSF based tools demonstrates a means whereby CASE tools may be developed for an Open Systems framework, without limiting its openness.

Adding Control Integration to PCTE

Huw Oliver

Hewlett-Packard Laboratories

Bristol BS12 6QZ, England

e-mail: heo@hplb.hpl.hp.com

Abstract

The PCTE interfaces provide data-integration services. In a good Software Engineering Environment (SEE), however, more is needed: control integration to automatically start tools and share services. We report on our intermediate practical experience of adding control integration to PCTE. More precisely, we show how Broadcast Message Services can be layered on the PCTE platform thus forming a SEE framework that spans the tool integration dimensions.

Keywords: CASE, Software Engineering Environments, PCTE, Soft-Bench.

1   Introduction

The computer support environment provided for software engineering today typically consists of a set of standalone tools. These tools are monolithic. These tools do not usually cooperate. They cannot access each other's functionality. They have no access to each other's data (and would not be able to understand it if they could). Their user interfaces differ widely.

The tools are monolithic in that they provide many of the services more naturally provided by the framework within which they operate or by other tools. For instance, some document processing tools today offer version control even though it is also provided by configuration management tools. Such tools provide so much because the tool providers have no way of composing tools from small modular pieces.

We are interested in how the framework can provide different types of composition or integration services. These integrating services would help tools to be smaller, more modular and built into the support environment as needed by the software engineer.

A complete support environment for software engineering will be a large, complex system. Neither the high level of financial resources nor the wide range of expertise required to provide all the elements of a support environment will be found within a single organisation. The use of open standards for these elements is an essential enabling factor for the production of quality SEE implementations.

We have looked at two technologies which provide elements of a support environment and investigated how they might be combined. The technologies are SoftBench [2] [4] and PCTE [7] [8] [9].

SoftBench is a product of Hewlett-Packard. It consists of an integration framework and an integrated set of tools.

PCTE stands for "a basis for a Portable Common Tools Environment". PCTE defines an interface to support CASE tools and development environments. PCTE itself does not provide any tools: it is a framework on which to build and integrate tools. The development of the interface has culminated in the ECMA PCTE abstract specification [9] which the ECMA general assembly adopted as an ECMA standard in December 1990.

We have undertaken a prototyping activity to show how these components can be combined. The goals of our prototyping activity are to investigate how to construct a support environment, to learn how to use it and to examine the benefits of working with it. We are using an implementation of version 1.5 [7] of the PCTE interface in our prototyping activities. We report here our intermediate technical results from constructing the prototype SEE framework in the HP research laboratories.

2   Integration Services in an SEE Framework

The ECMA CASE environment framework reference model [1] identifies and defines integration services that a framework may provide to support a SEE, and groups related integration services together. Figure 1 shows the overall structure of the reference model (this is an conceptual architecture not an implementation architecture).

The reference model (RM) can be used to categorise the services offered by an SEE framework. Although the ECMA RM activity was spawned from the ECMA PCTE Standards committee, the RM is completely independent of PCTE. The RM can be used to position standards proposals and commercial products, and helps to understand the relationships between different framework offerings.

This section quickly sketches the services required of an SEE framework in terms of those detailed in the RM.

The RM identifies three main aspects of tool integration:

- Data Integration (addressed by the data repository plus data integration services) is the sharing of data and descriptions of that data (schemas) between the users and tools of the support environment.

- Control Integration (addressed by the task management plus the message services) is the management of cooperation between independently developed tools to achieve a coordinated effect.

- User Interface Integration (addressed by the user interface services) is a common look and feel for tools.

2.1   Data Integration

The maintenance, management, and naming of data entities or objects and the relationships among them is the general purpose of the data repository services.

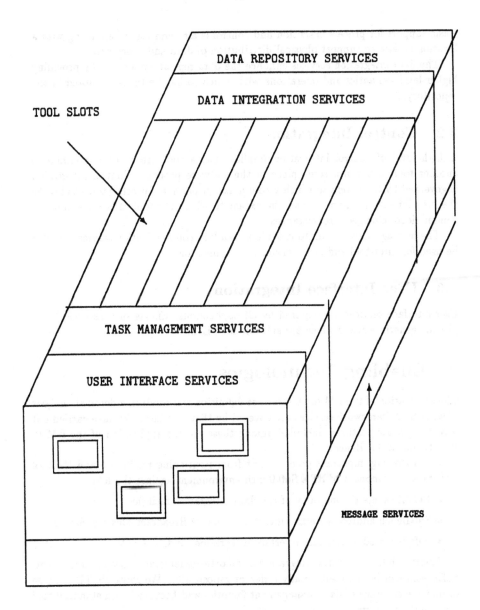

Figure 1: Reference Model Structure

Basic support for process execution and control is also addressed here along with a location service to support physical distribution of data and processes.

The data integration services enhance the data repository services by providing higher-level semantics and operations with which to handle the data stored in the repository.

2.2   Control Integration

A high level of control integration implies that a tool can invoke or stimulate another tool to perform some piece of the software process. Control integration is governed by the extent to which a tool makes it possible for other tools to invoke the functionality it provides, and the extent to which the tool calls other tools to communicate changed circumstances.

The message services aim to provide a standard communication service that can be used for inter-tool and inter-service communication.

2.3   User Interface Integration

User interface services are required by all applications. Efforts such as OSF/Motif provide generic services which are suitable for SEEs.

3   Enabling Technologies

The application of the RM to an interface definition will result in a detailed analysis of what SEE framework services are covered by that interface. We have carried out several such applications. Included among these are the application of the RM to PCTE and to SoftBench.

The following important points result from positioning PCTE 1.5 and the tool integration component of HP's SoftBench environment against the RM:

- PCTE covers the majority of the data integration facilities;
- SoftBench addresses control integration via its Broadcast Message Server.
- SoftBench addresses user interface integration via OSF/Motif.

SoftBench treats control integration as an orthogonal issue to data management. SoftBench can be used with many different repositories. We chose PCTE because of its wide coverage of data management facilities and because it is a standard tool portability platform.

From the point of view of integration technology, SoftBench and PCTE are complementary and add value to one another. This analysis encouraged us to investigate the combination of the SoftBench and PCTE integration technologies in practice. We next give an overview of each of SoftBench and PCTE and then describe our approach to combining them.

3.1   SoftBench

The SoftBench environment consists of a set of integration services and an extensible set of tools that communicate by sending and receiving messages. From the point of view of an environment builder, SoftBench consists of the Broadcast Message Server(BMS), the Execution Manager (EM), the user interface, support for distribution, the set of tools and the Encapsulator. The BMS and the Execution Manager are described in further detail by Cagan [2]. Further information about SoftBench tools can be found in Gerety's description [4].

3.1.1 SoftBench Integration Services

1. SoftBench's Broadcast Message Server (BMS) enables executing SoftBench tools to cooperate in supporting a software engineer to carry out tasks. Executing tools in SoftBench send a message to the BMS when they: require a service; have performed an action that may be of importance to others; or have a failure to report. The BMS forwards this message to all the executing tools that have registered interest in a "message-pattern" that the message matches (so the message 'broadcast' is in fact selective). Messages can be sent to the BMS by tools so they can register and unregister interest in patterns.

2. The Execution Manager (EM) in SoftBench keeps track of the tools that are executing. The execution manager cooperates closely with the BMS so that when a request message is received by the BMS, the EM determines whether a new tool should be started to service that request or whether the request can be satisfactorally handled by a tool that is already running. SoftBench tools are grouped into classes. Differing criteria can be applied for differing classes of tools. A class is a set of tools that provide equivalent services. Example tool classes are EDIT, COMPILE, or DEBUG.

3. All SoftBench tools have a common look and feel which conforms to the OSF/Motif [3] standard.

4. SoftBench is designed to operate over a distributed network of workstations, and offers distributed computing support of three kinds. Firstly, SoftBench can start tools and support transparent communications between tools executing on remots hosts. Secondly, SoftBench tools are built on the network transparent X Window System which means that programs can run on one system and display visually on another. Thirdly, SoftBench supports access to remote data.

3.1.2 SoftBench Tools

The initial set of tools delivered with the SoftBench product concentrates on support for developing, versioning, and debugging C and C++ programs. An increasing number of Encapsulated tools are available to extend the core environment, for example tools for configuration management, documentation, structured analysis and structured design, and testing.

Some fundamental SoftBench tools of particular relevance to our work to date are the Tool Manager, the Message Monitor and the Development Manager.

- The Tool Manager presents a way for a user to directly invoke tools. While this is useful at the start of a work session the user will later take advantage of the BMS and EM support for control integration. The user will normally be working within a particular tool (such as a debugger) and will be accessing the functionality of other tools from within that tool.

- The Message Monitor displays all messages that get sent in the environment.

- The Development Manager offers a view of the underlying file system, including an indication of the type of information held within the file (e.g. C source or build information). It also presents a set of operations available on those files (such as versioning). The set of operations made available dynamically matches the type of the file (e.g. it is not possible to even try to check-out a non-versioned file).

We see in section 4.2.3 how we have modified these tools to run on a combined SoftBench and PCTE framework.

The user sees tools working synchronously because cooperation between tools can be specified and the SoftBench system supports the execution of that cooperation. For example, should the user change the source code of a program while working in the static analysis tool, notification of those changes are automatically forwarded to any editor working on the source file for that code. The SoftBench user is also presented with seamless functionality (synergy) in that the services provided by one tool appear (to the user) to be available from several other tools also. For example, code can be recompiled through a user request to the debugger (which is automatically forwarded to the build tool via the BMS). The real benefit of SoftBench to a software developer is that it makes available these advantages of well-presented control integration.

SoftBench provides a further tool called the Encapsulator. This tool enables existing tools to be integrated into the SoftBench support environment without source code modification. It enables a wrapper to be developed for a tool so that its input and output is monitored. Suitable SoftBench messages can then be sent and acted upon by the encapsulated tool, and a SoftBench user interface can be developed so that the tool looks as well as behaves like a true SoftBench citizen (although this holds for a particular set of tools: those that can use standard input/standard output and that can be decoupled from any bitmapped screen handling they do).

3.2 PCTE Integration Services

A major contribution of PCTE is its Object Management System (OMS), designed to meet the data integration needs of CASE tools. The OMS provides the ability to model relationships between data objects, by supporting a variant of the entity-relationship-attribute data model. Object management facilities include typing, schemas and transactions to support data structuring and data sharing, and to maintain data integrity.

PCTE provides a complete interface for the tool writer, including process management and inter-process communication. PCTE provides synchronous and asynchronous calling of processes on local or remote hosts. The services provided are at a higher level of abstraction than those typically provided by the operating system. PCTE inter-process communication services are provided via the PCTE message queue. These services are closely modelled on the X/Open System V

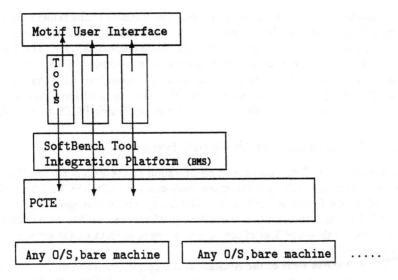

Figure 2: Prototype Architecture

UNIX[1] interfaces. These services are also at a higher level of abstraction than, say, socket based communication primitives.

The hardware architecture for a PCTE system is a network of bitmapped workstations connected by a high speed reliable LAN. PCTE is a distributed architecture, and all the object management and process management facilities are transparently distributed.

4 Prototyping Experience

In this section, we report on our intermediate results from building a prototype SEE framework.

4.1 Architecture

The architecture of the prototype is shown in figure 2. Because PCTE provides a complete interface for the tool writer and because the BMS control integration serives are at a higher level than the PCTE facilities, we have re-implemented the BMS on top of PCTE.

Each of the boxes shows one of the existing components from which we constructed the prototype. The arrows from the tools show which services were accessed by the tools. Thus the tools are linked in with and make calls to:

1. the Motif X Window libraries;

2. the BMS component of the SoftBench libraries;

3. the PCTE libraries.

---
[1]UNIX is a registered trademark of UNIX System Laboratories Inc.

It can be seen from the architecture that the SoftBench Tool Integration Platform only provides the BMS services. We are investigating extending this so that tools only access the PCTE services through this intermediate layer. This has the advantages of protecting the system from changes in successive PCTE versions and minimising the task of providing data integration in some way other than through the PCTE object base. It would also mean that existing SoftBench tools could be ported with a minimum of effort to the combined SoftBench/PCTE framework.

4.2 Description of the prototype

We are using the GIE Emeraude implementation of the PCTE 1.5 specifications known as Emeraude v12. It is a complete implementation of the PCTE 1.5 interfaces with additional Common Services (e.g. Metabase, Version Management).

PCTE's claim to provide a portability platform was verified by us when we ported several thousand lines of source code between workstations of different hardware from different manufacturers.

Figure 3 shows some of the elements of the prototype. The top box represents the BMS; the boxes in the second row represent class managers; the boxes in the bottom row represent instances of tools. All communication is via the BMS. We now describe these elements in more detail.

4.2.1 The BMS

The BMS runs as an PCTE process. The BMS communicates with all the tools through the PCTE inter-process communication mechanism of message queues. These replace the socket connections in the SoftBench BMS.

The BMS has an associated message queue whose whereabouts in the object base must be known by all tools. The message queue's location was (arbitrarily) chosen to be linked to the static context of the BMS (static context is the PCTE term for 'program'). Essentially the BMS maintains a 'pattern map' which is a map from tool identifiers to the set of message-patterns in which those tools have registered interest. It continuously reads from its message queue, suspending execution until a message arrives. The message will be forwarded to any interested tools or may cause the pattern map to be updated.

4.2.2 The Class Managers

Every tool belongs to a class. Each class defines the functionality which tools of that class will provide to other tools. This functionality is accessed by sending request messages to the tool. There is a class manager for each class. The class manager maintains a list of the running tools of its class and carries knowledge of whether there is a tool able to service any given request or whether a new tool needs to be started.

Each class manager runs as a PCTE process. They each have an associated message queue linked to their static context. Each class manager continuously reads from its message queue, suspending execution until a message arrives. Any request message will be forwarded to whichever tool is able to service it. All class managers are very similar except for the knowledge about when new tools should

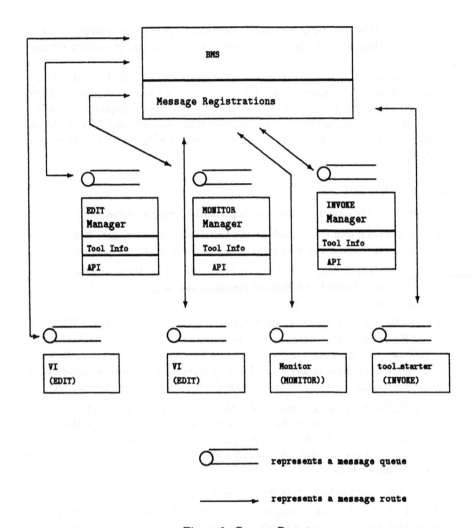

Figure 3: Current Prototype

be started up. This knowledge is more complicated in PCTE where objects do not have unique pathnames and where the context of a tool includes the working schema of that tool.

The amalgamation of all the class managers corresponds to the Execution Manager in SoftBench. By separating out the class manager processes we were able to make the decisions about whether to start new tools to handle requests specific to the class of the tool. In SoftBench the Execution Manager used the UNIX execution primitives. In our prototype these have been replaced with the PCTE execution primitives.

4.2.3 Tools

A number of simple tools have been put together for this prototype:

- The *INVOKE* tool corresponds to the SoftBench Tool Manager. It allows the user to select, start and stop tools of any of the available tool classes.

- The *MONITOR* tool corresponds to the SoftBench Message Monitor. It registers an interest in all kinds of messages and displays them. It provides a window onto the BMS activities.

- The *DM* tool corresponds to the SoftBench Development Manager. While the SoftBench development manager gives an interface to the UNIX file system, the DM tool gives a similar interface to the PCTE object base. This enables us to navigate around the object base. The tool includes some version management facilities using the common services provided with the Emeraude product.

- the DMGRAPH tool is a graphical interface tool to the PCTE object base. It navigates the object base via mouse selection of objects, displays the object graph to a user chosen depth, reorientates and manipulates the graphical representation and dynamically manipulates working schemas to provide views on the object base.

- The *EDIT* tool is for editing the contents of objects.

Each tool, like the class managers, runs as a PCTE process. They each have an associated message queue linked to their static context. Each tool continuously reads from its message queue (not suspending execution) until a message arrives. Any request message will be serviced in a tool specific way.

4.2.4 Additional PCTE features of interest

A PCTE installation will typically be distributed over a set of workstations connected by a local area network. The transparent distribution facilities provided by PCTE meant that we did not have to concern ourselves with distribution when designing the prototype. We believe that the SoftBench distribution facilities can be provided on top of PCTE with the added advantage of location transparent access to data.

ECMA PCTE implementations will provide more services than PCTE 1.5. One such service is the ability to respond to events such as access to particular objects in the object base. Adding such services to our existing control integrations services are of much interest and will provide further research directions.

We have not used the PCTE support for concurrency and integrity control and activities. We have not heavily used the schema management facilities.

5 Summary of What We have Learnt

Several points came out of our construction work with respect to PCTE:

- we found the PCTE interface useful in building the BMS and the prototype tools. It provided all the facilities we needed and many of the services were at a higher level than that provided by the operating system.

- PCTE is an effective portability platform;

- we found object identification somewhat confusing, having to switch between pathnames, internal references, external references and volume number, object number pairs. A clear notion of object surrogate would have simplified our task.

- documentation is needed to guide the tool writer through the many design decisions he needs to make. This should include a guide for data integration (how to use the schemas provided and how to write new ones, etc.), and a guide for control integration (how to use the interfaces exported by existing tools and what new message interface a tool should provide, etc.) ;

- a clear and well documented migration path from existing toolsets will be needed;

- The distribution facilities provided by PCTE meant that we did not have to concern ourselves with distribution issues when designing the prototype.

There are many software architecture decisions which should be made by tool writers even if PCTE is not used as the basis for the support environment (such as the production of appropriate schemas and the use of integrating service libraries which hide the underlying technology). These are generally good engineering practices but will protect investment in tools and will ease the transition to PCTE.

The prototyping work at HP Laboratories has proven the feasibility of adding a BMS to PCTE. We are starting a new prototyping phase to experiment with rehosting the SoftBench environment on PCTE.

References

[1] A. Earl. A Reference Model for Computer Assisted Software Engineering Environment Frameworks. Technical Report ECMA/TR/90/55, ECMA, 17 August 1990.

[2] M. R. Cagan. The HP SoftBench Environment: An Architecture for a New Generation of Software Tools. *Hewlett-Packard Journal*, 41(3):36–47, June 1990.

[3] A. O. Deininger and C. V. Fernandez. Making Computer Behaviour Consistent: The OSF/Motif Graphical User Interface. *Hewlett-Packard Journal*, 41(3):6–26, June 1990.

80

[4] C. Gerety. A New Generation of Software Development Tools. *Hewlett-Packard Journal*, 41(3):48–58, June 1990.

[5] F.Gallo G.Boudier and I.Thomas. Overview of PCTE and PCTE+. *ACM SIGPLAN Notices*, 24(2), February 1989.

[6] I.Thomas. PCTE Interfaces: Supporting Tools in Software Engineering Environments. *IEEE Software*, November 1989.

[7] Brussels Commission of the European Communities. PCTE Functional Specifications, Version 1.5, November 1988.

[8] Software Sciences Ltd. GIE Emeraude, Selenia Industrie Elettroniche Associate. PCTE+ Functional Specification, Issue 3, October 1988.

[9] Portable Common Tool Environment - Abstract Specification. Technical Report ECMA Standard 149, ECMA, Geneva, December 1990.

META-CASE TECHNOLOGY

Albert Alderson
IPSYS Software plc
Marlborough Court, Pickford St.,
Macclesfield, Cheshire, SK11 6JD, UK

1. Introduction

Meta-CASE tools are used to generate CASE tools. Meta-CASE tools have been available
for some applications for some time. Examples are compiler-compilers and Third and
Fourth Generation Language systems. Meta-CASE technology is now emerging that can
generate CASE tools which support software development methods. This technology is
capable of producing methods toolsets in time scales which are very short in comparison to
conventional development time scales.

In this paper the motivation for the development of this technology is discussed. The paper
then considers its conceptual basis and describes the ToolBuilder technology developed by
IPSYS Software.

2. Motivation

In a recent report from Butler Cox [1] the results of a survey of 600 projects were
presented. This survey found productivity lowered by 15% and error rates increased by
40% from the average for those projects using software development methods. To explain
this depressing fact, we must look at the place of methods in the software development life
cycle.

A software development life cycle is the process by which systems are conceived,
designed, implemented, maintained and decommissioned. The process contains all of the
necessary activities for software development. It describes how the development is
managed and gives the context in which all work is done. A method defines how to under-
take one or more activities of the software development life cycle and defines the inputs
and outputs of those activities. A method models part of the life cycle.

System development life cycles are usually discussed in terms of the conventional development "waterfall" model or the prototyping development "spiral" model. It is necessary to
recognise that these are just models. They do not represent actual software development
life cycles. They are not standards. Every organisation undertaking system development has
its own unique software development life cycle. This reflects the structure of the organisation, its management style, the relative importance it attaches to quality, timeliness, cost

and benefit, its experience and its general ability levels and many other factors. There cannot be and should not be any standard life cycle, because the uniqueness of organisations is the lifeblood of our competitive commercial system that drives continual improvement. These ideas are discussed at length in a report by Rock-Evans [2].

This of course is a source of great difficulty for method developers. A method models some part of a software development life cycle, but which should be modelled if there is no standard. Method developers have solved this by defining their method to fit some particular life cycle, usually their own. In the cases where the method fits the its user's software development life cycle productivity improves, otherwise it falls.

The ideal solution is to tailor the methods to their user's software development life cycle. But without the automation provided by CASE tools most methods are unattractive, and unfortunately the technology generally used to create the CASE tools does not permit such tailoring. Of course such a challenge and opportunity drives advances and the result is the methods meta-CASE technologies.

3. The Conceptual Basis of Meta-CASE

The intent of meta-CASE tools is to capture the specification of the required CASE tool and then generate the tool from the specification. Compiler-compiler systems, and Third and Fourth Generation Language systems are examples of meta-CASE technology. Compiler-compiler systems have been available for many years. Given a language syntax these will generate tables for the lexical and syntax analysis parts of a compiler. These tables parameterise a generic compiler to create a compiler for the specific language. The language syntax is described to the compiler-compiler using a meta-language. Third and Fourth Generation Language systems (3GLs and 4GLs) enable a user to specify a business application using the provided language or by updating the equivalent data model. The language system then generates parameterisations of a generic application composed of a matching teleprocessing monitor, database and forms manager. The challenge is to achieve equivalent results for methods tools.

A compiler is just one example of a tool that converts statements in a language into a data structure from which desired results can be derived. There is a duality between languages and data structures. The language syntax defines which data structures are legal for that language. The language semantics define the legal relationships between values of elements in the data structure. Equally a class of data structures can be represented by a language. These ideas allow us to think about methods tools in the following way.

A method is a number of inter-related techniques and notations for constructing a complex self-consistent information product. A method then may be based upon a data structure which embodies the concepts of the method. The user of the method enters values into the data structure to describe the system under development. The user enters these values by making statements using the notations (the languages) which the method provides. The correctness of those statements is checked according to language semantics defining the method. The results are generated as reports about the values held in the data structure.

At its very simplest we can see that we could use compiler-compiler technology plus report writing technology to generate a text based meta-CASE system. The input to the meta-

CASE system would be the notation and report definitions. However although this gives proof of concept it would not generate very attractive method tools. That requires good interactive data collection through diagrams, forms, text and so on. The most distinctive and attractive feature of methods are the diagrammatic notations that they use. Diagrams give a concise and accessible means of describing a system. However the problems of producing and maintaining these diagrams by hand are a great disincentive to their use. On-line diagram production and maintenance is an important feature of methods tools.

4. Meta-CASE for Methods Toolsets

The key breakthrough in meta-CASE for methods was the development of generic diagram editors. It was recognised that the diagrams used in methods generally take the form of a directed network of nodes and links which can be labelled with values and annotated with comments. Such networks can be represented by a very simple data model in which the nodes are entities, the links are relationships and the labels are attributes. Different kinds of diagrams are represented by different types of entities and relationships with their appropriate attributes. Extensions to the basic model are required for more complex diagram types, but a very wide range of diagram types can still be encompassed in a simple model.

The symbols and line styles used in a diagram are recognised as the lexis of a graphically based language. The legal uses of the symbols are the syntax and the legal relationships between nodes, links and the values of labels are the semantics. We can define a language in which to describe diagram types. The language is equivalent to the meta-language of a compiler-compiler. However rather than generate a compiler, we want to have the graphical equivalent of a syntax-directed editor. This has been achieved by constructing generic graphical editors which are parameterised by tables defining the symbols, line-styles, node, link and attribute types, and legal interconnections. The semantics are provided as functions. A number of such generic diagram editing systems have been built and used successfully. A detailed discussion appears in a series of papers by Beer, Welland and Sommerville [3, 4, 5].

Generic editing systems for forms, for structured text, for matrices and so on, have also been created. All can be created on the same general principles as the graphical editors.

The general form of a methods meta-CASE system can be seen as a specification capture tool which generates the parameters of a generic methods tool. To capture the specification of a method we must capture its underlying data model. The languages of the diagrams and other input types must be captured, as must the structure of the desired outputs of the method. From these inputs a meta-CASE tool can generate the data definition statements for any database used to hold the methods data structure, and the tables and functions required to drive the generic editors and output generations. The separation of the generation tool and the generic elements parameterised by its outputs allows concerns such as multi-user access, portability of the generated CASE tools, performance and other end-user issues to be dealt with independently of the method definition.

5. The ToolBuilder Technology

IPSYS have been creating a methods meta-CASE tool called ToolBuilder during the last 9 months. ToolBuilder is of the general form described in the previous section, having a method specification capture component (METHS), and a generic methods component (DEASEL) whose parameters are generated by METHS. This technology is based on the IPSYS Tool-Builder's Kit, TBK [6]. It is relevant to give a brief overview of TBK so that the construction of ToolBuilder may be explained.

5.1. The Tool-Builder's Kit (TBK)

TBK is an integrated collection of generic tools and function libraries aimed at solving the problem of building quality CASE toolsets quickly. It addresses issues of integration, compatibility with existing tools, portability across operating systems and hardware platforms, and openness to extension. TBK is formed as a series of layers of software, each addressing one of these concerns. Of relevance here are the Integration layer, which provides a database interface and a user interface management system, and the Generic Function layer, which provides generic diagram editing, generic structured text editing, generic plain text editing, and generic function interpretation. The Generic Function Layer is constructed using the Integration Layer.

The database of TBK has two-tiers. The first tier is at the level of directories and files and represents the coarse grain of data. The second tier is at the level of the contents of files and represents the fine grain of data. The database has a unified data model in which both the first and second tiers of data are represented. A Data Definition Language (DDL) is provided to define schemas. DDL allows definition of entity types with their attributes and relationships in both tiers of the database and includes relationships between entities at different tiers of data.

The database recognises two kinds of relationship, composition and reference, which may be single or multiple valued. As in PCTE [7], an entity only exists while it is the destination of a composition relationship. Reference relationships show how data is cross-referenced.

The Database Interface is based upon the functional model of data. Here, attributes and references are understood as functions of entity types. Data is accessed by functions or by functional expressions which use a notation highlighting that path names may be regarded as functional compositions. Functional compositions represent derived attributes.

The user interface management system, which is based upon OSF/Motif [8], provides a program interface by which an application may present information to a user and obtain input. The interaction style and layout are described by means of the Format Description Language (FDL) [9] which is interpreted by the user interface management system. FDL associates actions with the creation and the selection of each window, menu, button, and so on. These may be actions to make visible or invisible other interaction objects, to set the values of other interaction objects, to execute the actions of other interaction objects, to validate the input value, and so on.

EASEL is a simple, interpreted language for accessing various TBK interfaces. It has a particular affinity to the database using the same types. EASEL has a sub-language which is particularly suitable for defining the structure of reports. Many of the components of TBK have the EASEL interpreter built into them so that their functionality can be enhanced with ease.

The Design Editor is a generic diagram editor that can be parameterised by definitions of the graphical representations and the syntax of the diagrams of a particular method. The definitions are supplied as a script in the Graph Description Language (GDL) which is based on the premise that a design diagram is a directed graph which can be represented by nodes and links, which are both labelled. These represent the entities, relationships and attributes of the underlying data model upon which the method is based. The diagram editor displays these nodes and links as the symbols and lines of the method's diagrammatic notations. The Design Editor provides basic drawing operations which may be enhanced by functions written in EASEL. The Design Editor may be used in off-line mode to generate PostScript representations of diagrams.

The Structure Editor is a generic tool for displaying and editing structured textual representations. The user is offered a textual representation of the data that reflects the underlying data structure. The Structure Editor is parameterised by a layout written in Layout Language (LL). The layout defines the textual representation of the data structure, and the choices to be offered to the end-user when manipulating it. The Structure Editor provides basic display and editing operations which may be enhanced by functions written in EASEL. The Structure Editor may be used in off-line mode to generate text representations in file store, providing a flexible output generator.

5.2. The Generic Methods Component DEASEL

The DEASEL component of ToolBuilder presents the user of a method with diagram and structured text input capabilities for capturing the software definition according to the rules of the method. DEASEL can also be commanded by the user to generate the particular outputs of the method.

DEASEL is a single tool created from the TBK's Design Editor, Structure Editor, EASEL interpreter, and the database and user interface components. DEASEL presents two windows. In one, the Design Editor is used to present and capture information using the various diagrammatic notations of the method. In the other, the Structure Editor is used to capture textual information. The user selects a diagram or text frame by navigation between frames. Navigation is a hyper-text like operation consisting of selecting some entity which is on display and then choosing a diagram or structured text view of that entity. The required frame is displayed in the Design Editor or Structure Editor window.

The output generation aspect of DEASEL uses the Design Editor and Structure Editor off-line generation facilities in a framework provided by the report structure sub-language of EASEL.

DEASEL incorporates a multi-user access mechanism that allows concurrent access of a database.

5.3. The Methods Specification Component METHS

ToolBuilder models a method by a data structure into which users enter data about the software they are specifying or designing using the method. The data is viewed and edited through various diagram or structured text views. The outputs of the method are generated as reports on the values from the data structure. The methods specification component of ToolBuilder (METHS) therefore needs to capture five aspects of the method:

- the data model upon which data capture and output generation is based;
- the frame model upon which the views are based,
- the diagrammatic notation for each diagram frame;
- the textual presentation for each structured text frame;
- the structure of each report.

Since METHS is generating parameterisations of the DEASEL tool, and since DEASEL relies upon TBK components variously parameterised by DDL, FDL, EASEL, GDL and LL, the inputs to METHS are influenced by these languages.

5.3.1. The Data Model

The data model defines the collection of attribute types, entity types, relationships (both composition and reference) between entity types, and attributes applied to entity types. Entity types form a type hierarchy in which sub-types inherit attributes applied to their parent type, and so on transitively.

Reference relationships support the notion of the scope of the relationship. Relationships may be constrained not just by the types of the source and destination entities but by other relationships that the source and destination entities bear to each other. For example, relationships may be constrained to exist only between siblings. The scope of a relationship specifies such instance orientated constraints.

The data model supports derived relationships defined by aggregation, recursion or path specification over other relationships. Aggregation defines a derived multiple valued relationship as the collection of the values of a group of other single or multiple valued relationships. Aggregated relationships simplify functions in which a number of relationships must be treated in a uniform manner, or in which only one relationship may be selected from a group. Recursion defines a derived relationship by a recursive function over another relationship. For example, ultimate ancestor may be defined recursively over the parent relationship. A path derived relationship is defined as a composition of a sequence of relationships which may include recursive derived relationships. Each relationship contributing to a derived relationship may have a selection condition applied to it; only the selected values contribute to values of the derived relationship.

The data model supports derived attributes defined on other attributes by computation and/or path specification. A derived attribute could have a different type from the attribute on which it is based. A derived attribute and the attribute upon which it is based both relate to the same stored data value.

The data model is active in that triggers can be associated with events applying to attributes and relationships.

Triggers may be specified to be invoked whenever data changes. Each trigger is specified by a reference to the data of interest, the event, and the EASEL function to be invoked on occurrence of such an event. For a relationship, the event may be **creation**, **modification**, or **deletion**. For an attribute only **modification** is recognised.

A further event **on_creation** is recognised to allow an entity to be initialised on its initial creation.

Attribute types have the events **show**, **edit**, **validate** and **update** associated with them.. The **show** trigger allows a value to be manipulated prior to display to the user. This permits derived values to be displayed, for example, age rather than date of creation. The **edit** trigger allows a value to be manipulated prior to being presented for editing. So it is possible to present a mnemonic form rather than a full form. The **validate** trigger allows checking of the validity of a value that has been edited as a precondition to updating the database. The **update** trigger changes the database according to an edited value, for example, to convert a mnemonic value into full form. If a trigger is not specified for an event then a default appropriate to the attribute type is provided.

This association of actions with attribute types is important in reducing the amount of specification required to define the model of a method, since the functions involved apply to all attributes of that type.

An attribute may be specified as read-only, preventing direct changes through the editors. Changes can only be achieved as the side-effect of method-specific actions.

The data model is used to generate DDL and EASEL scripts for use by the DEASEL tool.

5.3.2. The Frame Model

The frame model relates to the user view of the underlying data model. Frames are structured collections of either graphical objects or text objects. These items are objects in the sense that they have an image on the screen, as either symbols or characters, and have actions associated with them. There is a default set of actions provided by DEASEL, but these may be overridden or extended by specifications supplied in the frame model. These actions are used to implement functions such as cut-and-paste, diagram tidying, checking of the view rather than validation of an individual value, and so on.

Some actions are navigations which enable the user to select particular views of particular objects. Given a view on display, the user may choose an object and then select any navigation action which that object has. As a result of the action the required view (diagram or structured text) will replace the previous (diagram or structured text) view on display. Navigations from diagram to diagram, diagram to text, text to diagram and text to text are all supported. Navigation is definable along any single valued relationship (usually a derived relationship).

Each frame may have further associated actions. Generally the list of such actions is presented for the user to make a selection. However the frame model includes the concept of a root frame whose actions are automatically invoked when DEASEL is invoked. No more than one initial navigation to a diagram frame and one to a structured text frame must be capable of invocation. When DEASEL is invoked this frame determines the initial presentation of information to the user. This mechanism can be used to provide context retention across invocations of DEASEL.

Any actions associated with the frame model or the data model which update data, cause the effects of such updates to be shown immediately in any frame which is on display.

The frame model is used to generate FDL, GDL, LL and EASEL scripts for use by the DEASEL tool.

5.3.3. Diagrammatic Presentation

The diagrammatic presentation specifies the shapes of symbols which represent nodes and the styles of lines which represent links in the diagrammatic notations of the method. A set of basic shapes is provided from which more complex sub-shapes may be defined. These sub-shapes may be combined, together with further basic shapes, to create the required symbols and link styles. METHS provides a diagram frame, the Shapes Editor, in which these shapes may be constructed.

Diagrammatic presentation is not limited to conventional diagrams. It has also been used for the presentation and editing of matrices, tables and maps.

The diagrammatic presentation is used to generate GDL scripts for use by the DEASEL tool.

5.3.4. Structured Text Presentation

The structured text presentation defines the concrete syntax of text objects. Capabilities exist to embed values extracted from the data structure within constant text and to generate punctuation. The embedded values are effectively text fields whose formatting (for example, right, left or centre aligned) may be specified.

Structured text presentation is able to handle table display and editing.

The structured text presentation is used to generate LL scripts for use by the DEASEL tool.

5.3.5. Output Definition

Outputs from a method need to cover reports generated for users of the method and inputs to further stages of the life cycle. These requirements place a need for great flexibility on the output generator. ToolBuilder output generation is character orientated. Reports with embedded diagrams are produced by generating PostScript [10]. Usually CASE tools accept text inputs (with the appropriate syntax) so generating inputs to further stages of the life cycle presents no general difficulties.

Customisation of generated outputs takes place at four levels. Each of these levels may be addressed independently.

First there is control over the sources of information for outputs. It is possible to gather information into a generated output from a variety of sources. For example, text from tools other than DEASEL may need to be included in an output, interspersed with information generated from different parts of the method database. At this level, the output generator may be seen as providing a crude form of integration.

Second there is control over the structure of generated outputs. Outputs are generated by executing scripts which navigate around the database, generating textual information themselves, or calling upon the Design Editor or Structure Editor, in off-line mode, to produce particular representations of the data. In order to make these scripts simple to maintain, they are generated from an appropriate high-level template language.

Third is control over the logical appearance of outputs. Output templates do not explicitly determine output appearance, since this would greatly increase their complexity whilst at the same time reducing their reusability. Instead, tagged output is generated so that the appearance is determined until run time.

Fourth is control over the physical appearance of outputs. This layer may process the tags directly to generate the final output or it may map the tags in the output onto those used by a publishing system's markup language, so that a variety of publishing systems may be supported.

5.4. Implementation of the METHS Component

The first prototype of METHS was created using elements from TBK. This has developed through seven versions to the point where METHS is now capable of specifying itself. (Again, this is a general meta-CASE property that the specification component is specifiable by itself. Compiler-compilers, 3GLs and 4GLs are often implemented using such bootstrapping techniques.) The ToolBuilder approach can be seen as a method of creating methods tools. This method has been specified using METHS and the appropriate parameterisations generated for the DEASEL component. METHS therefore is an instance of a DEASEL tool whose parameters have been generated using METHS.

This implementation greatly increases our ability to maintain and enhance the ToolBuilder approach. For example, it is intended to extend DEASEL to use the on-line help facility of TBK. This help facility enables navigation between frames of help text providing a hypertext like browsing capability. The help texts will be captured through METHS as part of the method specification. The appropriate version of METHS can be created by amending the current METHS specification and generating the new parameterisations for DEASEL.

6. Summary

Methods meta-CASE technology gives a new impetus to the use of CASE. It gives system developers opportunities to obtain the methods they want, to fit with their unique software development life cycle.

The first opportunity is to develop a tool supporting an existing method which has different facilities to existing tools for that method. This may be necessary where existing tools cannot (or will not) be extended by their developers.

The second opportunity is to amend and extend existing methods to obtain a better fit with their life cycle.

The third opportunity is to create entirely new methods to meet specialised needs. This can be a very attractive route for system developers with unusual requirements. For example, the UK Civil Aviation Authority is using the ToolBuilder technology to build a toolset for the SCAD method [11], specifically defined for maintaining and developing the UK's air traffic control system. This encompasses logical software and hardware system structure, physical hardware interconnection, and physical hardware location. It should be emphasised that the definition of a new method can be a complex undertaking, but meta-CASE technology can be used as a prototyping capability which reduces the cost and risk of such developments.

The fourth opportunity is to implement integrated sequences of methods to cover a number of phases of the life cycle in one toolset.

The strong emphasis on the data model of the method, together with generic output generation, allows a great variety of new outputs to be obtained from a method. A particular possibility is to generate inputs for existing CASE tools so enhancing integration. This includes the possibility of generating statements for different programming languages, 3GLs, 4GLs and database systems.

Experience of tool development with ToolBuilder has been very encouraging. ToolBuilder and the IPSYS SSADM tool began development in parallel. In a six month period DEASEL and METHS were developed, METHS was re-implemented using METHS, a demonstration tool for SSADM version 3 [12] was developed and a production tool for SSADM version 4 [13] commenced. SSADM version 4 is a very large method with around 100 frames which have complex data inter-relationships. The production tool will require about 2 man years of development. The SCAD method requires 20 simple frames. A prototype was developed in two weeks and the production tool will take about 9 man months. A prototype for the Information Engineering method [14] of 15 frames was developed in 2 weeks by external consultants with no previous knowledge of the ToolBuilder technology. Even the simple frames of the SCAD method represent a significant effort if they are hand-coded, so the ToolBuilder effort figures represent valuable productivity gains.

The power of this technology is not limited to methods. ToolBuilder has been used to prototype a change management system and a process modelling management system, as well as being used to implement itself.

However we should be aware that the meta-CASE tool itself is based upon a model and is limited by the concepts in that model. A meta-CASE tool is also limited by the facilities of the generic components which it uses to create the generated methods tool. For this reason ToolBuilder provides open access to the underlying facilities of the TBK software platform on which it is built. Openness is seen as a way to overcome the limitations of the model, and although this is less convenient than having the concepts built-in, it is preferable to being limited to the built-in concepts.

The argument for methods meta-CASE is discussed more fully in a report by Butler and Bloor [15].

The methods meta-CASE approach is a realistic option for systems developers who have a good understanding of methods and the development process of their organisation, and it is available now.

References

[1] Butler, M. and Cox., *Trends in Systems Development*, Butler Cox Productivity Enhancement Programme.

[2] Rock-Evans, R. and Engelien, B., *Analysis Techniques for CASE: a Detailed Evaluation*, Ovum Ltd., 1989.

[3] Beer, S., Welland, R.C., and Sommerville, I. "Software design automation in an IPSE" in *ESEC '87, Proc. 1st European Software Engineering Conference, Strasbourg, France, September 9-11, 1987*, ed. Nichols, H.K. and Simpson, D., Lecture Notes in Computer Science, Vol. 289, Springer-Verlag, 1988.

[4] Sommerville, I., Welland, R.C., and Beer, S., "Describing software design methodologies", Computer Journal, 1987, 30, (2), pp. 128-133

[5] Welland, R.C., Beer, S., and Sommerville, I., "Method rule checking in a generic design editing system", *Software Engineering Journal*, 1990, 5, (2), pp. 105-115.

[6] Alderson, A., Elliott, A., and Cartmell, J., "The Eclipse Programme" in *Proc. 1st International Conference on System Development Environments and Factories*, ed. Madhavji, N., Shäfer, W., and Weber, H., Pitman, 1990.

[7] *PCTE, A Basis for a Portable Common Tool Environment*, Functional Specification, Version 1.5, Commission of the European Communities, Brussels, 1988.

[8] *OSF/Motif*, Revision 1.1, Open Software Foundation, Cambridge, MA 02142, 1990.

[9] Smart, J.D., "A Man-Machine Interface Management System for UNIX", in *Uni-Forum 1986 Conference Proceedings, Anaheim, CA, 1986*.

[10] Adobe Systems Incorporated, *PostScript Language: Reference Manual*, Addison-Wesley, 1985.

[11] Jackson, K. and Bird, B., "SCAD-1 Formulation", SCAD Method Development Study Technical Note C22802/TN1/5, SD-Scicon UK Ltd., 1990.

[12] Longworth, G. and Nicholls, D., *SSADM Manual*, NCC Publications, 1986.

[13] *SSADM V4 Reference Manual*, NCC Blackwell Ltd., 1990.

[14] Martin, J., *Information Engineering*, Savant.

[15] Butler, M. and Bloor, R., *The Future of Software*, ButlerBloor Ltd., 1990.

Management Issues in Software Development

Rainer Burchett

LBMS PLC, Evelyn House, 62 Oxford Street
London W1N 9LF, UK

Abstract

There is a need to understand the overall environment within which methods and tools exist. This does not simply imply a complete view of the systems development life-cycle but more importantly the organisation itself, its management structure and the changes required to absorb and successfully use the growing array of tools and approaches available. This paper seeks to look in some detail at these management issues and present a view on their importance and impact on adapting a cohesive tools strategy. It is based around the experience gained by LBMS in introducing the first practical tools and methods within the UK market, but also looks forward to the rapidly evolving integrated solutions now appearing in the commercial marketplace across Europe.

Introduction

The problems of controlling the development of large scale computer systems are too well documented to need detailed repetition here. It is worth remarking, however, that management concerns extend beyond the confies of the traditional development life cycle and therefore, when considering the architecture and coverage of a tool-set to support system development, one has to consider some of the wider management issues for Information Technology as a whole.

In this paper I shall be concentrating on a detailed examination of the management issues and their influence on the LBMS I-CASE tool set. However, it is worth making the point that no matter how excellent the tool set, making effective use of it depends heavily on the organisation implementing new management disciplines and methods. Effecting cultural change and implementing new management disciplines is a major topic in its own right which could well form the subject for another paper.

After some 20 years experience of the methods and tools side of the IT services industry, I think the key management issues for the next decade are as follows:

- control over IT investment

- shortening the gap between the conception and implementation of IT systems (including enhancements)

- implementation of open system policies, avoiding dependence on proprietary technology.

This set of requirements is at too broad a level to guide the choice of architecture and approach when developing an I-CASE tool set architecture, however it is worth keeping the overall goals in mind.

Control over IT Investment

There are a number of areas in which organisations have experienced control problems. Examining these begins to set parameters for some of the facilities we need from our tool set. The key areas are the following:

- selecting the most beneficial areas to support with IT and supporting them in the right way.

  The most rapid development in the world is of little use if the wrong systems are being developed while areas that would yield great benefit are never tackled. The answer is to employ a strategic planning process that links IT planning with business objectives and business planning, ensuring that IT plans support business needs and that business plans take account of the potential benefit from IT applications. The amount of data to be gathered and summarised in such a planning activity requires the use of automated support, so the first requirement from the I-CASE tools set is that it should support IT strategic planning. It is also necessary to ensure that the key goals for the IT applications commissioned are followed through in the development process, so requirements traceability becomes another key feature in the tool-set.

- Keeping track of the whole IT Portfolio.

  This is the second area of control which has been problematic in the past. The 'IT portfolio' includes bespoke systems, application packages, software packages, mainframe hardware, minis, PCs and networks, and all of the projects and studies under way or planned. This needs more than a simple asset register, because the interrelationships and dependencies are as important as the base data. One multinational giant corporation found, through painstaking and time-consuming research, that the strategic planning study they were about to launch for a particular area overlapped with or impinged on 50 other studies and reviews that were already going on, few of which had any knowledge of any of the others. Such situations will never be brought under control without some form of corporate database or repository system. A repository system is also a requirement to support many of the life-cycle tools as we shall see later, but use as a corporate control mechanism for IT helps to dictate many of the necessary features.

- Project and Quality Management.

  Control of the allocation of resources and of the effectiveness of what is being done not only requires specialist tools, it requires that such tools are integrated with the other tools supporting the life-cycle.

Shortening the Gap Between Conception and Implementation

This is clearly the main area for the application of I-CASE tools supporting the traditional life cycle in the sense of requirements definition, design, construction, testing and maintenance. The emphasis is often put on productivity improvements, but while improving cost effectiveness is clearly always valuable, the real prize is faster realisation of business benefits.

Producing a tool-set to maximise effectiveness in this area is complicated because of the number of factors to be considered. Some of the most important are:

- the variety of project types and sizes

- the number of possible implementation platforms - including hardware, operating system, programming language or 4GL, DBMS, TP monitor and Data Dictionary as separate elements of the target platform gives a total number of possible targets running into several thousand.

- the natural desire on the part of client organisations to maximise the use of existing development methods and tools.

- the poor quality of both design, programming and documentation of many of the critical existing systems which need to be maintained and eventually migrated or redeveloped.

The tool developer confronted with this range of problems has two main choices: either to be a niche player targeting a narrow set of clients with particular types of project and particular environments (many 4GL suppliers fit this definition), or to provide a generally applicable tool set capable of meeting all or most of the wide variety of environments and project types referred to above. LBMS has made the latter choice, which implies particular approach to tool architecture and interfacing, concentrating on enabling technology and the use of standards, as a basis for the necessary flexibility.

Incidentally the user organisation has a similar choice, whether to select a large number of difference 'niche' tools for various purposes or to look for more of a 'one-stop shopping' approach, maximising the integration and commonality of the tool-set.

The more detailed description*) of the LBMS tool-set which follows this management introduction shows in some detail how these issues have been addressed. Some examples may, however, be useful here to illustrate the approach. There is no such thing as 'the project life cycle' - projects differ enormously in their size and complexity, trying to support them all in exactly the same way is as absurd as trying to apply the same technology to building sky-scrapers as one would use for garden sheds. A very small project consists largely of coding and testing (70 % plus), while a large project consists mainly of administration and communication with coding and testing only being some 10 % of the total effort. For small projects one needs powerful prototyping and code generation facilities on a single work station and not much else. For large projects one needs a complete integrated project support environment, including project management tools, word processing, graphics, spread-sheets, electronic mail, diary facilities etc. etc. in a multi-user configuration supporting effective team working.

The key is modularity, flexibility and the use of interface standards. By providing the central CASE tool in single and multi-user form and by using the Windows standard to link a variety of third party products dynamically into a single integrated tool-set, LBMS can meet this wide variety of needs in a cost effective manner.

The wide variety of target environments can also be catered for efficiently by careful architectural design. The first principle is that the CASE tool must be capable of containing a complete logical representation of the system specification, including full details of both the data definitions (down to data item level) and of the processing logic (expressed in a Systems Design Language or pseudocode). This approach enables the same system to be targeted at multiple platforms, whether simultaneously or for later migration.

Of more immediate importance for many clients, it also allows a choice of construction approaches. Many clients prefer to stay with third generation languages such as COBOL, PL1 or C. For these clients can use the LBMS code generator, a closely integrated companion product to the CASE tool which expands the logical

---

*) not included here

specification to the target language and takes account of the other elements of the target environment, such as DBMS and TP monitor.

On the other hand, many other clients use or wish to use 4GLs or other application generation technology. Another element of the enabling technology which permits this is the transformation system which enables the relevant elements of the specification. (e.g. menu structures, screen and report layouts, data definitions and processing logic) to be converted into the relevant syntax for the target 4GL or other generator. LBMS have taken the approach of building transformation technology which is sufficiently powerful that most new targets will only need a few days work, and sufficiently easy to use that user organisations who find that their preferred target has not yet been implemented, can write their own interface. In this way a growing library of interfaces will be built up very quickly, with a combination of LBMS' own development efforts and those of its clients.

The final example is the issue of methodology support. This is an area where there is more work to be done, a fully sophisticated and generalised approach may not be possible for another two or three years.

The problem is how to meet client requests for full tool support to home grown methods or method variants. There is no difficulty in providing for user specified diagram types and user specified design objects in the sense of being able to capture, store and report on the design data entered and the relationships between different types of design object. Configurable tools of this nature have been available for some time. The difficulty comes in carrying this information forward to code generation. To be able to generate 100 % of the code for a working system from a logical specification, requires a degree of precision and completeness in that specification, and therefore in the graphical and textual syntax it uses, which is not present in many 'home-grown' methods. At present the choice is thus to use a method which includes the essential elements for code generation supported by the CASE tool, accepting some restrictions on the variants that can be introduced by the client, or to provide full configurability without code generation.

In future it should be possible to include, perhaps with the aid of artificial intelligence techniques, a methodology validation facility which enables the user to elaborate the syntactical and definitional elements to the point where enough rigour has been introduced to allow code generation to take place. The code generation mechanism itself would be specified and generated as part of the same activity.

Another challenge for the I-CASE tool developer is to provide useful facilities to help maximise the use that can be made of the investment in existing systems, no matter how badly developed and documented. This is the area generally referred to as Reverse Engineering or Re-Engineering. This is the newest in I-CASE technology generally and will be the subject of intensive development for the rest of the decade. We are a long way from the dreamed of 'black box' that will instantly translate a million lines of 'spaghetti COBOL' into a well structured set of C programs running under a different hardware/software environment and with a relational DBMS instead of a flat file structure. There are indeed theoretical doubts as to whether such a transformation can ever be achieved fully automatically.

However, Reverse Engineering tools are increasingly emerging as part of the I-CASE toolset and can provide benefits. The unfamiliarity of this area means that a fully consistent and generally accepted terminology has not yet emerged. We find that essentially there are three things that clients wish to do:

- extend the life of existing systems and/or maintain them at less cost

- migrate an existing system to a new platform with no change of functionality

- redevelop an existing system with changed functionality, but capturing as much as possible of the existing functionality automatically to lessen risk and save analysis time and effort.

To support these differing aims, and to cope with the variety of existing languages and environments, once again a complex enabling technology is needed. There are basically three elements in the LBMS approach:

- code analysers to read existing source code and extract meaningful information

- an information system in which to store the information so that it can be interrogated to provide information to the maintenance teams

- a CASE transformer to move information back into the CASE tool to help regenerate or redevelop the system for new environments.

At present much of the higher level systems information has to be entered by those who know it, it cannot all be deduced from the source code. This is what prevents the technology at present from providing a black box solution. Over time it will be possible to generate more information automatically and thus have to do less by hand. As mentioned earlier, however, it may never be a fully automatic process.

Support for Open Systems

Increasingly organisations are reluctant to commit to proprietary products (whether hardware or software), which may lock them in to expensive suppliers in the future. Open systems to allow interfacing of a variety of components and easier migration to new platforms (ideally completely without effort) are the key features looked for.

For the tool vendor this has two main implications. Firstly the need to target open as well as proprietary platforms. Secondly the need to exemplify the move to open systems within the tool-set provided, ultimately facilitating even the migration away from that very tool-set. I have already dealt with the issue of targeting multiple platforms, it makes no difference to our tools whether these are open (e.g. UNIX) or proprietary e.g. IBM CICS COBOL. It is worth emphasising in this context the benefit of having a fully logical specification maintained in the CASE tool, so that the entire application can be generated for any target environment. Providing maintenance is done through the CASE tool, regenerating for a new environment will also not present a problem.

What has affected our thinking is the open architecture of our own tools, leading to the following features:

- participation in independent industry standards initiatives such as CDIF and IRDS. LBMS is not only committed to adhering to these standards and when they are published, we are active participants in the formation of the standards, particularly within CDIF.

- adherence to proprietary standards which have a large following. We are, for example, contractually committed to support the standards represented by IBM's AD/Cycle, which has a growing influence on the market. At the same time Microsoft Windows has a big following and we support as well. All our PC tools are or will be available with identical functionality under both Windows and Presentation Manager.

- our repository product is fully configurable without any need to program extensions. This means that, for example, should a user find after a few years use that he or she wishes to migrate to a different repository product, the LBMS repository can be reconfigured to mimic the structure of the new target in preparation for the move, and the standard import/export facilities can be used to effect the move. This means that all of the CASE information from the other tools in the set, all of which can be stored on the repository, can also be migrated through the same mechanism to other tools. The only restriction is the inescapable one that objects in one tool-set which cannot be represented in the new tool-set cannot be migrated. Otherwise both graphical and textual representations of objects and their relationships can be migrated.

Standardization of Software Development Enviroments

Adolf Peter Bröhl

Bundeswehrverwaltungsamt, Amt für Datenverarbeitung der Bundeswehr

Bonner Talweg 177, D-5300 Bonn 1

Objectives and Marginal Conditions

In the year 1986 a research and technology project called "Software Development
Environment for Information Systems of the German Federal Armed Forces" (SDE-IS[1])
was started. The objective of the project is defining general standards for software
development in the field of database-oriented DP systems in the German Federal Armed
Forces. These systems are characterized by a commercial environment, i.e. standard
hardware and software.

The technological developments, the change from data processing to information
processing and the often quoted development backlog required elaborating and defining a
uniform software development environment. The global objectives regarding the use of an
SDE are increasing quality and productivity, improving the transparency of development
processes and updating/maintenance as well as dominating the new technologies.

The levels of standardization within the scope of the SDE-IS are illustrated in fig. 1. The

---

1) SDE-IS stands for "Software Development Environment for Information Systems". The German
   term is "Software-Entwicklungs-Umgebung für Informations-Systeme" (SEU-IS)

top level represents the life cycle methodology (LCM), the next level holds the definition of methods, and the third level deals with functional requirements on the tools. These levels equally apply to the actual software development (SWE) as to all other project phases: project management (PM), quality assurance (QA) and configuration management (CM) incl. data administration.

Levels of Standardization

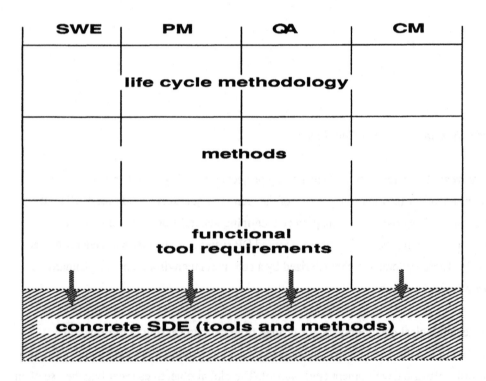

Fig. 1

In the view of the research project members, the realization of the actual SDE, including the choice of the corresponding tools is reserved for the individual project teams and is currently depending on the corresponding hardware and software environment.

Proceeding

The conventional proceeding, that starts with a detailed life cycle methodology, subsequently integrates the methods to be used and finally defines the tool requirements, was found not to be adequate. Experiences from former software development activities, as well as the fact that result and activity types of a detailed LCM are almost exclusively method-dependent, lead to a different basic approach. First, the methods to be followed were determined and agreed upon. Subsequently, corresponding tools were selected and tested in the sense of prototyping in order to specify functional requirements imposed on the tools. In a further step the LCM was revised. On the basis of a life cycle methodology for realtime-oriented system development, elaborated in a parallelly conducted project, the first standardization level was drawn up. This LCM is highly abstractive and thus valid as a standard for the entire software development activity of the German Federal Armed Forces.

Life Cycle Methodology (LCM)

The LCM is meant to be used as contractual basis with concise specification of scope of delivery and working method, as direction for execution and as communication platform for user and developer. It is limited to software development (no hardware development) and comprises regulations and standards concerning the four submodels and the interaction of these components.

The project flow is described in a "main activity/product-net" (types, no detailed specification) with the main activities, if required, being subdivided into partial activities generating corresponding partial products. The products are described with regard to their contents, but not to their explicit form. No persons or organization units are assigned to the activities, but roles. The role principle enables modelling of any organization you chose. Moreover, tailoring is described, the technique used in order to bring the LCM into line with the individual projects.

What is ruled by the LCM

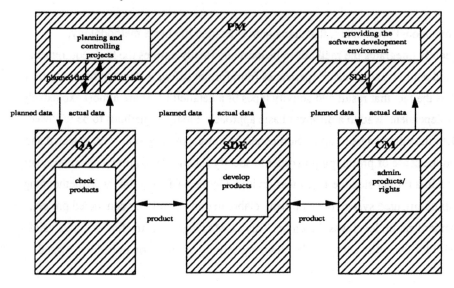

Fig. 2

The Ministry of the Interior is planning to issue the LCM as the basis for a standard, valid for the entire public sector. Moreover, this methodology in combination with the three-level-architecture of standardization will form the German contribution to the project "Euromethod" of the European community.

Method Definition

The second level of standardization describes method modules (in the sense of integral parts of market-relevant standard methods) and detailed procedural rules which are then applied to the corresponding submodels.

For the submodel SWE the method ISOTEC (Integrated Software Technology) developed by EDV Studio Ploenzke was found to be adequate. Main feature of the method ISOTEC is the parallel information/function structure analysis.

The Elements of ISOTEC

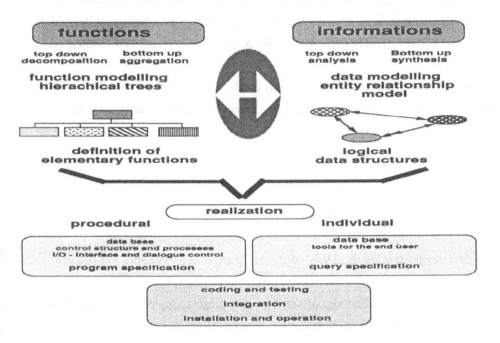

Fig. 3

To describe the method modules, the logical design of the SDE was developed using the elements of the method itself. In this meta level, the functions describe the corresponding steps of software development and the data describe the different sights on a development database. Bringing together these two perspectives forms a description of the development database meta structure.

This database represents the central part of the SDE and is to hold all results important during software development. Its functions are to facilitate communication and interaction between the different components as well administer various kinds of objects. Physically this development database is represented by the repository with the object administration system. One essential demand on the functionality of the object administration system is, that it must be able to administer complex objects. This feature is indespensible to allow flexible integration and combination of the single development steps and to enable application under the aspects of project management or quality assurance and facilitate further processing.

Logical designs in terms of this meta level also exist for the submodels "Project Management" and "Configuration Management". Concerning project management, specifications for network planning and project expenditure estimation were defined, the latter based on IFA (ISOTEC-based, function point analysis-oriented cost estimation).

The elaboration of the standardization study for the above described submodels will be completed in 1991, logical design and the standards for quality assurance will be elaborated in the year 1992.

Functional Requirements on the Tools

For the description of the third level of standardization, an architecture was planned first.

Objective of such architectural considerations is to present a logical architecture based merely on functional aspects, abstracting e.g. specific functions and tasks of software developers or tools as well as the actual distribution of functions within the network.

The architecture, which is drawn using so-called service units, is supposed to represent the framework for the specification of functional requirements on the tools and provide guidelines for the design of the concrete SDE.

On the basis of the function complexes the sevice units identify non-overlapping, self-contained rather compact service ranges of defined granularity. Thus the service units may be seen as basic modules building up the architecture. In the concrete SDE these modules are to be DP-technically replaced by tools.

While in a concrete SDE a module can only be represented by exactly one tool, the tool or the tool environment (integrated CASE solution) respectively can and preferably should cover several performance units, especially for minimizing interface development expenditures.

The elaboration and completion of performance unit requirements is planned for 1992.

Tool Prototyping

With regard to methodical definition for analysis and design within the software development process, criteria for tool prototyping in an IBM-oriented environment were defined.

First, a catalog of the general criteria to be collected was worked out and 144 companies were selected from ISIS catalog, tool studies and market examination by the specialized external project participants; those selected companies were referred to with a preliminary questionnaire and asked to specify a criteria catalog according to their tool. About 60 companies returned this questionnaire and were examined and evaluated by the SDE team. 12 products were left to choose from. The next step was the elaboration of a weighted detailed criteria catalog.

On the basis of this criteria catalog an application example was developed, which at the end of 1987 was tested for the offered products at the site of each tool producer/seller. Thus, one part of the detailed criteria could be verified. Verification and evaluation of the other criteria were done together with a technical representative of each company.

Based on the results of this verification process IEW (Information Engineering Workbench) from Knowledgeware and EPOS (Development and Project Management Oriented Specification System[2]) from GPP were selected for tool prototyping.

An operational DP project was chosen to test these tools.

The objective of this testing phase was evaluating the functionality of both tools and realizing parts of the selected pilot project - from design to realization of databases,

---

2) EPOS stands for the German term "Entwicklungs- und Projektmanagement-Orientiertes Spezifikationssystem"

dialogs and programs. Moreover, the tools were to be compared to each other in order to formulate a recommendation for the project developing sectors. In addition, the experiences made during the testing phase with regard to practical handling should be taken into consideration when defining the functional requirements on the tools.

A development project in the area of organization principles, at that time in the conceptional phase, was selected to be the pilot project. Target language was to be PL/1 and database system was to be DB2 with IMS-DC monitor. The time limit was set to 9 month and the team consisted of 6 to 8 members, with two method/tool specialists of the SDE team and one representative of the enduser department being available for supporting this test. Tool prototyping was completed in April 1989.

The following experiences were made:

The application of the method ISOTEC for analysing the DP system was approved by the enduser department as well as by the DP specialists. Especially the graphic models provide a common platform of problem understanding and as an image of the real technical situation they form the basis of the planned DP system. Investing high efforts into this early phase of analysis guarantees that the resulting product will meet the expectations of the user. In addition to user training it was regarded as very essential to have integrated a method/tool specialist into the project team. His tasks lay in the transfer of know-how on methods and tools as well as acting as a moderator. Such moderator function was of considerable importance in an area of tension between enduser and DP department. Moreover, the integration of a representative of the enduser department into the development team was found to be necessary to have someone representing the user side being available all the time. The method was classified as easy to learn.

When using the method, a great deal of informations are collected that need to be registered and administered. Changes, especially in graphic representation, can - at acceptable expenditures - only be handled using a corresponding CASE-tool. The tools also support input data consistency and thus result in higher quality. An essential feature of design tools is, that the input information can be subsequently worked with during physical realisation, for example when implementing the databases. The test of both tools has lead to the conclusion that the provided storage facilities are not sufficient to replace a data dictionary.

The test of IEW focussed on the Analysis Workbench and parts of the Design Workbench. For EPOS an ISOTEC-conform part of an EPOS-S application installed in a credit institute was tested.

In the course of the pilot project it showed to be appropriate to input results only after they had been verified to a certain extent. The first results were elaborated with the help of interviews and the corresponding display facilities. This method helped, especially in the starting phase - to achieve a common knowledge platform of the whole team and to coordinate the results with the superior decision-makers. Great importance was attached to teamwork and the resulting group-dynamic aspects. The moderator again played an important role at this point. In the course of the project and for upcoming changes the documentation facilities of the tools themselves were applied more and more also for team coordination.

If more than one PC-configuration is used in a project - which may be regarded as the normal case - consistancy of the data held in the different configurations must be assured. This proves to be not only a technical problem, that could be solved by installing a network system and using distributed databases, but also calls for organizational measures. This especially applies to the tested tools which were employed as "stand-alone" tools (possibilities of synchronization via host were not yet tested). In the project a data administration must be integrated with the objective of defining and monitoring the use of special terms to assure that no homonym and synonym problems occur and that project standards are observed. The expenditures for data administration increases with the number of configurations combined in the project. It is therefore recommended to minimize the number of configurations. In the pilot project two installations were employed with the project database results being merged every evening.

Transformation of Standardization Results

The following steps were made for the transformation of the R + D project results in an area where information systems are developed on the basis of a DP infrastructure characterized essentially by the use of IBM-computers:

The application of the LCM was simulated in a developed process, in order to elaborate specifics for information systems and to test applicability. Currently a pilot project for tailoring and project standard development is executed. This project also elaborates standards and guidelines for project management.

The tool environment in the SDE architecture is based on the IBM concept AD/Cycle.

In accordance with the methodic standard of ISOTEC, the tool IEW is meanwhile used in 18 projects and currently the MVS host component ist tested.

The LCM was automatically registered in the tool "Application Development Project Support" (ADPS) by IBM and the tools "ADW" (OS/2 version of IEW) and "Cross System Product" (CSP) as a generator were integrated. To support project management the host/workstation solution "Project/2-QWIKNET" by PSDI is tested currently . For the year 1991 testing of further tools is planned for example test installations of the "IBM-Repository" by IBM and the AIX-based "Object Management Systems" (OMS) by Softlab.

Experience shows that apart from the costs for tools expenditures are necessary for definition and monitoring of standards as well as for training and introduction in order to reach the high goals we set for productivity and quality of software development.

A SOFTWARE DEVELOPMENT ENVIRONMENT FOR CIM APPLICATIONS

Lothar Köhler
Software Engineering and System Technics, Continental AG
Königsworther Platz 1, D-3000 Hannover 1

INTRODUCTION

The Continental Corporation is the leading manufacturer of tyres and industrial rubber products in Germany. In the tyre sector, the corporation ranks second in Europe and fourth on the world market. The tyre sector, which consists of the brands Continental, Uniroyal (Europe), Semperit, and General Tire (USA), produces the bigger part of the turnover.

To meet the requirements of modern production (just in time, JIT) and rising quality demands (computer-aided quality, CAQ), it was decided in 1986 to force the automatization of production with Digital's VAX/VMS computers. Typical computer applications are production planning systems and storage systems. Part of the decision to implement computer-integrated manufacturing was the intention to use software engineering methods.

After joining Continental in spring 1988, I became responsible for selecting and implementing a computer-aided software engineering tool. The tools in use at that time were COBOL and FORTRAN compilers, Digital's VAXset for lower-CASE, and Digital's relational database management system VAX/VIA, including Rdb and the data dictionary CDD and CDD/Plus, respectively. The software had to be developed according to COMET, a waterfall model with seven phases.

GOALS FOR OUR SOFTWARE ENGINEERING

The main goal was to improve the quality of our software products, including not only programs but also the complete documentation. The sooner a bug is discovered in software development, the cheaper it is fixed. This translates into improved quality and cost savings. In the worst case, a wrong or missing requirement is discovered while the software is in use.

The second goal was to increase the productivity of software development. The engineering approach to software development is the only way to get rid of the rising complexity of applications and systems. There are more and more interfaces to other programs as a result of the growing integration of applications. These interconnections must be carefully documented. If software is developed according to software engineering methods, then there should be fewer reasons for maintenance. If maintenance is necessary, it should be supported by up-to-date documentation generated by CASE tools. As a result, we expected higher cost savings in the area of maintenance. We knew that software engineering methods would increase the efforts during the phases analysis and design and that these phases would have to be supported by a CASE tool to limit the additional expenses. For this reason, software developers have to learn the methods and the tool simultaneously. In addition, more hardware power is needed to run the CASE tool.

SELECTION OF THE CASE TOOL

The analysis of our software development process revealed that the phases analysis and design had to be supported by a CASE tool, and that the available software tools had to be used more consistently.

We decided to use the following software engineering methods:

ANALYSIS:

- Structured Analysis (De Marco)

DESIGN:

- Stepwise Refinement
- Entity Relationship Model
- Module Design with Information Hiding and Data Encapsulation (Parnas)

REALIZATION:

- Structured Programming

This list clearly shows one problem:

There is no one method, which supports the whole software development life cycle. But many methods are needed; each very valuable in the proper phase. The transition from one method to the next is a problem, especially the transition from analysis to design.

The requirements for the CASE tool were defined in cooperation with the leaders of the software projects.

The main items were the integration of the CASE tool with the available tools, the support of the maintenance phase, graphical documentation, and the support of the whole life cycle of the software, with regard to the fact that each phase in software development will not only be passed once, but again and again during maintenance and extension projects.

We had to observe the constraints of the project: The budget and the available hardware, the VAX cluster computers, and the lack of workstations, which seem to be required for graphical interactive software design. We decided to test three tools based on our experience, a market study, a visit to a fair, documents and presentations of tool manufacturers. At last, we decided to implement the tool EPOS of GPP (Gesellschaft für Prozeßrechnerprogrammierung).

IMPLEMENTATION OF EPOS

While we were looking for an upper-CASE tool, a Software Engineering Environment was built, during a second project, which integrated the available tools of lower-CASE. We managed to integrate EPOS in this environment with little effort. Thus, we now have a software engineering environment consisting of EPOS, the language-sensitive editor LSE, the version control CMS, MMS for the generation of programs, and the data dictionary CDD/Plus. In addition, we enhanced Digital's LSE to support EPOS's input language.

A well-funded pilot project is the usual way to implement software engineering. However, the results of such a pilot project are of little relevance to the usual projects. For this reason, it was decided to start immediately with software engineering in two projects.

Training for the use of the tool is needed. Much more important, however, is the training of the methods. But even training is not sufficient. It is necessary to form a group of experts, experienced in the use of software engineering methods, to support the software developers as soon as questions arise. This could be done by an external consultant as well, but more expensive.

PROBLEMS

The major problems did not arise from the tool itself but from the application of the software engineering methods. Most of the software developers were not familiar with these methods. The training examples were small and of no relevance to the real projects. What seemed to be easy during training, became complicated during the real projects. Thus most software developers became suspicious as to whether these methods were useful. Timely consulting is needed for every problem.
Another problem was that software developers felt that their "creative liberty" was

limited by the application of the software engineering methods.

If a developer absorbes one method, it is possible that the method is misused; for example structured analysis is used in design or design methods are used down to the COBOL statements. Generally, the phases analysis and design will last longer because they are more carefully carried out.

FIRST SUCCESS

The whole software life cycle is supported by the methods and tools. EPOS analyzes flaws in the analysis and the software design and, as a result, we create better designs. It is possible to present the customer with results of the analysis and the design through graphical documentation. The documentation is up-to-date at all times. The implementation of the first project, which was built with the help of the software engineering environment, showed that the quality and performance of the software had improved. A change in project staff was easier because of the good documentation. Quality assurance methods can be applied, which is nearly impossible without requirements and formal specifications.

Our experience demonstrates that it is not only possible, but necessary to implement software engineering methods and tools now. Despite of all the problems connected with the implementation, it proved to be advantageous and, with respect to maintenance, profitable to implement software engineering.

REFERENCES

R. J. Lauber and P. R. Lempp, EPOS Overview, Gesellschaft für Prozeßrechnerprogrammierung mbH, Kolpingring 18a, D-8024 Oberhaching.

S. L. Pfleeger, Software Engineering, Macmillan Publishing Company, New York, 1987.

A REPOSITORY AND OTHER TOOLS IN A COMMERCIAL DEVELOPMENT CENTER

Dieter Steinbauer

D A T E V   e G, Nürnberg

Paumgartnerstraße 6-14

0.   Introduction

The objective is clear. It is to improve the productivity
of software development, maintenance, operation and
replacement. In practice, all four parts of the life cycle
are of great importance when very large information systems
are involved. However, in the following discussion I will
focus on development and maintenance.

Fig.1 'Vicious Square'

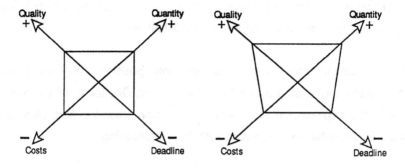

Productivity claims for software maintenance in CASE
environments are usually not based on existing systems
developed using different tools.

1. The Present Situation

In order to clarify what a large software house requires of a software development environment and especially what CASE expects from a repository, I would like to say something about the context into which it is introduced.

1.1 Application Development and Maintenance

Who are the people, and what are the software systems which a CASE environment is intended to support? As an example, let us take the systems which make up a financial accounting system. This is a very large information system. In our computer center, this system handles many tens of thousands of businesses.

Fig.2a 'Integrated Financial Accounting'

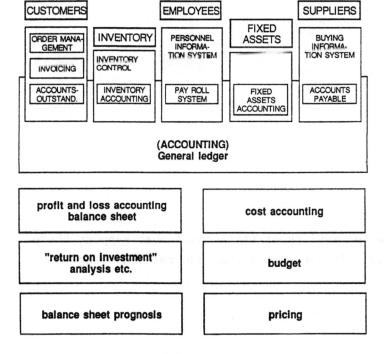

The existing system comprises a number of communicating
subsystems, each with hundreds of programs and data
elements. The system is not static, since it is continually
being developed, modified and new components are added.
Changes in legislation and other functional modifications
have to be integrated frequently. Amendments are also
required by the changing technical environment. Over the
years, the system has evolved into a large distributed
system in which thousands of PCs handling individual
functions communicate with the central system on the
mainframe.

Fig.2b   'Distributed Applications'

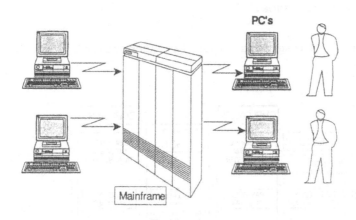

The software development environment must support these
aspects of software engineering and reengineering.

1.2 Software Engineering Tools

Regarding usage, we must differentiate between three different classes of tools:

- Tools which represent prototypes for software engineering methods under research;

- Tools available on the market, which implement a specific state of the art;

- Tools which the developer uses daily to help him in his work.

Until recently, commercially available tools had the following characteristics:

- They were oriented towards the classic life cycle (or waterfall) model;

- They were methodoligically immature;

- They paid insufficient attention to the support of different technical platforms;

- The system architectures were not sufficiently open;

- Software development was viewed as a manufacturing process;

- Performance aspects were neglected.

The tools presently in use being used are oriented towards results and support pragmatic methods with inadequate methodology. The emphasis, for example, is on support of quality control or implementation or debugging. Present tools are also directed at auditing requirements.

Fig.3   'Tools in the DATEV Context'

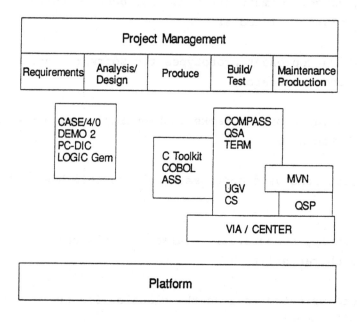

Both in the research arena and in the marketplace, there is
a lack of tools that support maintenance "on a large
scale". Tools which cover more than one part of the life
cycle are designed from the point of view of forward
engineering. It is only recently that commercial tools have
supported migration of data into new structures.
Frequently, maintenance is considered as working in an
existing tool environment - not as the development or
modification of existing systems originally developed
without the aid of those tools.

1.3 Systems Documentation during Development

The situation concerning systems documentation during
development, as practised in a commercial environment, is
reminiscent of the transition from file-oriented
application to database applications. The output from

bases, knowledge bases or encyclopedias specific to the tool. The form in which the results are stored is based on the requirements of the tool - not on the development result. In practice, the results of the software development process include very different structure elements. Functional design, for instance, contains SA-diagrams, ER-diagrams formatted text, free text, free graphics, user interface prototypes, and so on. During the development process we want to access previously created elements relating to a subsystem. This is supported by dictionary systems, which manage the interdependence between the individual components.

Fig.4   'Tool-Oriented Documentation'

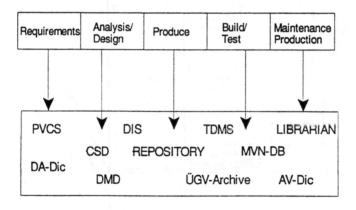

Many tool suppliers wanted to upgrade their data bases to form universal platforms, making them available to other tools. This approach aimed at an integrated software development environment based on a platform designed by one supplier. This could only work if other suppliers were prepared to take up this offer.

2. The Idea and the First Steps

Every large development center has its own model of software development. With AD/Cycle, IBM took the first step towards standardization. The market situation has also changed, in that many independent tool suppliers claim to be compatible with AD/Cycle or to support AD/Cycle.

Fig.5   'AD/Cycle Cube'

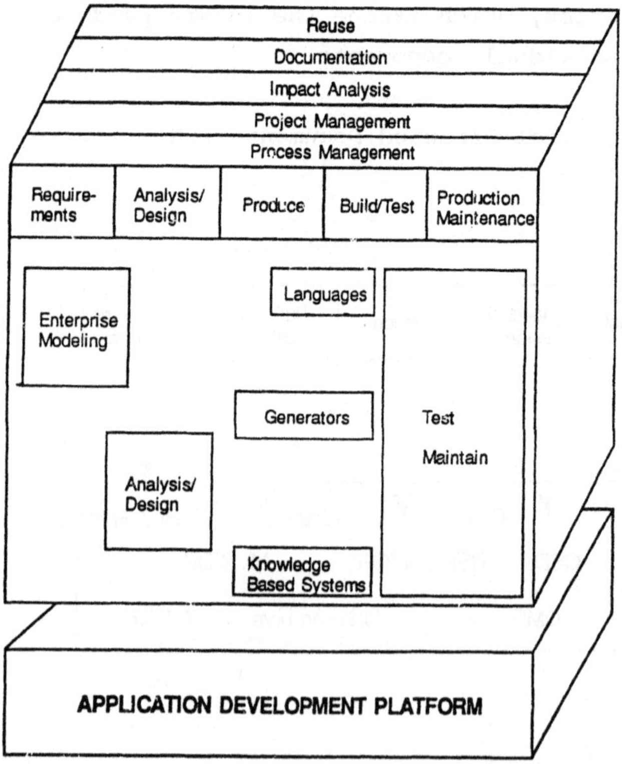

Reuse
Documentation
Impact Analysis
Project Management
Process Management

Require-ments	Analysis/Design	Produce	Build/Test	Production Maintenance

Enterprise Modeling

Languages

Analysis/Design

Generators

Test

Maintain

Knowledge Based Systems

APPLICATION DEVELOPMENT PLATFORM

The platform for integration within AD/Cycle is the Repository.

2.1 The Repository

The Repository is the universal storage system for development results in the software life cycle. The

Repository functions as a central store for documents or at least as a list of contents. All results are managed in such a way as to be non-redundant, consistent, re-usable, retrievable and so on. Consequently, development results can be controlled centrally. All tools store their results in the Repository. Tools used in subsequent phases of the life cycle can use the results stored in previous phases. Thus, the Repository satisfies the requirements for a non-standard database system since it manages different objects and structures.

Fig.6a   'Repository in the Life Cycle'

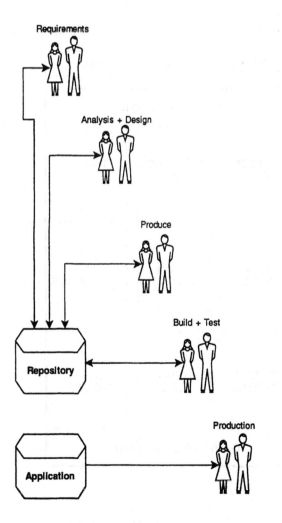

The problem is the Repository's information model. This could be called the meta data model for development results. The information model specifies what the development results are and how they are structured. The tools must agree on this structure if they are to make active use of the repository.

Our software development model defines a documentation structure. This model lays down the results of the development process and their structure.

Fig.6b   'Documentation Structure'

	FUNCTIONS	APPLICATION	DATA
C O N C E P T U A L	ORGANIZATION		
	FUNCTION MODEL	INFORMATION FLOW	DATA MODEL
L O G I C A L	SYSTEM STRUCTURE	FUNCT. STD / DATA UTILIZATION / DATA STD	DATA STRUCTURE
P H Y S I C A L	PROGRAM SYSTEMS	SYSTEM FLOW	DATA STORAGE
	CONFIGURATION		

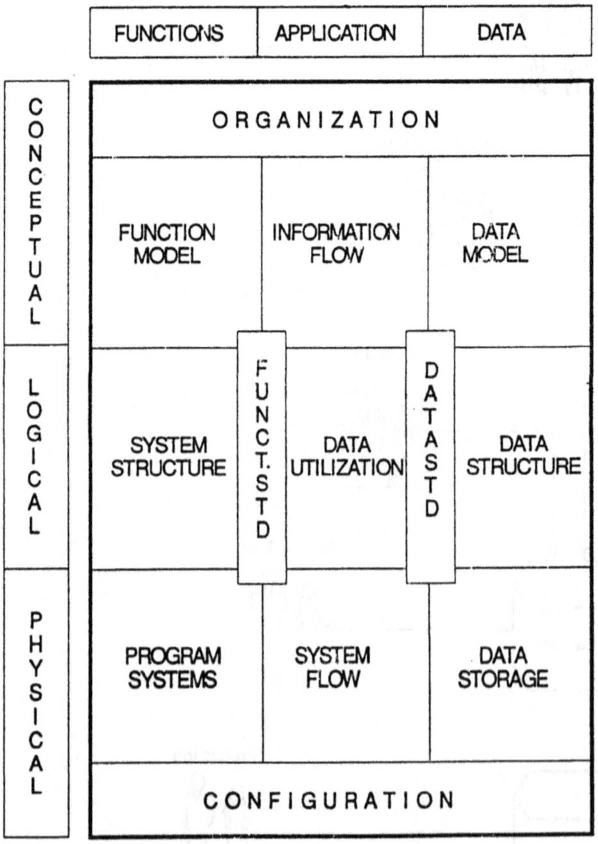

During integration of the Repository we have to check to what extent our model is compatible with Repository's information model. At present, we have the impression that the information model of the IBM repository is defined in large measure by the tools which it now supports.

Making a de facto standard of these structures would, in my opinion, cause severe restrictions in the future. Implementing our documentation structure one-to-one by extending and adapting the standard information model, would reduce the Repository to a mere data storage tool. This is not in our interest.

2.2 Life Cycle Tools

If the life cycle tools were to interface with the Repository and if the structures in the Repository were standardized, there would be two main benefits for a software development environment:

- It would be possible to exchange the individual tools for producing the results

- There would be no problem passing results from one tool to another.

This is the future. In reality, we have different tools. The first step towards integration is for them to be compatible from the methodological point of view. Care must be taken to ensure that the different methods used in the software development process are compatible with each other. The tools used must support only those methods which fit in with the software development environment which we are striving to achieve.

At present, the AD/Cycle tools available on the market do not cover all of the results and activities required in the software development process. This means that there are gaps which can only be filled by "methods" and we have to resort to structured texts or graphics for tool support. We see this for instance in system design.

2.3 Integrated Tools

Just two comments on this class of tool. I do not think much of process or project management tools which tell the developer exactly what to do. These control systems destroy creativity and often merely give management a false sense of security.

I am very much in favour of quality assurance tools which test the quality of results during the development process. Tools developed in-house should be used increasingly to test for consistency, completeness, performance, correctness, and so on. At present, there is very little from the tool suppliers in this field.

3. Experience

Our experience to date gives hope for the future. There are still a number of problems. We now have to do what is possible to achieve the greatest possible benefit. Future trends must be taken into account to avoid getting trapped in a dead-end.

3.1 Benefits

At present the AD/Cycle idea in conjunction with the Repository only provides very limited benefits. It has strengthened the trend towards an open repository on the part of the tool suppliers. It has strengthened pressure towards standardization. For certain results, there have been attempts to define interfaces which can be used by different tools.

The benefits to be expected if the Repository is a success are self-evident. A central information base for the results of the development process would facilitate:

- Reusability

- Clarity

- 'Open' tools.

This central information base would enable the results to be stored for the future in a form independent of the tool. The results produced by one tool could be processed by subsequent tools. If the Repository includes the data dictionary used in the first stages of development, the enterprise data model would available for all design tools, which would have a standardizing effect. The synergy effect on applications development would be enormous. The Repository would allow the meta information on application data and functions to be used directly in the development process.

3.2 Problems

There are very many problems, mostly resulting from the currently available methods and tools in the marketplace. Some of them are as follows:

- The Repository needs sophisticated version management. We know that database systems currently provide inadequate version management.

- Tool interfaces must be active. The repository must not be used as a long-term archive. The problem of replicated and distributed data in an active development environment must be addressed by the Repository.

- The standardization of the results, methods and tools in regard to their structure and interfaces needs further work.

- The performance of the Repository could be better and storage requirements could be smaller.

- The information model of the Repository is not yet complete.

- There is a lack of "suitable" tools in the analysis and design phases.

- Introduction of a repository means reengineering of existing archive systems, also involving migration of data.

These are only some of the unanswered questions, when migrating to a new universal platform.

3.3 Migration and Integration

The migration strategy must be developed before introducing the Repository. We have the following strategy for using the Repository and its functions as a general platform:

- Definition of an information model for software development using existing tools;

- Integration of existing tool user interfaces, where possible using the SAA standard;

- Becoming familiar with the Repository information model and comparing it with the existing model;

- **Assessing the impact of differences;**

- Choice of pilot applications taking into consideration:

  o Benefits and improvements for the developer
  o Stability of the information model in the area chosen
  o Conformity with our own model
  o Stability with the methods used in this area
  o Resource usage and timing for first productive use.

We are at present engaged in our first pilot project. We are importing information on data structures from old system designs. The existing documents are characterized by a degree of standardization. This means that the migration can be semi-automatic. We can, therefore, dispense with some of the old documents.

The second pilot project is in the planning phase. It will involve importing structured information from the analysis stage. Because of the tool being used at present, we are faced with the question of replicated data.

4.   Prospects

The greatest problem is that the Repository and the tools are evolving as applications are being developed. There are always applications which are based on the newest technology or methods. For these applications, the tools are not available commercially and the Repository is not yet adequate.

Bearing in mind that we are writing object-oriented applications using presentation manager and OS/2, where are the tools for object-oriented design?

5. Bibliography

<1> Carlyle, R.:
Is Your Data Ready for the Repository? Datamation
1990, No 1, 43 - 47.

<2> DATEV eG (Hrsg.):
DASEM - DATEV-Modell zur Software-Entwicklung,
Handbuch, 1989.

<3> Dennert, E.; Hesse, W.:
Projektmodell und Projektbibliothek: Grundlagen
zuverlässiger Software-Entwicklung und
Dokumentation, Informatik-Spektrum, Bd.3 (1980),
Heft 4, 215-228.

<4> Farle, G.:
Rally Round the Repository,
C/A/S/E outlook, No. 4, 1989, pp. 5 - 13.

<5> Humphrey, W.S.:
Managing the Software Process,
Addison-Wesley, Readings, Mass., 1990.

<6> IBM (ed.):
AD/Cycle Concepts, Systems Application
Architecture,
Report, GC26-4531-0, 1989.

<7> IBM (ed.):
Repository Manager/MVS, General Information,
Version 1, Release 1, Report GC20-0001, 1989.

<8> Mecurio, V.J.; Meyers, B.F.; Nisbet, A.M;
Radin, G.:
AD/Cycle strategy and architecture,
IBM Systems Journal, Vol.29, N.2, 1990, pp. 170-
188.

<9> Nagl, M.:
Softwaretechnik: Methodisches Programmieren im
Großen, Springer Compass, Springer Verlag, Berlin,
Heidelberg, 1990.

<10> Ortner, E.:
Ein Referenzmodell für den Dictionary-/Repository-
Einsatz in Unternehmen, Universität Konstanz,
Informationswissenschaft, Bericht 1/90, 1990.

<11> Österle, H.(Hrsg.):
Anleitung zu einer praxisorientierten Software-
Entwicklungsumgebung,
AIT-Verlag, Hallbergmoos, 1988.

<12> Sagawa, J.M.:
Repository Manager technology,
IBM Systems Journal, Vol.29, No 2, 1990, pp. 209-227.

<13> Summerville, I.:
Software-Engineering, Addison-Wesley, Reading,
Mass, 1989.

<14> Zgraggen, P.M.:
Ein Vorgehensplan zum Technologiewechsel,
in Thurner (Hrsg.): Reengineering,
AIT-Verlag, Hallbergmoos, 1990, pp. 101-113.

LESSONS LEARNED FROM DOMINO AND GRAPES

Johann Wagner
Application Software and Projects, Siemens-Nixdorf AG
Otto Hahn-Ring 6, W-8000 Munich 83

Introduction

The fascinations of computing have helped to write these lines, and have outweighed the frustrations connected with the birth of a new technology.

Software technology has become one of the key technologies of our industry /EIRMA 89/, and its impact may be compared with that of automotive transport or wireless transmission techniques.

It will, like the other technologies, change the relations and the self-understanding of nations again.

Software was formerly a necessary appendix to hardware. Today this relation is reversed. Software has become an industrial product. Higher productivity or lower costs and the mastering of its complexities have their origin in the simplification, standardization and reliability of components. Software standardization, however, is only in its beginnings.

Because of the nearly unlimited range of creativity which is allowed software developers, it can hardly be expected that standards arise for reasons of their usefulness and clarity. Massive economic interests clearly dominate the scene, even if the phenomenon of UNIX may make one reconsider or even reconcile oneself with actual trends.

Animated by parallelisms in mechanical industrial production, concepts of semi-finished and finished products keep turning up: building blocks, subsystems, component libraries, software ICs and open integration platforms. Along the same lines of continuous mounting of finished components (waterfall model) the process of industrial software manufacturing has been viewed for a long time. From it are derived the phase models of all software process orders which have been developed up to now. This model is useful but is in discussion.

The concept of "software engineering" has been in existance for nearly 20 years, the concept of Computer Aided Software Engineering for the past five years. CASE was to be the method of industrial production of software. It was the answer of the United States and Europe to a Japanese challenge. Today we have to ask ourselves if we can be satisfied with what has been achieved. We are not alone if we now review results critically /DB&D 90/.

The CASE balance sheet

The roots of CASE

In the middle of the 1980's, at a time when the development of software was usually done by external software development companies, and when it became clear that the covering contracts were based on trust rather than on concrete requirements, pioneers of CASE like Yourdon and DeMarco observed that the developers produced graphical diagrams during the planning and coordinating sessions showing: function blocks, storage (in the shape of tubs) and lines of communication (in the form of lightning bolts).

Flow charts and state transition diagrams had been used for some time, but for abstract representations of systems the corresponding formalisms were lacking. At the same time, the first graphical workstations, and soon after the first graphic PC's evolved, which could be used as a means of drawing diagrams. The graphics tradition from the CAD field also had an influence on the efforts to use graphical languages for software design. Oddly, however, at the same time in hardware development, due to the rising complexitiy of the designs, the use of textual representations, e.g. ADA dialects, was spreading.

CASE was connected with the belief that with the aid of graphical representation software designs might be more easily understood, and therefore more easily checkable. The blueprint-based reviewing of software began. The appeal of the CASE gurus was mainly directed towards the management of the companies. Introducing CASE became a company goal, it was a question of prestige.

Today, according to the latest statistics /OVUM 90/, only about 4% of the software-producing companies use the classical CASE tools for system analysis. About 40% companies have acquired such tools. So most of this tools became what is called "shelfware".

Is CASE therefore the washout of the eighties? What are the underlying reasons hampering the spread of CASE and thereby of software engineering?

The intentions of CASE

Scientific and industrial progress is interwoven with the development of linguistic means of description of the relevant objects. This is also true in software development. Beyond this, as an activity based on the division of labour, software development needs linguistic means of description of the components which the participating individuals have to contribute, as well as for agreement on proceeding and the actual process itself.

CASE is a child of industry, and therefore a means of productivity improvement. The demand for software is growing continuously, and although the reuse of existing software is desirable, it fails for several reasons. Software is difficult to describe verbally. Reuse causes additional project costs. Reuse also generates dependencies from suppliers which may not be desirable. Still, for many system components like operating systems, data bases and more recently graphical systems, a far-reaching standardization and reuse was reached. Within individual companies, however, in most cases a giant potential for rationalization still exists.

In this way, CASE increases public access to the ideas of others
and decreases privacy. If this social or ethical reason were the
only reason for the failure of CASE, management would have to be
blamed.

We should, however, take into account some other underlying
problems of CASE before speaking of our own experiences and trying
to show some ways out of the CASE dilemma.

The opposing forces

Software development is a creative, skilled and courageous explo-
ration of new solutions. Every piece of software which is written
is something basically new. The important question is if the procedures recommended by present CASE methods conform with the
habits and possibilities of the human mind.

Thus one should rather mistrust people who recommend a strictly
top-down procedure. Recent field studies showed that even in the
early stages of a project, detailed information is of eminent
importance and that imagination oscillates between various levels
of abstraction rather than progressing continually. The human mind
possesses the ability of abstraction, which makes it possible to
accentuate important parts which are in a special situation and to
document them for others.

The levels of abstraction or refinement demanded by CASE are
levels of documentation. Would we not, in proceeding top-down,
document things we do not yet know or things we have already
completely mastered, because we have experience with them ? Would
we not, in effect, put the cart before the horse?

As a means of analyzing existing organizations the value of CASE
methods is indeed proven. Finding the data objects and process
hierarchy is still done by analyzing events ("What happens if"-
questioning) rather than by performing some mysterious top-down
data flow analysis.

After the documentation of the present state of a system by means
of CASE, the next phase is the most painful for CASE prac-
titioners. Some concepts of the new system become vaguely
discernible and, at the same time, many many other alternatives
exist. Many projects, even those with only a few participants, are
hanging in this state of contrary opinions.

Who is able to decide with certainty whether the chosen
architecture is right? Who will accept the responsibility? A
stagnation like this may result in the termination of a project
unless an experienced team member takes over the leading role and
presents a proposal for the architecture of the new application,
for example a structure of the data management. This very often
makes a top-down architecture (such as an existing organization)
obsolete and thus usually causes violent protests.

This critical phase in system development, which also contributes
to the result that the application of CASE does not reduce costs,
puts the developers into a kind of quarantine. The validation of a
proposed solution is done only by reasoning about it.
A kind of prototyping is done in the mind, comparable to the
"desktop-test" in the era of costly computer time, but now for
much larger systems. This leads to increasing demands for
executable specifications. This implies a demand of prototyping or
simulation for error detection in a concept at an early stage. For
this however, the quality of the linguistic means for designing is
absolutely decisive.

CASE in its present form is an exceedingly abstract documentation
aid for concepts of software systems. Did we expect more? If not,
why was CASE not accepted earlier?

CASE at present is too abstract and its aim too widely spread.
CASE requires training to comprehend its way of thinking. CASE as
a concept comprises more than the variety of CASE tools we use for
drawing and which we love or hate.

For a programmer, CASE is something unfamiliar and therefore not
considered necessary. The programmer knows the jungle of the
application which he is concerned with, the traps of the language
in which it is written and the confusion his predecessors left to
him. His knowledge, however, is rather intuitive and topo-
logically oriented. He may be compared to an expert who cannot
pass on his knowledge and has never learned a language in which to
do so. CASE has never found the right language for the average
programmer, for instance a COBOL programmer in a bank. Company
analyses by means of CASE confirm this strongly.

CASE, today, is a means of expression for trained engineers. CASE
for specific applications does not yet exist. Company models are
still in development.

Software makers of today (there are about two million COBOL
programmers) shy away from abstraction. Abstract reasoning is
repulsive to many and implies too much aesthetics or even good
taste.

To someone who completed an apprenticeship in pure CASE the
inconsistencies of a software product with which he is in daily
contact seem strange. A first attack of rage is followed by
lasting frustration. A single person is insufficient for the
repair of a large system. The first impetus also fades because the
necessary revision of a working system is often regarded as "apple
polishing".

CASE is meant to bring clarity into architecture and thus to
produce systems which are maintainable over a long period of time.
But who really wants that? The speed with which the so-called
fourth-generation-languages gained a market shows that there is an
interest in short-term solutions. The productivity of these
languages is considered to be fabulous. As to the maintainability
of the programs written in them, there is dead silence.

None of these languages has grown into a standard. Still the
influence of these languages signals a need for limited, and
thereby simple but powerful linguistic means.
If software is not lasting, and if commercial software is always
developed along the same lines, what purpose will CASE serve ?
What means CASE ?

Shortly after he had sold his company, Ed Yourdon said that CASE
was good only for the domination of the "Mongolian hordes" when
they attacked the Department of Defense.

CASE standardization efforts

CASE is also a means of partitioning of work. Any project in which
more than one person is concerned is forced to divide the work.
Larger projects cannot be carried out without a partition of the
necessary efforts, that is without structuring the sub-systems and
programs which have to be written.

In all tenders for large engineering or electric projects the
design is a part of the contract. So far in software projects this
part was represented by the requirement specification and at best
some structure planning. Architectural design and the completeness
of the solution could not be checked. What was finally delivered
consisted of a rough solution and many later additions. For this
reason, CASE plans are now demanded as part of the tender,
especially in public tender offers.
This is carried to the point that CASE designs are accepted only
from persons who have graduated from an official CASE school.
Efforts to standardize unified and therefore comparable CASE
methods are in full swing in view of the Single European Market.
Siemens-Nixdorf participates in the development of the CASE method
for the Single European Market, which is called EUROMETHOD.

The Software Engineering tradition at Siemens
(now Siemens-Nixdorf)

DOMINO

In 1978 a set of rules, called Process Technology, which
introduced a product lifecycle, were installed at Siemens for the
professional development of application software.

We can state today that this Process Technology has proved its
usefulness and strength.
The essential point is the clear structuring of decision-making
and the steering of development through costs and quality. This
cost- and quality-consciousness is one of the most important
criteria in industrial production and development.

The decisions on the further advance of project are taken at well-
defined milestones by two persons on management level: one from

the technical and one from the marketing side. In this way, the project leaders are never left alone in their decisions. The parties decide on the basis of work results and have to come to an agreement.

The system of milestones, which at the same time represent the development and maturity of a product, is familiar to everybody in management and the development and production process. The expressions are: a product has reached T30 (end of the integration test), T50 (product release test), and "finally" B70, such as the release for customers.
This basic order for development is flexibly adapted to the needs of each project. For instance, in the deliverables of milestone T30, a performance description may not in some cases suffice. a function model of the intended product may be required.

When the first signs of the CASE era began to show it was recognized that our existing development methods were incomplete and that our tools supported software development on mainframes only.

Taking a new approach in 1985 DOMINO was introduced as a strategic product defining an integrated methodology for the development and the domination of complex information systems.

The first tools were nearly developed almost exclusively in-house. From the mid 1970's onward Siemens had departments that were chiefly occupied with the development of tools.

CASE in this context meant better support for the early phases of development and transfer of results into the realization phase, such as an integration into the existing tool set. "Design" meant the use of graphical plans and realization meant the use of standard programming languages like COBOL and C and subsystems like data storage and menue systems. The connection had to be a design language which was to be generally applicable and could be projected onto the paradigms of the target language. It also needed to contain the corresponding transformation tools (generators). This was the birth of GRAPES 86, (GRAPES = GRAPhical Engineering System) /GRAPES 90/.

GRAPES

Starting in the mid the mid 70's with intensive inhouse usage of Petri net, CCITT-SDL, Yourdon, HIPO and Refa techniques, IORL(Input Output Requirement Language) was considered. Long before the times of object orientation, the value of data encapsulation and the use of process objects acting independently from each other had been recognized in IORL. In contrast to other design languages developed in the field of Structured Analysis, it also contained a complete programming model. In addition, it was able to do simulations, and was therefore able to act as a prototyping language. This was both a blessing and a danger. The great scope of IORL, comming as close as it did to known implementation languages, threatened to overburden it with the peculiarities of these languages, and even to replace them.

The features for describing data models, important in business
programming but lacking in IORL were added. In addition several
models of interprocess communications were introduced.

Today developments appear to include object-oriented and knowledge
engineering paradigmes in the GRAPES language and therefore making
it conform more closely to the new programming paradimes.
The basic problem of the transformation of a design language into
a target system also exists in GRAPES, although even when IORL was
used, simulations were successfully done. At that time there was
much talk of "automatic programming". This vision, in reality, was
merely the search for a powerful programming language. This
desired language, however, may be hampered by the restrictions of
the planned target enviromnent. But within that environment a
dedicated CASE-language can be very helpful. I-CASE (Integrated
CASE), a more recent off-spring of the 4GL family, uses such
dedictated language forms.

Programming means to write down anything one likes, as long as the
prescribed constraints are not violated. Programming without programmers (James Martin) means programming with more powerful and
clearer programming languages. Finding this notation is the basic
task of CASE.

In the development it was recognized that there are basically
three aspects of dynamic systems: dynamic behaviour, data
structure and intercommunication of processes. These different
views are described with GRAPES in different types of plans, as
shown in figure 1.

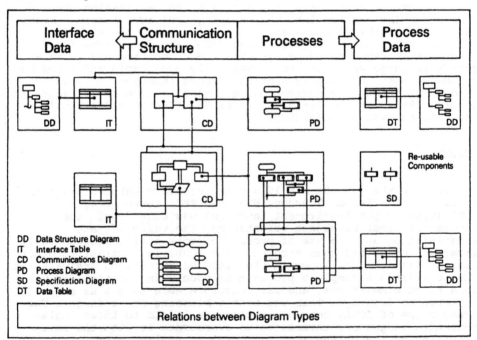

Figure 1: GRAPES 86, a Language for Executable Specifiations

Confusing these viewpoints was the cause of misunderstandings in many discussions in the past. Artificial constructs such as top view, front view or side view were used to make existing habits of thinking more receptive to a more abstract view of systems. At the same time the symbols of the graphic language were elaborated, taking into account the tradition of software engineering and general symbols of the daily life. The aim was to develop a blueprint language for the software engineer. A company of the size of Siemens regards contribution to standardization in the software industry as an obligation.

After continuous improvements, and above all continuous increases in precision, the GRAPES language has proved to be successful in many projects. Especially during analysis the three views of objects brought a great improvement over the previously used standard method, the Stuctured Analysis. The various inspection of a design from different viewpoints affected a mutual advance of the work under the other views. In this the interplay between data structure (objects) and process behaviour (methods) was found to be the driving wedge.
The communication relations followed as a consequence of each analysis step rather than determining it. GRAPES was also used for the post-documentation rather of existing systems with no major problems.

Still, there seemed to be no great enthusiasm for GRAPES and the CASE tools which had been developed in the meantime. The reason turned out to be that the software houses, which were approached, were more occupied with maintenance and extension of existing systems than with new developments for which CASE could have been used.
Was CASE too late?

We soon overcame growing resignation. The corollary to CASE was CARE - Computer-aided Reverse Engineering.

CASE & CARE

The EDP departments of present software companies had been suffering (and still do) from several constraints. The major one was the lack of trained personnel, the second was the pressure to come to solutions quickly ("Anything needing more than six months is obsolete when it reaches the market") and the immense effort required for the maintenance and adaptation of existing solutions. According to "Computerwoche" in March 1991, IBM estimated this to be 90 % of EDP budget.

So the task was clear. More had to be done for the long-neglected upkeep of systems. If existing systems could be made CASE-able, it would mean progress for CASE as well. In 1988/CARE 88, CARE 90/ we chose the name CARE for that dicipline. Meanwhile the name has become the name of an entire software discipline.

The success has been considerable. A fully automated procedure has been developed, allowing the restructuring of existing COBOL programs. Additionally, a comfortable browser interface for repository-oriented re-engineering was developed. We gained a lot of experience using the restructuring tools in customer service projects. The browser is now used as the user interface of our standard repository ERMS (Entity Relationship Management System).

The new COBOL 85 standard offered the chance to improve the maintainability of systems significantly. It could be shown that maintenance, that is the defined insertion of changes in structured code, can be done in half the time needed in non-structured programs.

In our work, which has given us a pretty deep insight into the existing COBOL culture, we also noticed that management meanwhile has learned to distinguish between short- and long-term program solutions. For the latter only standard languages are applied. This question has today become a question of the survival of software companies.

Despite the rather moderate initial success of CASE there is no reason for resignation. There still exists a great number of possibilities to achieve a better CASE technology. In the following we present areas of development which will, in our opinion, reward investments.

Further CASE-enabling technologies

Computer-aided reverse engineering

This offers enormous possibilities for development. The present metrics are totally insufficient as quality standards. They are at best a measure for the complexity of a program, but not for the understanding of an application. A theory of comprehension is still lacking. Such a theory would not only be useful for the inspection before the re-engineering of a program system or for controlling of the maintenance quality (the factor of source ergonomy), but also for the development of the future CASE language in conjunction with the as yet unknown interface between this CASE language and the user.

The development of a restructuring technique could in the end be done not only within one language paradigm, but also permit the change of paradigmes. In our restructuring work we have found old COBOL programs from the 1960's which one would today undoubtedly implement using decision tables. Transformations of this nature are not yet possible.

The field of controlling program terminology and the system-wide updating of program names is not completely undeveloped anymore. Names are the key to understanding the functionality of a program. As we know from our large collection of programs from all over Europe, most sins are committed in this respect. Finding good

names is not easy, but indispensable in a program with any life
expectancy.

Today we have powerful parser generators. Together with dialog
programs like browsers they can help to reedit entire systems.
This also obviates the reams of paper which in the past were
produced when a program was analyzed.

CASE repository

Nowadays even application programs are becoming so large that it
is impossible to understand their specifications at a glance, let
alone work with them. Many program specifications are described in
several places, several times, and by several authors, leading to
redundant code. The problem is not dealt with by simply storing
the specification in their present form in a central register, the
repository. The repository of the future, from which CASE expects
to profit much, should not be abused as a refuse dump.

A meaningful use of a repository depends to a large extent, on the
quality of the piece list structure of the elements. Here however,
no clear statements about the meaningful and economically
justifiable depth of resolution of the development documents can
be made at the moment, because of the performance problems which
have to be expected.

Using the repository as a platform for tool integration is a
useful proposal from a technical point of view. The problems of
performance and communication are not simple but solvable in
principle. Much greater difficulties arise from semantic problems.
Trying to integrate tools with different semantics and from
different suppliers, in this respect, might be compared to the art
of mixing a good cocktail. Without agreement on the methods used
by the tools a sufficient advantage for the customer cannot be
reached.

Furthermore, one should not underestimate the influence of a
repository on the structure of a company. In this, the strategy
followed at its introduction is decisive. It starts with the
choice of the repository itself. One should not adhere to the
belief that a totally integrated repository is possible or even
beneficial for a company. In no case should the expectancy of a
repository (the "final company model") lame all development.

The future development of display technologies for the presentation of large amounts of data seems to be decisive for a
efficient use of a repository. Work is going on /BYTE 91/ which
confirms our developments. This work extends the possibilities of
the orientation of the user by projecting the information into a
three-dimensional space and using rotation as a means of accessing
information.
Our way of thinking includes the space around us. This is known to
any programmer who, doing something completely different at a
different place, suddenly realized why a program did not work.
Inversely we should increase the use of this tie of knowledge to
space when designing the layout of graphical interfaces.

Next to the form of the representation is the possiblity of rule-based abstraction of structures, that is the derivation of coarse-grained from fine-grained information. This will prevent the user from drowning in the flood of information. In these techniques Knowledge Engineering will have to be applied in connection with Hypertext functions. They will prepare the way for a new generation of databases, the Intelligent Data Bases /IDB 89/.

Information models

CASE today is too abstract. The development of business models and business rules, will presumably bring the necessary application-oriented specialization. Today already 50% of all program systems in use in the USA are standard solutions. This trend might extend to proprietary solutions as well. A uniformity of the economy is not be feared, but should lead to a more frictionless business life.

In software development this standardization will lead to a significant reduction of demands on programs. Today the surroundings for which a function is to be written have to be explained verbosely to the programmer by the organizer. This leads to huge piles of paper which nobody can find his way through. The future programmer will grasp things much more easily due to the capabilities of company models.

Object-oriented design

Although still in its infancy, but already considered a deliverance, the first experiences with the paradigms of the object-oriented (better called simulation friendly programming technique) give rise to new hopes. This is a way of designing which at first glance appears to be more understandable than many of the previous, as it allows the consideration of systems as a whole from the viewpoint of the data (objects and functions). Using this programming paradigm, productivity rises as a result of the re-use of so-called class libraries. These allow the quick adaptation of a certain type of program to the actual demands. The advantage of classifying functions (methods) according to the data schemes results in a remarkable reduction of code. The classifying hierarchy, however, narrows at the same time the view of the data itself. For example for one peson a Mercedes may be a car, for another a status symbol, depending on their different views.

Hardly anybody will now dispute that object-oriented means of programming are useful for the development of tools in the CASE and CAD(Computer Aided Design) areas. They are applied if the corresponding data re-positories are available.

Their use in commercial applications is at present under investigation in pilot projects. A use of this paradigm in a large project is not known so far.

Multilanguage paradigms

The babylonian confusion of tongues, which the multitude of
programming languages can be considered, is an obstacle only in so
far as even with the most common languages a simultaneous use in
one application gives rise to great difficulties.
Here lies a great need to catch on for the standardization of communication models within different programming paradigms. Such an
effort would undoubtedly have repercussions on the development of
a future CASE language, which would have to take into account such
principles of communication and provide a continuous specialization in the direction of such paradigms.

Process structure

As development from scratch becomes less and less necessary, the
adaption of existing software by either reuse of parts or by
generation will become more important and there must also be an
influence on the process structure of software development.
Presumably in the future even the smallest changes will have to be
approved by a "Technical Director", who will of course be
supported by a staff of experienced personnel. There will be
departments that specialize in the maintenance of components and
do not work on functional extensions of the systems.

Process management

The reduction of production cycles for software, demanded by
management for economic reasons, has advantages for development
with a corresponding marketing strategy, as it makes it easier to
find out much earlier what is really wanted. Thus, one only has to
have the courage to turn away from wrong system structures.
The constantly improving user interfaces allow almost any
intelligent layman to design his own user interface. More information than for the common spread-sheet technique is not
required. Prototyping may be shifted more and more to the pro-
spective user. The prototype of the user will be an important part
of the requirement specification.

The process of software development will not only lead to a new
product, but also to the capture and inspection of new re-usable
software components. The life-span becomes a cycle.

CASE training

Decisive for the success of CASE is the training of the developers. A first reading of the CASE manual brings no enlighten-
ment, because experience only grows from application. Regrettably,

training costs time and money. We are not yet trained to recognize good software design, and for this reason some managers adopted the CASE way of proceeding with some suspicion and tended to become impatient the nearer an agreed deadline comes. CASE therefore can only be introduced by performing pilot projects. And this demands a decision from the higher levels of a company.

The development of a CASE culture

CASE is a child of industry. It is a challenge for computer science. Many have regretted that computer science was put next to mathematics and that far too little was done for the applicability of its achievements. Most frequently this is heard from mathematicians themselves, who have landed in industry.

We established with some effort, lectures on CASE (DOMINO and GRAPES) at local universities.

The division of computer science into the branches of theoretic computer science and software engineering is long overdue.
CASE points the way.

Literature:

WEINB 71:	G. M. Weinberg, The Psychology of Computer Programming, Van Nostrand Reinhold Inc, New York, ..., 1971 ISBN 0-442-29264
EIRMA 89:	European Industrial Research Management Association EIRMA Workshop Technology '99, Paris 11-13.10.89
DBP&P 90:	J. F. Palmer, CASE: The Good, the Bad, and the Ugly, DATABASE PROGRAMMING & DESIGN,Vol 3, No 10, Oct. 1990
OVUM 90:	R. Rock-Evans, K. Hales, Reverse Engineering: Markets, Methodes and Tools, Vol 1, Ovum Ltd, London, 1990
GRAPES90:	G. Held, Hrsg., Sprachbeschreibung GRAPES, Syntax, Semantik und Grammatik von GRAPES-86, Berlin, München, Siemens AG, 1990, ISBN 3-8009-1581-2, (soon available in English)
CARE 88:	J. Wagner, Graphic Computer Aided Reverse Engineering(CARE), Second International Workshop on CASE, Proc. Voll. 1, Boston, July 12-15 1988
CARE 90:	J. Wagner, Computer Aided Reverse Engineering(CARE), der Weg aus der Wartungskrise, ADV-Kongreß, Wien, March 1990
BYTE 91:	M.A. Clarkson, An Easier Interface, Xerox PARC, in BYTE Febr. 1991, S. 277-282
IDB 89:	K. Parsaye et al., Intelligent Databases, Object-oriented, Deductive Hypermedia Technologies, WILEY, New York,.. 1989 ISBN 0-471-50346-0/2

Should CASE be application dependent?

Peter Hruschka
Systemhaus GEI
Pascalstr. 14
D-5100 Aachen, Germany

1 Introduction

Back in the early '80s, when GEI started its CASE activities, two of our original
goals were formulated in the following way [Hru82]:

Our [life cycle covering CASE-] solution should be
· general enough to be applicable to a wide variety of applications, but
· specific enough to be efficient and helpful in each different application

The words "general enough" and "specific enough" indicate the old dilemma
between general purpose solutions and specific solutions. In this paper we want
to discuss where CASE in general and GEI's solutions specifically stand today
within this spectrum.

From programming languages we know the overall trend from application
independent solutions (like the first machine codes and assembly languages) to
more application specific solutions (like COBOL for commercial applications or
CHILL for telecommunication applications), and on to even very specific application generators (like many of the VHHLs).

We will summarize our observations during the last ten years, the adaptations
and refinements that GEI made in its product strategy, and our plans for the
future by approaching the topic from two different perspectives: from a user's
point of view and from a developer's point of view. We will try to answer the two
questions: 'Does the user need different CASE components for different applications?' and 'How are CASE builders influenced by different application areas?'
(An overview of GEI's CASE strategy can also be found in [Ktg91].)

2 CASE from a User's Point of View

Users perceive CASE as methods and tools supporting various activities they
have to perform when they develop a new system. Let us take this list of activities
as a basis for discussing, whether CASE today is application neutral or applica-

tion specific - and if so, how much. Although more sophisticated process models are known today, let us look back to the waterfall model as a basis for discussing the status of CASE with respect to applications in the various phases. We will consider

- Requirements Capture, Analysis
- Design and Implementation
- Maintenance and Reengineering

Such rough categorizations are not only given by the waterfall model, similar ones can also be found in the CASE frameworks of the leading hardware manufacturers. Therefore, they are still considered to be state of practice.

2.1 CASE supporting Requirements Engineering

Looking into the process of requirements capture and systems analysis we could observe a clear shift over the last 15 years in methods and CASE tools. In the late 1970s and the early 1980s system analysis and the supporting tools were clearly application domain specific: on one side function driven methods and tools were used for more process oriented applications. Examples are Structured Analysis (SA), SADT, and various other derivatives. We mainly supported SA with our environment ProMod/SA. On the other side, for more information system oriented applications, data driven methods and tools were used. Examples are the many alternatives based on Entity Relationship Modeling [Che76].

By the mid 1980s applications in the real-time and embedded (RT&E) systems world demanded and developed specific enhancements to existing systems analysis methods [W&M86, H&P87]. These enhancements allowed systems analysts to express their requirements more adequately. Tools supporting the new ideas soon followed: ProMod/SA was augmented by ProMod/RT already in 1987 and among the first to support the integrated SA/RT-method. Other CASE tools followed.

In the late 1980s both application domains (i.e. the IS-oriented and the RT&E-oriented) discovered the usefulness of the "other" approach for their own systems. When RT&E systems became more complex they needed more and more integrated data bases. IS-systems discovered more and more important functional and control aspects. Convergence of ideas in analysis methods started. The three basic views (function view, data view, and behavior view) are now considered necessary, independent of the application domain. Just the amount of time spent for one or the other view still differ. Again, some CASE tools supporting the integrated views became available; among them GEI's ProMod/SA, /RT and /IM on UNIX and VMS-platforms, and ProCycle/SA and /IM on OS/2 platforms.

Using these application independent kernel methods and CASE tools has shown success in various kinds of application domains. We have used this approach for industrial automation projects as well as for big administration management projects. The next step is now, to make it "specific enough" to be even more efficient in the different application areas. To achieve this goal, different extensions to the requirements tools are made.

For the RT&E world, behavior modeling is extended by methods and tools to make the dynamic behavior visible. Requirements models are animated and simulated. Data flow diagrams, state transition diagrams, and process specifications are "executed", the execution is visualized in terms of system mockups, which the analyst can build from predefined building blocks, like instruments, buttons, gauges, etc. Thus, the user can detect a new category of errors in this very early stage of a project. Tools supporting this animation and simulation have left the labs and are already available as products, tightly integrated with the basic modeling tools. With ProMod/SA and /RT the tool "ShortCut" is used to shorten the development cycle.

For the IS-world mainly the data models are extended by tools supporting the prototyping of user interfaces, screen layouts and report generators. The goal is the same as in the RT&E world: using the basic model for a more extensive feedback from the user. By not only showing "paper models", but letting the user play with a prototype of the final system, the development risks should be reduced.

Summarizing the evolution we have observed in requirements engineering we could say that we have reached a stable basis, from the methods and the CASE tools, by supporting the 3 basic views (function, data and behavior), on top of which we can now add more application specific features.

2.2 CASE supporting Design and Implementation

While we can see the common basis in the area of requirements engineering, we feel that the worlds of designers are still far apart. Depending on their final application domain they tend to use very different working styles, methods and tools.

In the world of commercial systems, design is very much data driven. The structure of the data base within an application determines the design style. As soon as this structure is designed, the major work is done. The rest is considered to be mostly clerical work. All the functionality is often purely formulated as queries of the data base or as triggers within the data base. The behavior of the system under construction is described in sequences of screens, that the user will finally see and use.

In more technically oriented applications the functionality of the planned system still drives the design. Many surveys among designers show, that function-oriented design methods like Structured Design [P-J88] are still most popular. Advances in modularization techniques as advocated by D. Parnas since nearly two decades gradually begin to creep into practice. Modern languages like Ada or new buzzwords like object oriented design help in this process. As soon as the designers have found an overall modular architecture of the planned application, the necessary data are localized inside the modules, behavior is implicitly given by the use-relationship between the modules.

GEI decided to support both strategies by specialized products. The starting point is the common requirements model as described in the previous section. For data-base driven appliations one can generate physical data base structures as design skeleton. The starting point is the conceptual information model. Using the tool ProFace for this transformation, the data structures are normalized, entities and relationships are resolved into simple DB-relations. The designer can then use the 4GL environment UNIFACE to add transaction desriptions, triggers, screens, report layouts, etc. From all this information the final application can be generated for a wide variety of existing data base systems.

On the other hand one can transform the complete requirements model into a first cut hierarchical module structure. The major sources for this transformation are the hierarchy of data flow diagrams and the control structures of the real time model. The ProMod-transformer suggests modules, interfaces and the use-structure of the overall architecture. The design structure is then iteratively improved and augmented with more detailed module bodies, local data, function descriptions, etc.
This dichotomy for the different application domains is shown in figure 1.

Design and implementation today are conceptually already much closer and more tightly linked than requirements and design. How is this reflected in CASE-tools? There we have to be more realistic: If every developer of technical systems would be using modern languages like Ada or object oriented versions of C and Pascal, then tools could provide a tighter link between design and the final code, since the design concepts and the programming language concepts can be nicely matched.

If every developer of data base systems would already use E-R-modeling as basis and generators based on such design concepts, the final code would have an identical structure as the design.

The fact stays, that most systems in the IS-world are still coded in COBOL. Also for RT&E-systems we feel, that we will still have to live with Fortran and C code for a long time to come. So, the best thing tools can do today, is generate code frames and skeletons from the design. GEI provides such generators for various languages in the Pro/Source parts of ProMod/SI (source code interface).
In many cases it is up to the project manager to ensure (through organisational means) that design and code do not diverge. This issue automatically brings us to the next topic: maintenance and reengineering.

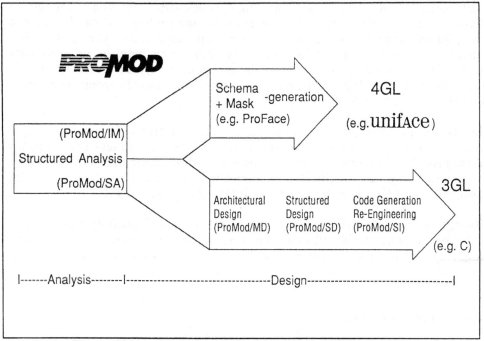

Fig. 1: Alternative solution for design with 3GL and 4GL

2.3 CASE supporting Maintenance and Reengineering

For developers maintenance is an old and sorrowful topic. From a CASE viewpoint this topic has been ignored for a long time. Only recently many activities have been started in the CASE world to not only support the creation of new systems from scratch, but also to continue working with existing systems, especially with such systems, that have not been created using CASE-technology. Reengineering is the magic word for this technology.

Because of this newness of reengineering, CASE solutions today are not yet as sophisticated and not as widespread as forward engineering solutions. Nevertheless they provide valuable help for maintenance personnel, in any case more than they have had available some years ago. If the level of expectation is not too high (e.g figure out the requirements from this 150000 lines of spaghetti assembler program) CASE solutions can be found today.

Similar to the design and implementation task, the reengineering technology heavily depends on the target programming language and the target environment. Therefore, GEI offers specific reengineering solutions for different starting points today.

In the commercial world, the world of COBOL and mainframes, the reengineering tool VIACENTER allows to dive into the complex structures and to reengineer COBOL systems. The emphasis is more on human understanding of large and complex existing COBOL programs than on automatic restructuring. The tools help the developer to understand complex interactions between program logic and data structures. This is achieved by bringing the typical CASE work style (i.e. interactive working, ergonomic user interfaces) to a world, where block-mode 3270 terminals are still standard.

In the technical world, the world of Fortran, C, and Ada, GEI provides tools to recover the structures embedded in the code of these languages and translate them prback to functional dependencies and module structures. The reengineering parts of ProMod/SI (Re/Source) perform that link from source code to the design tools, so that systems can be maintained on design level.

Reengineering is a still a very young research area. Hopefully the different strength of todays tools will soon converge, so that we can trace the structures and ideas within systems not only back to the design level, but also to the level of requirements.

2.4 Where do we head?

For the CASE tools that a user can see and work with we can say, that methods drive the tool developement. Whenever a better understanding of the underlying methods is achieved it only takes a short time before tools are available to support these new ideas. Some years ago every method and every tool claimed to be applicable for any kind of system development. Today, we can already see a bifurcation in a more technical oriented branch and a more commercially oriented branch. Various industry reports on CASE published in the last 12 - 24 month also indicate this trend. Several CASE conferences have split their programs to either attract one or the other kind of audience.

GEI has performed a trend study covering software engineering and CASE evolution over the next 10 years. This study resulted in the projection that out of the two branches today there will be more specialization for different application areas within this time frame. Not every single applications will have its own methodology and tool set, but major application domains, like car manufacturing, insurance industry, telecommunication industry, etc. will have specialized methods and tools. This trend is portrayed in figure 2.

3   CASE from a Developer's Point of View

From a user's point of view the further development of software engineering methods has the strongest influence on the evolution of CASE. And methods tend

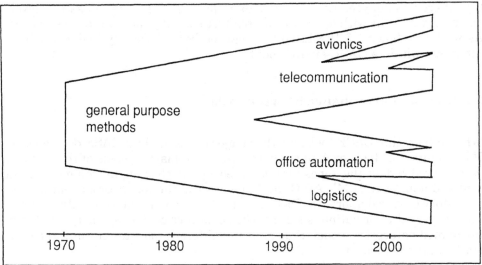

Fig. 2: From general purpose method towards specialization

to become more application domain specific as indicated in chapter 2 above. From a CASE developer's point of view other factors are much more important: hardware platforms, operating systems development and data base (or repository) progress. Let us discuss how much these factors make CASE application dependent or application independent.

Since we have left the decade, where single tools were used to solve isolated problems during system and software development we have to look into integration strategies for CASE tools.

3.1 User Interfaces

One major kind of integration strategy is integration on the user interface level. Today we have already reached a point, where this problem can be considered as solved: all the big hardware vendors provide user interface management systems (UIMS) with the basic software or operating system. Whether it is called DEC-Windows, OpenLook or Motif does not matter too much for the user: support of multiple windows, mouse driven operations, context switches between different tools are available in second generation tools.

For a CASE developer there are mainly two alternatives: either ignoring the vendor specific UIMS and implementing a uniform user interface for different CASE tools or equipping the CASE tools in conformance with the UIMS and style guides of the different hardware manufacturers. GEI has chosen the second approach in order to offer the well known look and feel to users of a certain hardware platform, independently whether they are currently working with a CASE tool or with other packages available on this machine. While users perceive the differences between the various UIMSs just as syntactical nuisance, developers have to fight with the internal architecture differences in today's UIMSs. As we have shown (cf. [K&L91]) they can be harmonized by higher levels of interfaces within a CASE-environment.

3.2 Information exchange between tools

When integrating CASE tools, another major question for a CASE developer is: How do different tools exchange information. Two major schools of thought can be observed today: the repository centered approach and the communication centered approach. IBM's AD/Cycle framework is the major proponent for the repository centered approach. Tools are implemented around the central repository, where all information is stored. The semantics of the tools is based on the predefined enterprise model, thus allowing different tools to interpret the data stored in the repository.

The other school of thought is represented e.g. by the Eureka Software Factory (ESF) concepts. Tools are built along the central "software bus", exchanging information on this communication channel, independent of the place, where information is stored. HP-Softbench is another example for a communication based architecture for CASE.

DEC's Cohesion concept has features of both schools: With CDD and RDB a repository is available, which can be accessed by CASE tools though the object-oriented interface ATIS. On the other hand the NAS-architecture allows for communication oriented exchange of information between tools.

As of today we can say, that most of these architectural issues are still in the research and testing phase. Looking into todays practice (i.e. products, that are available on the market) we can find that different tools are not integrated at all, or they communicate through data integration on company private data base structures. GEI's ProMod also has its proprietary object management system (ProMod/OMS) as central repository, through which the analysis, design and code generation tools communicate. However, the architecture of the single tools is already structured in a way, that will allow integration of these tools into a repository centered or communication oriented framework. Already today each tool is internally structured in 3 layers, a user interface component, a service component and a data base component. This architecture allows us to insert the communication layer between the user interface and the service component. So the major part of the tool could be executed on a central server, only the user interface part is working on the networked clients. It also allows us to insert the communication part between service component and client, such that the majority of work is performed on clients and only for repository accesses the server is needed.

What does all of that mean for the user of CASE? Will it be application dependent

151

or not? From a developer's point of view we can see the same kind of application domain dependency that we discussed in chapter 2. This time there is a different reason for it. While we stated above, that the user will need specialised methods for specific domains, the argument here is as follows: Since users in a commercial, data driven environment will want to hold their company data in a centralized repository (as many of them already do it today, even when they are working without CASE), they will provide a larger machine holding the centralized repository. So they have to have CASE tools, that can be integrated via such repository concepts, working on their company-wide data.

On the other side, many projects in the RT&E industry will not require that many central data. But they might require heterogeneous network hardware structures, anyhow (if, e.g. processing is done in various places in a manufacturing company, or little specialized processors are placed in various places in an airplane); therefore the CASE solutions for such applications will have to provide commmunication based information exchange.

Also the latest kind of integration strategy - tool interaction controlled through process models - will result in application domain specific process models and therefore in application domain specific CASE environments.

4 Summary and Trends

Today, many CASE environments could be classified as not *application* dependent, but *application domain* dependent. As a trend we currently believe that we have reached a point in CASE, where more application dependent specialization is asked for by the users and more standardization is asked for by the developers. This is not necessarily impossible, as the following thoughts show.

From a user's point of view we feel, that the time has come to provide application domain specific additions to the agreed basic tools for requirements engineering and design. One focus of our current research activities is on RT&E systems: Within the Eureka Software Factory project we try to build "FERESA", a first ESF-factory for real-time and embedded systems applications. Various tool integration mechanisms, especially communiation oriented architectures are testet to integrate tools from different European manufacturers. Also process models for RT&E-applications are investigated. The ESPRIT II project COMPLEMENT (COMprehensive Large scale Engineering MEthodologies aNd Technology transfer) goes one step further: within this project existing industrial practice, methods and tools in the area of RT&E applications are investigated, gaps identified and closed, and the resulting approach to RT&E systems will be transferred to the developers through multiple media, like books, seminars, common training centers, etc.. We believe that both activities will lead to good, specialized methods and tools for this application domain.

From a developer's point of view are trying to structure the overall tool architecture in a way, that allows us to provide uniform interfaces to repositories and communication based frameworks. Within these two different frameworks the architecture of CASE environments will become better standardized and application independent. However, the tools embedded in the architecture will become more application dependent.

So, the need of the users and the needs of the developers can be brought together towards more application domain specific, but nevertheless more standardized CASE environments.

Acknowledgment

I am indebted to my collegues of the ProMod team at GEI, especially to Matthias Hallmann for the helpful discussions on this subject.

Literature

[Che76]   P. Chen: *The Entity-Relationship Model - Towards a Unified View of Data,* ACM Transactions on Database Systems, Vol. 1, No. 1., March 1976

[Hru82]   P. Hruschka: *ProMod - Motivation and Introduction,* GEI internal publication, 1982, reprinted in German in: P. Hruschka: *"Mein Weg zu CASE",* Hanser Verlag, München, 1991

[H&P87]   D. Hatley, I.A. Pirbhai: *Strategies for Real Time System Specification,* Dorset House, New York, 1987 (German Edition: Hanser Verlag, München, 1991)

[Ktg91]   H. Keutgen: *CASE - eine unendliche Geschichte,* in: P. Hruschka (Ed.): *CASE in der Anwendung, Erfahrungen bei der Einführung von CASE,* pg. 65-84, Hanser Verlag, München, 1991 (in German)

[K&L91]   U. Krapp, J. Lieven: *Entwicklung Style-Guide-konformer portabler Dialoganwendungen,* Systemhaus GEI, 1991, submitted for publication (in German)

[P-J88]   M. Page-Jones: *The practical guide to StructuredDesign,* 2nd edition, Yourdon Press, Prentice Hall, 1988

[W&M86] P. Ward, S. Mellor: *Structured Development for Real-Time Systems,* Vol. 1-3, Yourdon Press, 1986

Utilizing Fifth Generation Technology in Software Development Tools

Wolfgang Henhapl, Stefan Kaes, Gregor Snelting

Praktische Informatik

Technische Hochschule Darmstadt

Magdalenenstr. 11c, D-61 Darmstadt

email: {henhapl, kaes, snelting}@pi.informatik.th-darmstadt.de

Abstract. Software developers express a desire for more intelligent support for all phases of the software development process, but current CASE technology does not fully utilize the advancements which have been achieved in fields like automated deduction or specification languages. It is the aim of this paper to demonstrate how such techniques can detect and even prevent errors and inconsistencies much earlier than conventional tools. We describe inference-based support for interactive configuration management, interface checking, component reuse, and intelligent browsing; furthermore, we present a programming environment for rapid prototyping based on a lazy functional language. All tools make heavy use of automated deduction techniques such as order-sorted unification or AC1 unification, and are parameterized with language-specific information such as type inference or module dependency rules.

1 Introduction

In a recent paper on the management of software projects, P. Elzer [El89] reports on an inquiry among the participants of a software engineering conference, who were asked for their wishes with respect to future software development tools. The majority of the interviewees voted for *intelligent tools*, but only a minority believed that such tools could be realized in the near future.

The aim of this paper is to demonstrate that software tools which are far more intelligent than those currently available can indeed be constructed and be the basis of a software development environment. These tools are developed as part of the ongoing research activities at the Technical University of Darmstadt.

We will present

1. an interface checker which is incremental and can handle incomplete or inconsistent software component libraries
2. support for reusable, polymorphic components even if the underlying programming language is not polymorphic
3. an interactive configuration management system which can handle partially specified configurations, infer missing information, and automatically construct makefiles
4. an intelligent retrieval system which allows to search library components by usage patterns
5. a programming environment for rapid prototyping, based on the lazy functional language SAMPλE.

The first four tools belong together; we call them the *intelligent software component library*. The last system is a stand-alone implementation of SAMPλE which is also called the *prototyping environment*.

All tools stick to the common principles *ambiguity tolerance* (they can handle incomplete and infer missing information), *fault tolerance* (they temporarily allow inconsistent information), *incrementality* (they allow fast and comfortable interaction), and *generateability* (they are parameterized with language-specific information). This is in contrast to most existing environments, since currently available tools for the above tasks are either not interactive, unable to cope with missing or inconsistent information, or unable to be parameterized with language-specific information. Our inference-based tool kit can automatically complete information which has only partially been given by the programmers. Hence, our tools can check consistency much earlier than traditional approaches, and can detect errors as soon as the globally inferred information becomes inconsistent. To achieve our goals, we make heavy use of artificial intelligence techniques, especially techniques from automated deduction.

The work described in this paper evolved from an earlier project, where we developed a generator for language-specific programming environments. This system, called PSG [BS86, BS91], generates a language-specific hybrid editor and an interactive interpreter from the definition of syntax and semantics of a programming language. PSG already sticked to the above principles and utilized inference-based mechanisms for static program analysis. Our excellent experiences in using these algorithms finally led us to believe that they can be applied to support programming in the large. The SAMPλE system also benefits from the PSG project, since the SAMPλE editor was generated by PSG.

2 Inference-based Interface Control

Our tool set is centered around a library of software components. This is common practice, and it is standard that for components or modules which depend on each other, interfaces must be checked in order to guarantee correct component interaction. Traditional approaches support only a fixed language and are entirely batch-oriented, whereas more modern software engineering environments are interactive and integrate interface checking into system development, or are even generic tools which are parameterized with language-specific information. But none of the current approaches can handle incomplete or inconsistent interface information.

The intelligent component library uses an active, unification-based mechanism which not only checks interfaces, but also can infer interface information which has not (yet) been provided by the programmers. The mechanism is based on the notion of *context relations*. Context relations have originally been introduced as a device for incremental semantic analysis of incomplete program fragments. In contrast to traditional techniques (e.g. attribute grammars), they can handle and infer missing information and guarantee the detection of errors as soon as a fragment cannot be embedded into a correct program. An elaborate theory and implementation exist, but due to lack of space we can only give some general remarks. The interested reader is referred to [BS86] for conceptual and methodological foundations and to [Sn91] for the underlying theory and optimal incremental analysis algorithms.

Relational analysis associates sets of attributes with nodes of a given abstract syntax tree. Attributes are terms of a free order-sorted algebra with sorted variables, where the signature of the algebra is language specific and therefore must be given by the language definer. Generally speaking, the use of an order-sorted algebra has the big advantage that many context conditions can be expressed as sortal constraints: for example, requirements like "the operands of an addition must have arithmetic type" or "the object on the left side of an assignment must be a variable" can easily be formulated.

Conceptually, context relations are very similar to the relations known from relational database theory. The main difference is that order-sorted terms are used as tuple components, which may contain sorted variables (expressing that certain (sub)attributes must be equal). A join operation has to *unify* corresponding tuple components instead of just testing them for equality. For purposes of semantic analysis, the domain of a context relation is always a set of syntactic entities and program objects respectively. A relation which contains more than one tuple describes overloaded objects, which may have several (still possible) attributes. The language definer has to specify *basic context relations* for all terminals and rules of the language's syntax. A basic relation specifies sets of possible attributes (namely order-sorted terms according to the attribute algebra) for syntactic entities. It can be seen as an inference rule describing all context-sensitive constraints which apply to the syntax rule or terminal. A fragment can then be analysed by joining all basic relations of its constituents; the resulting relation describes exactly the (incomplete) semantic information associated with the fragment. As soon as a fragment is erroneous, that is, cannot be embedded into a correct program, an intermediate relation will become empty, signaling a semantic inconsistency. Usually, the analysis is an active process which can very well infer (still) missing attributes of e.g. (still) undeclared variables from its uses (*type inference*).

In the intelligent component library, interface information is described by context relations. An interface relation of a component contains the attributes (as inferred so far) of those objects which are relevant for the library. Typically, these are exported and imported objects, as well as (still) undeclared objects which could be declared outside the component or module in question. An object attribute contains object class and type. For procedures, a list of argument types and a result type is given.

Imagine a stack module which exports e.g. procedures "push" and "pop", as well as other objects. Since the module is under development, some of its text is still missing, or even purposefully left open, e.g. the concrete representation of stacks. Below, we present a typical context relation which describes the interface of this module, as inferred so far. Variables are written in uppercase letters (possibly with an additional index), where for simplicity a variable's name also gives its sort. Use of variables state that certain (sub)attributes must be equal (e.g. the stack's element type and the argument type of procedures "push" and "pop"). The presence of variables in a relation indicates also incomplete or polymorphic information (in the example, we assume that the stack type is an opaque type, and that the element type of the stack has not yet been declared and is thus still unknown).

stack	(module, __)
elementtype	(typeconst, TYPE)
StackId	(typeconst, opaque(117))
newStack	(procedure, (< >, opaque(117))
push	(procedure, (< opaque(117), TYPE >, __))
pop	(procedure, (< opaque(117) >, __))
top	(procedure, (< opaque(117) >, TYPE))
isEmpty	(procedure, (< opaque(117) >, bool))
isFull	(procedure, (< opaque(117) >, bool))

Now we imagine two hypothetical clients, which import objects from the stack module and use them. The local component analysis will infer possible types for the imported objects from their uses, despite the fact that the stack definition module may contain definitions of these types. For example, relational analysis of the first client might infer that the stack's element type must be an arithmetic type, because an arithmetic operation is applied to an object which afterwards is pushed onto a stack. Relational analysis of the second client might infer something different, namely that the stack has elements of type char. The clients thus might have the following interface relations:

stack	(module, __)
StackId	(typeconst, TYPE)
newStack	(procedure, (< >, TYPE))
push	(procedure, (< TYPE, ARITHMETIC >, __))
pop	(procedure, (PARMLIST, __))
isFull	(procedure, (< TYPE >, bool)

stack	(module, __)
StackId	(typeconst, TYPE)
newStack	(procedure, (< >, TYPE))
push	(procedure, (< TYPE, char >, __))
pop	(procedure, (PARMLIST, __))

These relations contain a number of uninstantiated (sub)attributes, probably due to the fact that the components are still quite incomplete. But even at this stage, our system can detect a global inconsistency.

In the first client, the procedure "push" has argument type "arithmetic" (which again is not fully instantiated), in the second client, this procedure has argument type "char". Remember that in the definition module the element type of stacks has been left open and is thus still unknown. But nevertheless, we detect an inconsistency because the interface checker tries to unify the attributes of all occurrences of "push" in the three components. This unification fails, since "arithmetic" and "char" are not unifyable. Thus, whatever might be inserted later for the stack's element type, it will never lead to a correct library. Hence, our system has anticipated an error which classical methods would detect much later!

Although our example is very small, it fully scales up to real-world situations. Since efficient algorithms for order-sorted unification are known today, inference–based interface checking is hardly more expensive than conventional techniques. During editing of a component, only local consistency will be checked; as soon as the component is written back to the library, interfaces to all neighbour components in the component dependency graph are checked or inferred.

3 Improving Reusability

Only some years ago, programming languages have been enriched with concepts which support reusability of software components. Two examples are generic packages in ADA and polymorphic functions in ML. Both concepts allow to fix the final types of e.g. function arguments not at definition site, but only at the usage of a package or function. This provides for reusable software components, which can be fed with objects of many different types (but these types must stick to a common pattern). Hence, such reusable components can be used in different contexts – but the security of strong typing is still guaranteed. Some authors go even further and propose to use not complete function or package definitions, but *program schemes* or *templates* as basic software components, which must then be filled in and completed by the programmers. [En88] argues that a combination of template-based libraries with good retrieval techniques is the most promising approach for the future. But current tools cannot guarantee consistent use of such schemes, because incomplete programs cannot be analysed.

We have seen above that library components may be incomplete and may have an ambiguous or overloaded interface. As we shall describe below, such components can easily be made polymorphic and reusable. Our approach therefore opens the door to generic or polymorphic program templates with secure interfaces even for languages like C or Pascal which do not explicitly support polymorphism. Furthermore, library components are named; they can be used by other components simply by providing their name. Thus, components may be decomposed into named pieces. In addition, we provide for components that are *parameterized* in the sense that named "holes" (missing parts of a fragment) can be *instantiated* by the user of a component; this is done just by providing program text or component names.

If an interface relation contains uninstantiated variables (due to missing information), the component can be made polymorphic simply by ensuring that different clients may instantiate missing interface information differently. Thus, every client must stick to the pattern specified in the interface relation, but different clients may instantiate this pattern differently. Technically speaking, we avoid that attributes of *all* occurrences of an object are unified; instead, each attribute of an object's use in a specific client is unified with a (conceptual) copy of the attribute from the supplier's interface relation.

In the above example, both clients of the stack definition are consistent with its supplier, because "type" and "arithmetic" is unifyable as well as "type" and "char". Thus, if we omit the requirement that all occurrences of global objects must have unifyable types, and only insist on the weaker condition that every client must be consistent with its supplier, we can use the stack definition module as a generic, reusable component: the stack's element type is purposefully left open, in order to allow programmers to use this stack definition as a program scheme, where the element type must be filled in. But even in this situation, consistent use of schemes can be guaranteed. Hence, a slight change in the analysis algorithm results in reusable, polymorphic components: the programmers need only state which objects or components should behave polymorphically! In fact, we obtain a reusability mechanism for (almost) free which is very similar to ADA or ML, but useable for languages which do not support reusability explicitly.

4 Inference-based Configuration Management

Configuration control deals with the management and consistent configuration of system families, whose members differ only in some components (variants); it has recently received much attention. Most of today's tools are extensions of Make [Fe79] or RCS [Ti85]. The shape system [ML88] allows variants for Make targets; additional attributes can be used to specify a particular configuration thread. A different approach can be found in [Est88]: here, component dependencies are computed (rather than specified) from language-specific rules; additional attributes are then used to compose a particular configuration. Again, all these approaches are batch oriented and neither incremental nor ambiguity tolerant.

In our system (which has first been described in [Sch89]), any library component may exist in several variants. A *variant editor* is used to visualize the system dependency graph. Dependencies are determined by the system, hence no specification (e.g. a makefile) is necessary. For each component, the editor will offer the available variants in a menu, thus the user may interactively construct a particular configuration. Although the basic dependency graph cannot be modified (dependencies are computed by language-specific rules and thus cannot be changed arbitrarily), the editor allows to compose or decompose a component into named subcomponents and to add or delete variants. As in the above-mentioned systems, we use additional attributes to distinguish variants of a component. By using these attributes, the editor can check immediately whether a configuration is consistent. The consistency check in the variant editor makes again use of context relations, and this has some important consequences:

- The editor can partially infer attributes itself: if, for example, one variant with the attribute "X-Windows" (in contrast to "SunView") has been selected, the unification-based mechanism will conclude that all relevant clients and suppliers also must have this attribute.
- Inconsistencies can be detected even if a configuration thread is not completely specified: if in the above scenario a user tries to select a "SunView" variant, this inconsistency will be detected even if other attributes are still unknown.
- By filtering the menus for variants with respect to the attributes inferred so far, the editor can even guarantee that inconsistent configurations cannot be constructed.

According to the calculus of context relations, attributes may be structured and grouped into conceptual classes. This is a simple consequence of the use of order-sorted terms and imposes a taxonomy on variant attributes. For any library, inference rules must be given which describe constraints on the variant attributes of dependent components. Such inference rules are just basic context relations; if the system structure changes, new basic relations must be provided.

Note that attributes used for variants and attributes used for interfaces are different and in principle completely orthogonal. For practical reasons, it is even necessary to allow that different variants of a component have different interfaces. In such a case, the interface analysis will first filter out all variant combinations which have inconsistent interface relations. The variant editor will then display only variants which passed this test; the variant attributes are used as an additional device. Once a (partial) configuration has been determined (because attributes have been supplied or inferred), the editor can automatically generate appropriate makefiles.

We demonstrate our concepts by extending our small example library. We introduce a variant attribute

stack-organization = dynamic | static

A component may exist in two variants, or may have an uninstantiated variant attribute, indicating that it can (as yet) be used in both variants. Variants with attribute "static" realize an array implementation of the stack, the variants with attribute "dynamic" realize a linked list implementation. It is a perhaps wise technique not to have a component itself available in two or more variants. Instead, variant-dependent parts of a component exist as subcomponents, and each subcomponent exists in the required variants. This minimizes duplication of code and avoids the well-known difficulties with redundant program text.

The variant editor will display the component dependencies either in graphical or textual form. The editor offers menus for all (sub)components which exist in variants, and the user can choose between "dynamic" or "static". In our example there is an additional inference rule (realized as set of basic context relations) which states that the variant attribute of all variants of a configuration must be equal. Thus it is sufficient to select just one menu item: once the "static" variant of some (sub)component has been selected, the editor knows that all other fragments must be static as well. All remaining menus are filtered such that the "dynamic" item can no longer be selected: the editor guarantees consistency of the configuration. Note that our example is very simple; it is possible to use more than one variant attribute and to specify dependencies between attributes. It is also possible to store (partial) configurations and load them when the variant editor is invoked, thereby establishing working environments. Such environments can be named (e.g. "fast access" for a partially specified "static" configuration), hence a configuration with certain global characteristics can be made available immediately.

The interface analysis treats variants as overloadings of fragment interfaces. The relational calculus allows to describe such overloadings in a natural way, and the analysis will automatically filter out inconsistent variant combinations – which is actually the same as overloading resolution, a standard relational facility. The library is considered globally consistent as long as there is at least one consistent configuration possible.

Assume that a new subcomponent (realizing an additional function) is added to the stack definition module, which exists only in the static variant and implies that the stack's element type must be "arithmetic or set". Since the second client needs element type "char", the system will infer that it can only be used in a "dynamic" configuration, because otherwise an inconsistency in the interface relations would emerge. Consequently, the static variant will not be offered by the variant editor, and any attempt to use the additional function in the second client will cause a complaint.

5 Improving Component Retrieval

Component retrieval in a library deals with effective search procedures for components which obey a certain given (possibly incomplete) specification. Two techniques have recently been proposed to obtain more intelligent retrieval. The first approach tries to (hand-)construct a taxonomy of software components in a library. This allows to build special expert systems, which can find components with given characteristics or attributes. The second approach evolved in the world of functional programming: here, some systems allow to search for functions not by name or attributes, but by usage patterns, thus using a type scheme as a search key. The type scheme is inferred from intended uses of a function, and the retrieval component will find function definitions with equal or similar type characteristics [RT89, Ri89]. It turned out that usage patterns are a much better filter than one might think, and we therefore generalized the approach to arbitrary languages.

The general idea is to allow context relations as search patterns. Such relations can be supplied by the user, or computed by the system itself. For example, a list of all library objects which can be used at a given point in a fragment can simply be achieved by inferring the attributes of the object at the point of use, and unifying this information with attributes of objects available in the library. The former attributes are a by-product of local relational analysis, and the latter are part of interface relations. If the unifications do not fail, the library object is added to the list and can be displayed to the user. It is also possible to search for combinations of attributes: "give me all pairs of functions, where either the result type of the first is equal to the argument type of the second, or the second has five parameters of type real". Hence we can use polymorphic or overloaded search patterns, by simply coding them as context relations.

Imagine a user who thinks that our sample library contains something like a "stack", but does not know the names of the corresponding functions, not to speak of parameter types and order. However, he believes that there are two functions "add an element" and "remove an element", which both take an argument of type "stack", and the first one takes an additional argument, the stack element. The user does not know anything about the realization of stacks, all he knows is that both functions must accept an argument of the same type. This rather unprecise search pattern can be described by the following context relation:

"add"	(procedure, (< TYPE_2, TYPE_1 >, __))
"remove"	(procedure, (< TYPE_1>, __))

Although the user has mixed up the order of parameters, the relational inference engine (enhanced with AC1–unification [Fa84] for parameter lists) will find the module "stack" in our sample library, since the interface relation for "stack" has columns for "push" and "pop" which contain attributes compatible with the search pattern. The corresponding module and procedure headers are displayed to the user.

Component search directed by usage patterns will usually find more than one candidate, and in order to increase accuracy, it can be combined with traditional retrieval techniques. Our retrieval component also offers searching for component names, text fragments or variant attributes. Interface information, inconsistencies, inferred attributes of program objects etc. can be displayed conveniently. In addition, the fragment mechanism gives us hypertext-like cross-referencing for free: as described above, fragments may refer to each other, and a mouse click onto a fragment reference immediately shows its definition.

6 The SAMPλE Prototyping Environment

Functional programming has gained widespread acceptance as a tool for specification and rapid prototyping of complex software systems, because functional languages have powerful and flexible type systems, simple semantics, do not require user implemented storage management and permit better program structuring techniques due to higher order functions and lazy evaluation [Hu89].

However, the actual use of functional programming systems has lagged somewhat behind its acceptance as a useful paradigm. One of the reasons for this, as we feel, unfortunate situation is the lack of adequate development tools for functional programs. Currently available tools are either batch oriented, like e.g. the Lazy-ML compiler [AJ89], or offer only a primitive command line oriented interpreter interface, like e.g. Miranda [Tu85] or the various Standard-ML systems [AM87, Ha86]. None of these tools offer help for interactive type error correction or debugging, a problem that needs special attention for lazy languages.

The programming language SAMPλE and its progamming environment adress this situation; they are the outcome of the DFG-project "Umgebung für konstruktive Spezifikationen". The primary goals of this project were the design of a high level functional programming language and the implementation of a programming environment to support the development of large systems written in that language. Additionally, it was deemed necessary to provide an efficient implementation for executing and debugging lazy functional programs.

System Overview

Unlike most other functional language implementations SAMPλE is embedded into a language-dependent, fully integrated, interactive programming environment. The environment's components are a hybrid editor, an inference based type checker, an interpreter, a compiler, a debugger and a library system. All components share a common user interface which exploits the possibilities of modern workstations, such as bitmap-oriented displays, pointing devices, windows and menus (see figure below). The editor has been partially generated with the PSG-System, all other parts are specific to SAMPλE. Management of module dependencies, type checking, compilation, updating and maintainance of all files is fully automated.

Language Design

The design of SAMPλE has been influenced by many other (functional) programming languages, most notably Miranda, Lazy-ML, Standard ML, HOPE [BMS80], and META-IV [Jo82]. SAMPλE is a modern functional language based on a lazy semantics which, among having other advantages, enables the programmer to describe and use infinite data structures very naturally. Moreover, lazy semantics is absolutely essential for the use of SAMPλE as a description language for denotational semantics. Pattern matching can be used to define functions or to extract subcomponents of arbitrary data values. SAMPλE provides concise notation for the definition of lists, sets and finite mappings through an extension of ZF-expressions, which were first introduced in Miranda. Abstract datatypes can be specified by writing a signature and providing a concrete model for an implementation. The development of large systems is supported through a simple module system which allows the export and import of arbitrary language objects across module interfaces. A font with the most commonly used mathematical operators and the possibility to define prefix, postfix and infix operators greatly increase the notational expressiveness of SAMPλE.

The following program to compute the thousandth prime number illustrates some of the SAMPλE language features. It consists of three definitions. First, the infinite list of odd natural numbers is defined as the number 1 concatenated with an application of the higher order function *map* to the increment function (+ 2) and the list of odd natural numbers (note the recursive definition of an infinite list!). Second, the predicate *relprime x l* is defined to be true if x and all numbers p in the ascending list of primes l that satisfy $p * p < x$ are relative prime. The list of primes *primelist* is then defined to consist of the number 2 followed by all members p of *odds* save 1 that satisfy *relprime p primelist* (again a recursively defined infinite list). Finally, the thousandth prime number is extracted from *primelist*. This program works only because lazy evaluation will automatically stop computation of more primes after the required prime has been found.

module primes
definitions
```
odds ≡ 1 ^ map (+ 2) odds
relprime x l ≡ ∀ p ← l, p * p ≤ x : x mod p ≠ 0
primelist ≡ 2 ^ ⟨p | p ← tl odds; relprime p primelist⟩
eval primelist ↓ 1000
```

In designing SAMPλE we have not taken the approach of the functional purist, i.e. we have included non functional language features, such as updateable variables, assignments and traditional control structures. Although this results in a loss of referential transparency and proving programs with side effects is in general more difficult than proving pure functional programs, there are also good reasons for this approach: Referential transparency in itself is not the reason why functional languages are preferable over imperative ones. Instead, functional languages offer new ways of program modularization by means of higher order functions and lazy evaluation and provide much more expressive type systems than conventional languages. None of these advantages is offset by the introduction of side effects. Second, some algorithms can only be awkwardly expressed in pure functional notation. Third, to our knowledge it is still unknown whether all imperative algorithms have a functional equivalent of the same time and space complexity. But, most importantly, incorporating side effects into the language enables reasoning about them within the language framework and thus allows the stepwise refinement of functional specifications down to imperative implementations.

Another feature which sets SAMPλE apart from other functional language implementations is the provision of a general interface for functions written in imperative languages. Any function or data value and even abstract data types can be declared external, provided an implementation is given in the external language (currently only the use of C is supported, but an extension to other languages poses no problems). The interface is seamlessly integrated in the SAMPλE environment, i.e. the user of a function cannot see any difference between pure SAMPλE definitions and externally implemented functions. Referential transparency and type safety can of course not be guaranteed across such an interface. However, if the system is to be used for the development of real prototypes, it needs an interface to the underlying operating system and other widely available software packages, like numerical libraries, window or database systems. It would be very undesirable and extremely uneconomical to fix the knowledge about these packages at the language design level.

The Type System

SAMPλE has a powerful type system with an extended concept of polymorphism, which allows the usage of sorted type parameters and recursive types. The notion of parametric polymorphism has been combined with the concepts of overloading and coercions for predefined operators and data types. The next version of the language will even permit user defined overloading and coercions. The main properties of the type system are:

- Every typable expression has a unique most general type.
- Every possible type is an instance of the most general type.
- The most general type can be inferred from the program text.
- Typeability prevents type errors at runtime.

In a pure parametrically polymorphic type system the principal type of any expression can be expressed as a type expression over unsorted type variables. For example, the expression

$$twice\ f\ x \equiv f\ (f\ x)$$

has the unique principal type

$$twice : (\alpha \to \alpha) \to \alpha \to \alpha.$$

twice maps arbitrary functions of type $\alpha \to \alpha$ to functions of type $\alpha \to \alpha$ for *any* type α.

The addition of abstractable overloadable operators and implicit coercions destroys this property: in SAMPλE, the principal type does in general depend on a set of coercion and overloading constraints [Ka88]. In our system the function *twice* has the most general type

$$(\alpha \to \beta) \to \alpha \to \beta \mid \beta \triangleleft \alpha .$$

twice maps functions of type $\alpha \to \beta$ to functions of type $\alpha \to \beta$, provided values of type β can be coerced to values of type α. Thus *twice trunc* has the type $real \to int$. Overloaded operators are treated similarly:

$$double\ x \equiv x + x$$

has type $\alpha \to \alpha \mid \alpha\{+\}$, it can be applied to values of all types which are allowed as arguments of the addition operation. Coercion and overloading constraints can depend on each other: the function

$$add1\ x \equiv x + 1$$

has the most general type

$$\alpha \to \alpha \mid \alpha\{+\},\ int \triangleleft \alpha.$$

The function *add1* can be applied to values of type α, if α admits addition and integers can be coerced into values of type α. Therefore both *add1* 3 and *add1* 3.5 are valid applications of *add1* with types *int* resp. *real*.

Type Error Correction

Polymorphic type systems complicate the correction of type incorrect programs, since types are inferred rather than declared by the programmer. The source of type errors usually cannot be confined to a narrow program region. In most cases, only an analysis of all participating program parts can reveal the real cause of error. Implicit coercions, overloaded operators and recursive types aggravate this problem: even small progams give rise to complicated type structures and it is not clear which of the many inferred types should be presented to the programer for error correction.

In order to make the decisions of the type inference component transparent and understandable, the system remembers for each program subexpression the computed type and other useful information such as cross references to definition and uses of identifiers, identifier classes and declaration type. These informations can then be interrogated by the programmer through a simple mouse click on the relevant subexpressions. Therefore it is possible to restrict the amount of information contained in error messages to the absolute minimum necessary. This technique enables novice users of the language to ask for more information, whereas experienced programmers often spot the problem without this additional information. Our experiences with the SAMPλE environment show that this approach yields much higher productivity than traditional terminal oriented methods.

Execution and Debugging

For program execution we have developed a variant of the SECD-machine supporting lazy evaluation and "flat" environments. Modules can be compiled either into abstract machine code, which is then executed by the interpreter, or can be compiled into native code of the host machine in order to speed up execution. Modules in abstract code can be arbitrarily mixed with native code modules and can be linked to produce a stand-alone program runnable outside the development environment.

The current version of the execution component supports debugging only for abstract code modules. However, modules which are in the development and test phase are usually compiled into abstract machine code only. This reduces compilation times significantly (compilation rates for typical modules, including type inference and strictness analysis without subsequent assembly pass, are between 30 and 70 lines per sec. cpu time on a SUN-3/60). At the same time, the possibility to use native code allows efficient execution for approved modules. Additionally, modules of a program under development are kept loaded during a single system session in order to keep the time needed for linking at a minimum. After successful compilation new versions of recompiled modules are incrementally relinked into the still loaded program. This method leads to extremely fast response times comparable to a pure interpretative system while keeping the advantages of compilation techniques.

Debbuging aids are indespensable for the development of large and even medium-sized programs, no matter how abstract the notation. The first level of debugging present in SAMPλE is strong static typing, a sometimes underestimated advantage of modern functional languages. The second level consists of a runtime debugger which has been specifically tailored to the lazy evaluation mechanisms of the SAMPλE execution component and represents a major technical achievement of the SAMPλE project.

Computations in imperative languages are defined by the sequence of assignments to program variables regulated by control flow constructs. The resulting state change over time can simply be visiualized through the insertion of input and output statements at the appropriate places in the program. Debugging tools can simplify this process since they avoid the need for explicit insertion of IO statements and additionally allow the computation to be interrupted at arbitrary program points, possibly followed by inspection and/or updates of program variables.

In a pure functional program, control flow is hidden in the data dependencies that exist between the result and the arguments of a function call. With lazy evaluation, arguments of functions or locally defined values are only evaluated if and when they are needed. Thus, even if it is possible to insert output statements into function definitions, the resulting output is usually very difficult to understand. Moreover, adding trace output statements can influence the evaluation order, possibly changing a terminating into a non terminating program!

The SAMPλE debugging system solves these problems by providing a box model similar to some Prolog systems. The smallest observable actions in this model are function calls and the evaluation of yet unevaluated expressions. Functions can be entered through several ports, one for each definition clause. Evaluation of function arguments or locally defined values leads to an exit from the function box. Boxes can be identified by function name and lexical scoping. Unevaluated expressions are represented by their defining program text together with an assignment of values to free variables.

The current implementation provides menue and/or program triggered debugging actions such as break points, tracing, single step and control over the amount of debugging information presented to the user. Furthermore, the interpreter offers support for profiling: for each function, the number of calls and cpu time spent can be displayed as well as number and size of allocated memory cells. A detailed description of the SAMPλE debugger can be found in [GKT90].

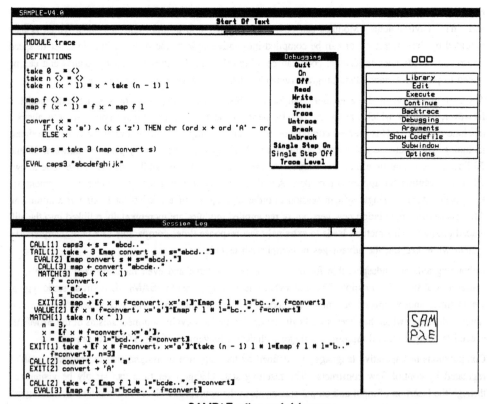

SAMPλE editor and debugger

7 Conclusion

In this overview article, we have presented two strains of current research at the Technical University of Darmstadt, namely the intelligent software component library and the SAMPλE prototyping environment. Development of the intelligent library has just begun, whereas SAMPλE is in everyday use at our laboratory. It was not our intention to present an in-depth technical description of the elaborate underlying theory; such descriptions have been published elsewhere. Nevertheless we hope that the reader has got an impression how unification technology can improve software development tools, and how research on lazy functional languages can increase the usefulness of rapid prototyping environments. Many aspects of what people call fifth generation software technology are by now well developed, and time is ripe to utilize them in the software development process.

Acknowledgements. Thanks go to M. Gloger, F.J. Grosch and U. Schroeder for their very active participation in the development of the concepts and tools described in this paper.

The development of SAMPλE has been funded by the Deutsche Forschungsgemeinschaft, grants He-1170/3–1 and He-1170/3–2. Development of the intelligent component library is also funded by the Deutsche Forschungsgemeinschaft, grant He-1170/4–1.

8 References

[AM87]   Appel, A. and MacQueen, D.: A Standard ML Compiler. Proc. FPCA 87, LNCS 274, pp. 301 – 324.

[AJ89]   Augustsson, L. and Johnsson, T.: The Chalmers Lazy ML Compiler. The Computer Journal 32, 2 (April 1989), pp. 127 – 141.

[BS86]   Bahlke, R. and Snelting, G.: The PSG System: From Formal Language Definitions to Interactive Programming Environments. ACM TOPLAS 8, 4 (October 1986), pp. 547-576.

[BS91]   Bahlke, R. and Snelting, G.: Design and Structure of a Semantics-based Programming Environment. International Journal of Man-Machine Studies, to appear.

[BMS80] Burstall, R., MacQueen, D. and Sanella, D.: HOPE: an experimental applicative language. Proc. Lisp Conference 1980, ACM.

[El89]   Elzer, P.: Management von Softwareprojekten. Informatik Spektrum 12, 4 (August 1989), pp. 181 – 197.

[En88]   Endres, A.: Software-Wiederverwendung: Ziele, Wege und Erfahrungen. Informatik Spektrum, 11, 2 (April 1988), pp. 85 – 95.

[Est88] Estublier, J. : Configuration Managment. Proc. International Workshop on Software Version and Variant Control, Grassau 1988.

[Fa84]   Fages, F.: Associative-Commutative Unification. Proc. 7th CADE, 1984, LNCS 170, pp. 194 – 208.

[Fe79]   Feldmann, S. I.: Make - A program for maintaining computer programs. Software Practice and Experience, Vol. 9, April 1979.

[GKT90] Gloger, M., Kaes, S., and Thies, Ch.: Entwicklung funktionaler Programme in der SAMPLE Programmierumgebung. Report PI-R3/90, Technische Hochschule Darmstadt, Fachbereich Informatik, June 1990.

[Ha86]   Harper, R.: Introduction to Standard ML. Report ECS-LFCS-86–14, University of Edinburgh, November 1986.

[Hu89]   Hughes, J.: Why functional programming matters. The Computer Journal 32, 2 (April 1989), pp. 98 – 107.

[Ka88]   Kaes, S.: Parametric Overloading in Polymorphic Programming Languages. Proc. 2nd European Symposium on Programming, LNCS 300, pp. 131 – 144.

[ML88]   Mahler A. and Lampen, A.: An Integrated Toolset for Engineering Software Configurations. Proc. Practical Software Engineering Environments, SIGPLAN Notices 24, 2 (February 1989).

[RT89]   Runciman, C. and Toyn, I.: Retrieving Re-usable Software Components by Polymorphic Type. Proc. Functional Languages and Computer Architecture, ACM 1989, pp. 166 – 173.

[Ri89]   Rittri, M.: Using Types as Search Keys in Function Libraries. Proc. Functional Languages and Computer Architecture, ACM 1989, pp. 174 – 183.

[Sch89]   Schroeder, U.: Incremental Variant Control. Proc. 2nd International Workshop on Software Version and Variant Control, Princeton 1989, pp. 145 – 148.

[Sn91]   Snelting, G.: The Calculus of Context Relations. ACTA INFORMATICA, to appear.

[SGS90]   Snelting, G., Grosch, F.J., and Schroeder, U.: Inference-based Support for Programming in the Large. Report PI-R13/90, Technische Hochschule Darmstadt, Fachbereich Informatik. Submitted for publication.

[Ti85]   Tichy, W. F.: RCS - A System for Version Control. Software Practice and Experience 15, 7 (Juli 1985), pp. 637 – 654.

[Tu85]   Turner, D.: Miranda: A non-strict functional language with polymorphic types. Proc. FPCA 85, LNCS 201, pp. 1 – 16.

Integrated Software Components :
a Paradigm for Control Integration

Dominique Clément
Vincent Prunet
SEMA GROUP Sophia-Antipolis
Francis Montagnac
INRIA Sophia-Antipolis
INRIA, 2004 Rte des Lucioles,
F-06565 Valbonne Cedex, France

Abstract

This report describes how control integration between software components may be organised using an encapsulation technique combined with broadcast message passing : each software component, which is encapsulated within an *integrated software component* (*IC*), communicates by sending and receiving events. Events are emitted without the emitter knowing whether there are any receivers. The proposed mechanism can be used for intertool communication as well as for communication within a single tool.

This programming architecture frees the code from dependencies upon the effective software components environments, and simplifies its extension.

1   Introduction

Intertool communication is a very general issue within software systems. Recent work indicates that a good approach to achieve tool integration is to let the control of information be external to the tools. Hypertext systems are more or less based on this principle : communication is expressed by external scripts. Some programming environments are organized around a distributed architecture using message-based communication techniques [16,5,10]. But control integration is not limited to communication between tools. It is also a matter of concern within a single tool.

We propose to organize control integration using an event programming technique : objects communicate by sending and receiving events. Our approach is to use a notion of observers familiar in concurrent languages [13]. The capability of a software component

---

[0]This research is partially supported by ESPRIT, N. 2177.

to communicate with the external world is characterized by a set of inputs and outputs. Inputs correspond to the primitives provided by the component. Outputs correspond to the messages — we call them signals — that the component can emit. Note that signals can carry a value. Inter-component communication is then described as a network of connections between components.

In the following we present the *integrated software components* architecture. We start with a quick discussion on the advantages and disadvantages of an object oriented approach to tackle the control integration issue. Then we show how an encapsulation technique solves most problems of control integration. Finally we illustrate our approach on some examples. We conclude with a discussion and related work.

2 An Object Oriented Approach

One possibility for organizing communication within a tool is to use an object-oriented approach. In object-oriented architectures, message passing provides abstraction and modularity. Abstraction comes from class definitions together with *generic* methods. Modularity comes with the possibility to add new elements within the type hierarchy. Furthermore it is possible to specialize a method according to the types of its input parameters. To organize communication between tools the standard message passing technique appears to be insufficient. Consider for example the coupling of a scrollbar and an object that one wants to scroll over. Clearly the scrollbar must be able to communicate with the object, i.e., to send a "scroll" signal to that object. Here message passing seems to provide the necessary independence between the scrollbar and the scrolled object, since one can argue that the scrollbar must know how to find the object [14]. The situation is less clear if the object can scroll by itself (for example, if it is a text editor). In that case the object must be able to communicate with the scrollbar. It's not clear how to establish that communication. Ideally, one does not want the object to know whether or not it is controlled by a scrollbar.

A standard solution is to use the existing object structure as a vehicle for messages. In our example, the object could send a "scrollbar" message that propagates over the structure in which the object and the scrollbar are combined. We propose to use a message passing technology where messages are emitted without the emitter knowing whether there are any receivers.

We propose to organize control integration using an event programming technique: objects communicate by sending and receiving events.

Consider the case of a type-checker which reports errors. To integrate this type-checker within an interactive environment, we need a mechanism to couple the type-checker output, i.e., the errors, with a browsing facility. Here, we are concerned with the communication between a source window and an error window. For example, after running the type-checker on a program perhaps the list of errors and warnings appears in a separate window on the screen. When moving from error to error, by selecting the error of interest, one induces a selection in the source window. Conversely, from the source window, one may ask what error message corresponds to a given selection in the source.

Note that at the time the error window is associated with the source window, it is likely that the latter is already connected to other objects. Of course, we do not want such connections modified. Further this new connection should not interfere with existing ones.

3 Definitions and unformal specifications

In this section, we describe the connection of software components using an encapsulation technique. The names we use to describe this "software integration" of components are based on an analogy between the described model and electronic boards and components.

The connection of software components, the run-time message broadcast system, and a control integration service component are described.

3.1 Encapsulation of components

At the application level, a software component is called an *external component* (*EC*). External components are not constrained to fit any specific programming concept: their behaviour is not described within our model.

To be connected to other components, an *EC* is encapsulated within an *integrated software component* (*IC*), which provides the interface between the *EC* world and the *IC* system. There is no particular interface requirement for an *EC* to be encapsulated within an *IC*. Such an *atomic IC* provides the necessary interface adjustments.

The external interface of an *IC* is static : each *IC* is given a type at creation time. An *IC-type* is defined by a *name*, a list of *input* ports and a list of *output* ports. A subtyping mechanism is provided to ease the definition of new *IC-types*. The interface is a property of the *IC-type*, not of its instances.

Communication between *IC*s is achieved by plugging them in a common *local bus IC* (*bus*). A *local bus* is a higher order *IC* which itself can be plugged in a nesting *bus IC*. A *bus* specifies both the connections between its elements and an interface with the external world. The *bus* wires are dynamically extended: they do not have to be defined.

Within a *local bus IC*, the ports of an *IC* are connected to the *bus* wires, provided that the ports and the wires have the same name (this restriction can be relaxed using port renaming). Of course a bus wire can be connected to input ports of several *IC*s, i.e., signals may be broadcast. In principle, a port of an *IC* can be connected to several wires.

To summarize, we have defined two different kinds of *IC*s : i) when an *EC* is stored within an *IC*, this *IC* becomes *atomic*; ii) when an *IC* has other *IC*s plugged in, this *IC* is called a *local bus IC*. *IC*s are structured into trees, whose nodes are *local bus IC*s and leaves are either *atomic IC*s containing an *EC* or empty *local bus IC*s. Finally, an *EC* can be stored within several *IC*s, but an *IC* can be plugged in at most one *bus*.

3.2 Broadcast Message Passing

Communication between *IC*s is asynchronous. For example, if an *IC* has an input port connected to several wires, the *IC* receives several signals through its input port, each one with its own value. Note that the signals that are neither input nor output ports of a *bus IC* are local signals, whose communication is limited to within the bus. We briefly describe the principles of the implementation.

An *IC* can emit any signal provided that the signal's name belongs to the *IC-type* output list. An *IC* can receive any signal provided that the signal's name belongs to the *IC-type* input list. Except for *atomic ICs*, the behavior of an *IC* on receiving a signal on a port is to broadcast that signal to all the *ICs* that are connected to it.

An *IC* can emit a signal using the "emit" primitive:

```
emit <object> <port> <value>
```

where the `port` corresponds to an output port of the *IC* and `object` is either an *EC* (when the *IC* is *atomic*) or the *IC* itself. When `object` is an *EC*, the `port` argument must be prefixed by an *IC-type* (because of possible multiple encapsulations of the *EC*). Except for *atomic ICs*, an *IC* can also emit a signal because it exports one of its wires.

When a signal is output from an *IC*, it is propagated on the wires the output port is connected to. On each wire, the signal is selectively broadcasted to all *ICs* connected to the emitting wire.

An *IC* can receive a signal on an input port in two different cases : i) the signal is carried by a wire of the *bus* the *IC* is plugged in (the wire being connected to an input port of the *IC*); ii) the signal is emitted — with the *IC* emit method. In such a case, the *IC* needs not be plugged in a *bus*. This feature is often used while testing an *IC*.

When an *IC* receives a signal on an input port, the performed action depends on the *IC* status. A *bus IC* propagates the input signal to a wire of its internal *local bus*. Every *IC* plugged in the *bus* and connected to the given wire (on an input port) receives the signal (the name of the signal is the name of the input port, not the name of the wire which may be different). For an *Atomic IC*, the method associated with that input port is called. Here it is necessary for an *atomic IC* to have access to its associated *EC*, because the action to be executed belongs to the external component's address space.

3.3   Control Integration Service Component

In the context of a distributed architecture it is also necessary to have a mechanism to connect different tools. This kind of intertool communication can be achieved using a broadcast message server as in [16,4]. We propose to use the above described broadcast message passing technique to implement a control integration service component (*CISC*) based on tool encapsulation. Here we assume that the tool one wants to encapsulate provides a programmatic interface which includes primitives one can call from outside the tool but also some mechanism for the tool to report information to the external world, for example a callback mechanism.

For each tool, its interface is defined by an *IC-type*. When encapsulating the tool with an *IC* it is necessary :

1. to bind input ports to the primitives the tool provides;

2. to make sure that the tool callbacks are bound to the *IC* output ports to be transformed into appropriate signals.

These two bindings are done using a predefined application interface which implements tool encapsulation.

Within the *CISC*, tools are represented by *remote ICs* (*RIC*). A *RIC* is just like a local *IC* except that it encapsulates an external tool : it is not possible to "pair" the *IC* with the tool itself. However, the *RIC* must behave like would do a local *IC* : the tool must receive signals comming from the *CISC* through its input ports and output signals must be emitted within the *CISC* whenever they are emitted by the tool.

We propose to modelize the connection of the *CISC* with a client tool using a notion of *dual IC-type*. A *dual IC-type* is obtained from an *IC-type* by exchanging input and output ports : the dual of an *IC-type* has the *IC-type*'s inputs as outputs and conversely the *IC-type*'s outputs as inputs. Then, the connection of a tool with the *CISC* is achieved by creating a *dual IC* within the encapsulation interface of the tool and by linking that *dual IC* to the tool *IC*. Note that within the tool space, this *dual IC* is a *RIC*. This is depicted in figure 1.

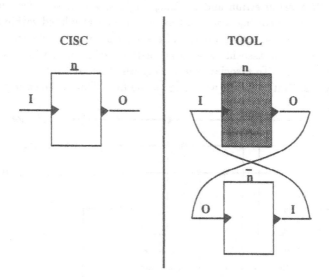

Figure 1: Tool integration

All the output signals emitted by the tool *IC n* are received by the *dual IC $\overline{n}$* which is connected to the *CISC* in a manner that these signals are emitted on the output ports of the *RIC n*. Conversely, all the input signals received by the *RIC n* within the *CISC* are transmitted to the tool encapsulation interface to be emitted by the *dual IC $\overline{n}$*, and then received by the tool *IC n*.

Note that the connection between a *remote IC* and its corresponding *dual IC* is implemented using TCP-domain sockets.

4 Examples

We illustrate our control integration method on three examples: an editing assistant tool, a user interface dialog component, and finally on a distributed programming environment.

4.1 An Editing Assistant Tool

Let us illustrate the principles of using our control integration mechanism within a software system to couple an editor with an editing assistant tool. By editing assistant tool we mean any tool which implements functionalities similar to "template editing" provided by some programming environments [19], [8]. Typically, a menu of possible templates is proposed to the user, this in function of some contextual information (for example the kind of the object denoted by the current editor's selection). When a menu item is selected by the user some action is called, for example the current object is replaced by the selected template.

To simplify, assume that we have an editor which is encapsulated within an *IC-type*, say a view, with a *set-selection* and a *change* inputs, and a *selection* output. Then, assume that we have an editing assistant tool which is encapsulated within an *IC*, say an editing-assistant, with a *selection* input, and a *set-selection* and a *change* outputs.

Initially, the editor is associated with an instance of a view, which is connected to other *IC*'s within a bus. To associate the editing assistant tool with the editor, one only has to plug the assistant tool's *IC* within the same bus. This is shown in figure 2.

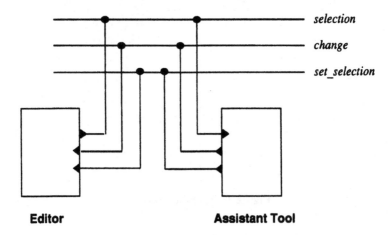

Figure 2: Editing Assistant Tool

Every time the editor emits a selection signal, for example as the result of some action of the user such as pointing at an object within the editor, the editing assistant tool receives that signal (through a bus wire) and updates its list of templates (e.g., using the object type). Then upon user request, for example by selecting a menu item or an element within a choice list, the editor selection is replaced by the selected template. This because of the change signal which is emitted by the editing assistant tool. Possibly, a *set-selection* signal is also sent to move the editor selection on a sub component of the supplied template.

4.2 A Read Dialog

This example illustrates the use of our communication method on the control integration between an application and its user interface. Here we assume that the application is completely isolated from any graphical operation of the user interface, typically by the use of an application interface layer. Also we assume that a dialog toolkit is available.

Suppose we want to create a **read** dialog, which one uses when the application needs to read a user specified file. From a purely functional view point, the read dialog returns the name of the file one wants the application to read.

In terms of encapsulation, we can define a read *IC-type* with only one output port, i.e., *read*, which carries a string value. Clearly, we have to associate the read dialog with some user interface widget, typically a button. For this we can use a predefined button dialog: it is an *atomic IC*, of type button, with only one output, *activate*. Let us assume that we include such a button *IC* in a *bus IC*, which is an instance of the read *IC-type*. Next, we can choose another element in the dialog toolkit to be activated by our button. A natural candidate is a file selector dialog: it is an *atomic IC*, of type file-selector, with an input, *activate*, and an output, *ok*, which carries a string. We include this in the read *bus iC* after renaming the *ok* output to *read*. The final read dialog is shown in figure 3.

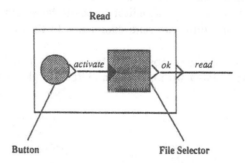

Figure 3: Read Dialog

It is the responsibility of another software system, e.g., a user interface toolkit, to associate the appropriate widgets to dialog fragments. In our example, a button widget to the button *IC* and a file selector widget to the file-selector *IC*. This is done by associating *IC*s to objects as described earlier.

What is now the behavior of the read dialog? Initially, there is only a "read" button on the screen. The user depresses and releases the mouse within the button widget. This causes the button *IC* to emit the activate signal within the **read** dialog *bus IC*. On reaching the **file-selector** *atomic IC* this makes a file selector widget appear. The read dialog emits a *read* signal, as soon as the file selector emits its *ok* signal. This happens on some user action, e.g., selection of an "OK" button provided by the file selector widget. (Of course, the user also has to have selected some file name!)

Interestingly, if the file selector remains visible on the screen then it is possible for the user to read another file without using the read button; he only uses the file selector. Every time the "OK" button of the file selector widget is used, the currently selected file name is emitted through the *read* port of the **read** dialog *bus IC*.

Here it is important that the communication between the application and the user interface to be asynchronous. In the above example the user can continue interacting with the user interface even during the time necessary to read the selected file.

4.3 A Distributed Programming Environment

In that last example we illustrate the principles of using our *CISC* to create a distributed programming environment [7]. Today, most programming environments include a kernel for syntactic processing, language specific editing facilities, and semantic components such as type-checkers, interpreters, debuggers, etc. However tool integration is mainly achieved by the use of a common storage.

Here, we assume the syntactic kernel is a *server* which provides services that are solely syntax-oriented, such as the creation and the management of structured data. All other tools, e.g., parsers, evaluators, editors, etc., have access to abstract syntax objects through the services provided by the server.

Consider intertool communication between a parser, a syntactic kernel, an editor, and an evaluator. To simplify, the syntactic kernel needs to receive the parser's output to create a data which can be used by the editor to be displayed and by the evaluator to be computed. Of course, the editor can send commands to the syntactic kernel to modify the data.

First, we propose to use our encapsulation technique to modelize the control integration: each tool is encapsulated within an *IC* and *IC*s are plugged on a *bus IC*. This is shown in figure 4.

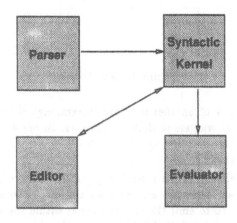

Figure 4: Intertool Communication

Second, we propose to create a distributed implementation of the above described control integration using our *CISC*. Each tool, as a separate process, is connected to the *CISC* using *remote/dual IC*s. This is depicted in figure 5.

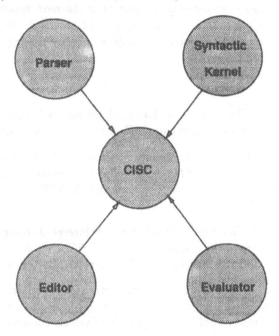

Figure 5: Distributed Programming Environment

5 Conclusion and Related Work

The control integration mechanism presented in this paper originates from current work on software development environments [4], [12], [18], [21], and from work in developing an environment generator [3].

Our main concerns are: i) to separate control from tools; ii) to make tool integration as easy as possible; iii) to make no assumption on the implementation (single process or multiple processes). iv) to make integration of technological changes as easy as possible. Note that the latter is a fulltime concern in our project [6].

This leads to a very open control integration mechanism which can be used to describe and implement intertool communication but also interobject communication within a single tool. Here, we claim that broadcast is the key concept. The notion of message based communication architecture commes from the Field Environment [16]. The notion of encapsulation comes from B. Fromme [9], revisited with concepts of concurrent programming. The notion of software bus commes from the ESF/Eureka project [20].

Note that we do not address the issue of data integration between tools, which has to be tackled with techniques such as full data integration in the spirit of PCTE [2], standardized protocol definition languages [22], [15], and data management [17].

The proposed control integration mechanism is currently used to implement modeless user interfaces (in the style of our read dialog example), editing assistant tools, and distributed programming environments, in particular the next version of the Centaur system. Finally, work has started within our project on the definition of the formal semantics of software integration based on broadcast message passing.

References

[1] G. Berry, G. Gonthier, "The Esterel Synchronous Programming Language : Design, Semantics. Implementation", *Comp. Sci. Prog.* 1989.

[2] G. Boudier, F. Gallo, R. Monot, I. Thomas, "An Overview of PCTE and PCTE+", *Proceedings of the ACM Software Engineering Symposium on Practical Software Development Environments*, SIGSOFT Software Engineering Notes, V.13 No.5, November 1988.

[3] P. Borras, D. Clément, T. Despeyroux, J. Incerpi, J. Kahn, B. Lang, and V. Pascual, "Centaur: the system", *Proc. of SIGSOFT'88, Third Annual Symposium on Software Development Environments*, Boston, USA, 1988.

[4] M. Cagan, "HP Soft Bench: An Architecture for a New Generation of Software Tools", *SoftBench Technical Note Series, SESD-89-24 Revision: 1.4*, Hewlett-Packard Company, Software Engineering Systems Division, November 1989.

[5] N. Carriero, D. Gelernter, and J. Leichter, "Distributed data structures in Linda", *Proceedings ACM Symposium on Principles of Programming Languages*, Jan 1986.

[6] D. Clément et al., "Technical Annex of the GIPE 2 ESPRIT Project", SEMA-GROUP, Paris, France, 1989.

[7] D. Clément, "A Distributed Architecture for Programming Environments", *Proc. of ACM SIGSOFT'90, Fourth Annual Symposium on Software Development Environments*, Irvine, USA, 1990.

[8] V. Donzeau-Gouge, G. Kahn, G. Huet, B. Lang, J.-J. Levy, "Programming environments based on Structured Editors: the MENTOR experience", *Interactive Programming Environments*, D.R. Barstow, H.E. Shrobe and E. Sandewalls (Eds.), McGraw-Hill, 1984.

[9] B. Fromme, "HP Encapsulator: Bridging the Generation Gap", *SoftBench Technical Note Series, SESD-89-26 Revision: 1.4*, Hewlett-Packard Company, Software Engineering Systems Division, November 1989.

[10] E. Golin, R. Rubin, and J. Walker II, "The Visual Programmers Workbench", *Proceedings of the IFIP 11th World Computer Congress*, San Francisco, USA, 1989.

[11] J.M. Hullot, "Ceyx, a Multiformalism Programming Environment", *Proceedings of IFIP 83*, R.E.A. Masson (ed), North Holland Paris, 1983.

[12] R. Ison, "An Experimental Ada Programming Support Environment in the HP CASEdge Integration Framework", *International Workshop on Environments*, Chinon, France, September 1989.

[13] R. Milner, "A calculus of communicating systems", *Lectures Notes in Computer Science*, Springer-Verlag, n. 92, 1980.

[14] C. Nahaboo, "The X11 Generic Window Manager", *GWM Manual*, BULL, 1989.

[15] The OSF Distributed Computing Environment (DCE).

[16] S. Reiss, "Integration Mechanisms in the FIELD Environment", *Technical Report No. CS-88-18*, Computer Science Department Brown University, Providence, Rhode Island, October, 1988.

[17] R. Snodgrass, K. Shannon, "Fine Grained Data Management to Achieve Evolution Resilience in a Software Development Environment", *Proceedings of ACM SIGSOFT'90: Fourth Symposium on Software Development Environments*, Computer Science Department Brown University, Providence, Rhode Island, October, 1988.

[18] R. Taylor, F. Belz, L. Clarke, L. Osterweil, R. Selby, J. Wileden, A. Wolf, and M. Young, "Foundations for the Arcadia Environment Architecture", *Proceedings of ACM SIGSOFT'88: Third Symposium on Software Development Environments*, Irvine, USA, 1990.

[19] T. Teitelbaum and T. Reps, "The Cornell Program Synthesizer: a syntax-directed Programming Environment", *Communications of the ACM*, vol. 24 (9), September 1981

[20] M. Verrall, "The Needs for Tool Integration Met by the Software Bus", *to appear in Proceedings of the Software Engineering Environments 1991*, Aberystwyth, 1191.

[21] J. Wileden, A. Wolf, W. Rosenblatt, and P. Tarr. "Specification Level Interoperability", *Proceedings of ICSE'12*, Nice, France, March 1990.

[22] CCITT Recommendation X.208 (Draft), *Specifications of Abstract Syntax Notation One (ASN.1)*. Gloucester, Nov. 1987.

Formal Methods in Software Development Requirements for a CASE

Dines Bjørner

Dept. of Computer Science
Technical Univ. of Denmark
DK–2800 Lyngby, Denmark

in collaboration with:

Søren Prehn
CRI: Computer Resources International
Bregnerødvej 144
DK-3460 Birkerød, Denmark

Abstract

We capture, define and analyse phases and rôles of computing systems development and developers. We examine the rôle of formal methods, and we set up requirements that a process model and a CASE ought satisfy. A reference process model is presented and a prototypical CASE system is outlined.

The RAISE[1] Tool Set is reviewed wrt. its conformance with the process model.

The paper delineates its subjects, proposes a taxonomy, gives tentative definitions, and outlines a programme of experimental research and development.

---

[1]RAISE: Rigorous Approach to Industrial Software Engineering, is a Method, has a wide-spectrum Specification and Design Language, RSL (RAISE Specification Language), and a Tool Set — and is available from CRI (Computer Resources International) Denmark.

1 Background and Introduction

The paper is based on work within the following projects: (i) RAISE, (ii) LaCoS[2], (iii) ProCoS[3], and (iv) RapID[4].

RAISE was, and LaCoS is, supported in part by the CEC ESPRIT I (315), respectively ESPRIT II (5383) phases, ProCoS is supported in part by the CEC ESPRIT Basic Research Actions (3104) programme, and RapID is supported in part by the STVF, the Danish Technical Sciences Research Board.

Mr. Søren Prehn has kindly co-operated in furnishing section 8.2. Mr. Prehn has since 1985 been a chief designer of RAISE, its wide spectrum language RSL, method and, in the last years also increasingly its Tool Set.

The subject of this invited position statement is that of software development: who is doing it, how, and for whom. The emphasis is on mechanical support. The thesis of the paper is that of basing so-called process models for software development on rigorous, precise and logical, that is: formal methods — to the extent where such is reasonable — and to have computer aided software environments, that is: CASEs, reflect such models intimately.

Without loss of generality we shall focus on software development for technological systems — such as embedded, real-time safety critical (ie. high integrity, dependable) computing systems. We do recognize that CASEs for to be used exclusively by non-EDP end users may pose different requirement problems. But we claim that an analysis, as carried out in this paper, and similar conclusions as here advanced, apply!

2 Project and Product Qualities

CASEs must help secure quality. Hence we need analyse facets of quality.

We examine requirements that the producer and consumer, the developer and the customer (or client) put to the development and use of complex systems.

Project and Product Components: We see the development of a computing system to consist of the development of: the problem-domain specific application, the base systems software that enables the development of the application, and the computer systems hardware that carries the development and deployment of the application.

---

[2]LaCoS: Large-scale Correct Systems using formal methods, a follow-on project to RAISE, involving BULL (Paris, France), Matra Transportation (Paris, France), Lloyd's Register (London, UK), Space Software Italia, Inisel Espacio (Barcelona and Madrid, Spain), TechniSystems (Athens, Greece) — as clients using RAISE, and with CRI (Denmark) as the main producer facilitating RAISE

[3]ProCoS: Provably Correct Systems, a joint project with computer science departments at the universities of Oxford, Kiel, Oldenburg, London, Manchester, Århus, and the Technical University of Denmark (the latter as main partner).

[4]RapID: fRAme Programme In Datatechniques

To carry such developments we require: a spectrum of mathematics based requirements definition and analysis languages, together with techniques anfd tools for their appropriate use, a spectrum of similarly based specification and design languages, together with techniques and tools for their appropriate use, and a spectrum of similarly based programming and machine languages.

The base systems software then includes development support systems and compilers that help develop requirements definitions into functional specifications, these into programs, and to compile programs into code.

In this position paper we shall only cover the aspects contained in the first kind of developments. The second and third kinds of developments contain facets all contained in the first item.

The point about emphasizing the above two-by-three items is that it is not enough for the application to be correctly developed. If the underlying systems software and hardware is erroneously developed then the whole thing is wrong.

Publications [6, 7] outline a project in which the above two-by-three facets are researched and advanced development prototype development studies are implemented. We also refer to a forthcoming set of 4 technical/scientific monographs, [41, 16, 55, 48], which will present emerging, appropriate development methods for applications and base systems software — the first two items of the first grouping and all the three items of the second grouping above.

Product Qualities: For a client to accept a product it must satisfy most of the below qualities: Fit for purpose: that is: Solves the problem; Operable: can be easily used; and Comprehensible: can be easily learned; Conformable: that is: Valid wrt. unformalizable requirements; Correct wrt. functional specifications; Reliable, Fault-tolerant and Secure; and Adaptable, Perfectable and Portable.

Project Qualities: For a developer to assume responsibility for the development of a product the ensuing project must satisfy all of the below qualities: Plannable and Estimatable; Expenses commensurate with Finances; Resourcable, Allocatable and Schedulable; Predictable; and Trustworthy and Enjoyable.

QA: Quality Assurance: QA is then about securing all of the above 4+5 facets: project + product qualities. We take the view that QA is not something that is done over and above programming, but that quality comes out "automatically" as a result of applying the formal programming activities — such as described in section 4.

3 Formal Methods

Formal methods are claimed to help guarantee qualities. Since CASEs shall help secure qualities we need, later, examine in what way formal methods influence the design of CASEs.

Hence we need understand what we mean by a formal method.

Method: A method is a set of procedures for selecting and applying — according to a number of principles — a variety of techniques and notations, using tools, in order to efficiently construct an efficient artifact.

We shall limit our artifacts to be software.

The procedures are to be performed by humans. Selection, among alternative techniques, notations and tools, is based on decisions (thus taken by humans). These decisions may be based on analyses also performed by humans and themselves using techniques, notations and tools.

Formal Method: Formal is a term that can be applied to notations and techniques. Unfortunately it is now being used in connection with methods. As we shall see techniques and notations can be formal, and tools can be based on formal foundations.

A notation or technique is formal if it is subjectable to mechanical manipulations according to some calculus, and if those calculi, notations and techniques can be understood mathematically.

The aim of formalism is rigour in reasoning as well as mechanical, computerized support. If a method uses formal techniques and/or formal notations, then it is called formal.

Examples of formal software development methods are: VDM (for Vienna Development Method) and RAISE — these are described in [8, 9, 14] — books to be published this year, 1991, as well as, for VDM, in [22, 23].

Mathematics and Formal Specification Languages: Mathematics and mathematically precise, formally explicable specification languages form an important basis for formal software development. As formal languages these have a precise mathematical foundation and consistent proof systems. These latter permit exact reasoning about formal expressions which state requirements, specifications, design and code — including formal proofs.

Tool Implications: Given such formal notations and given the ability to mechanically conduct and verify proofs, as well as 'calculating' executable code from abstract specifications, we find, increasingly, the need for CASEs to incorporate such tools. We go even further: we claim that the whole CASE architecture be completely rethought around such formally based tools. The RAISE Tool Set covered in section 8.2 is an example of what we aim at.

Caveats: As also carefully argued in [10] we are not claiming that formal methods assist in securing all facets, but we are asking that one examine carefully the potentialities of formal methods since they have been very successful in the areas to which they have currently been put!

Prof. Michel Sintzoff (of Univ. Cath., Louvain, Belgium) has suggested that instead of 'formal methods' we call the subject: 'precise or logical methods'. The reason is that informal methods are not scorned, whereas imprecise and illogical are!

4   Phases of Systems Development

A CASE is expected to support such phases of development for which it is reasonable to use CASEs. We therefore need examine all phases such that we can later assess proper rôle of CASEs and CASE tools for every phase: its techniques and notations.

We see four phases of systems development: the two development stages of requirements and software, and the two other phases of installation/use/- maintenance/discard, and — over and above it all — before, during and after: management.

4.1   Preliminaries

Example: We assume, for the sake of illustration, that we are to develop the computerized monitoring and control of liquid heating system. A liquid is housed in some container. You may assume, for illustration, that this container is located in the open. •

We see such a system as satisfying laws of nature (in the example: thermodynamics), being controlled according to some automatic control principle, instrumented in terms of (pneumatic) mechanical, electro-mechanical, and electronic components in addition to the computer system (hardware + software).

For the sake of illustration we shall focus only on the software part of the system — leaving all other components, including the computer hardware, to the environment.

The thesis is that we may potentially (soon) be able to guarantee the correctness of the software wrt. a number of assumptions about the environment and the functionality of the system as a whole.

These assumptions state that the software never fails, but that everything else may fail. In case of external component failure (single, double or multiple) the software is expected to force the system into a harmless repair-state.

Overview of Development Stages Based on the above delineation of the product development problem we see the development project to consist of the following parts:

1. Requirements capture, definition and analysis, with stages: problem domain model, control-theoretic model, system (environment + component + core) model, safety model, and performance model.

   This part is pursued primarily by mathematicians, control-theoreticians, operations research analysts, safety and performance engineers.

2. Software development, with stages: functional specification, stages of from abstract to concrete design, and coding.

3. Software commitment, with stages: installation, use, maintenance — which repeats all of the previous stages — and discard.

We now examine the first two stages in more detail.

4.2 Requirements Capture, Definition & Analysis

The requirements stage has as its first purpose to develop an mathematical understanding of the problem domain at hand, as its second purpose to develop a control-theoretic understanding of how it can be controlled, as its third purpose to develop a systems engineering understanding of the various components that enter the overall system, as its fourth purpose to develop an understanding of the safety critical aspects of the system: of all that may go wrong and of all that must go right, and as its last purpose to develop performance criteria based on all of the above.

The requirements stages alternate between capture, definition and analysis. Capture is usually performed in a linguistically controlled dialogue with problem domain and technology specialists. Definition is usually carried out formally. And analysis develops theories about the problem domain based on the definitions.

Problem Domain Model   The problem domain model reflects the laws of nature that determine an overall frame or setting for any solution. Such a model is expressed in mathematics, typically by means of sets of differential equations, and applies laws of physics and chemistry.

Example: In terms of our heating system example the problem domain model apply laws of thermodynamics and expresses such things as: the ambient (t_a), the heater (t_h) and the liquid (t_l) temperatures, the heat dissipation — cooling, possibly expressed in terms of external wind (w), humidity (h), radiation (r), etc. —, evaporation (e) of liquid, supply (s) of new liquid (of temperature t_n), etcetera. It is assumed that $t_l > t_a$.

The differential equations then state the relationships between the various measurable (eg.: $t_a, t_l, t_n, w, h, r, e$) and controllable (eg.: t_h, s) quantities. •

It may be that "the problem domain model" is in fact several models, ie. a set of models, with each model capturing its set of problem domain properties.

Control Theoretic Model The control-theoretic model first establishes criteria for and then means of control. Finally a mathematical model is established which focuses on the criteria, expresses the control principle, and which relate to the problem domain model.

Among criteria for control can be that certain of the measurable or controllable quantities are to follow certain ideals — say over time, and that certain other quantities, possibly not mentioned in the problem domain model, are to be optimized.

Example: In our continuing example we may find that the temperature of the liquid, t_l, is to stay close ($\pm \Delta \tau$) to an ideal, constant temperature, t_c ($> t_a$). •

Among means, or choices, of control we mention such which are based on stochastic, direct digital, "bang-bang", or other control principle.

Example: In our continuing example we may, for example, choose either to control the heating process by conducting heat "continuously", in "synchrony", ie. in "response" to continuous changes in the ambient temperature etc., or by supplying heat in "on/off" bursts. The latter can, for example, be accomplished by means of a full blast (on/off) flame being directed at the liquid container. •

This stage of development now constructs, based on the control criteria and principle, a control-theoretic, mathematical model which focus on the criteria, is expressing the control principle, and which can be shown to adhere to the mathematical problem domain model.

Like for problem domain modelling it may be that "the control-theoretic model" is in fact a set of such models — each model capturing further unrelated control facets.

System = Environment + Components + Core + Interfaces — including Operations : The system model first establishes the notion of a 'system' — as consisting of a 'core', (other) 'components', an 'environment', and 'interfaces' between the first three. Then the system model formalizes the interfaces in terms of 'assumptions' about the environment and the components upon which the core 'relies' in order for the component+core sub-systems to 'guarantee' adherence to requirements.

Environment: the environment is "that" about which we know "things" through reading 'sensor' values and which we control by means of 'actuators'. We are not designing the environment, it is given to us.

Example: The environment of our continuing example manifests itself through interface sensors measuring humidity, wind, radiation, ambient and liquid temperature, etc., and interface actuators. •

Component+Core: The components + core consists of that which we design, ie. over which we decide. The distinction between 'components' and 'core' is a pragmatic one — and is determined by who we are, by our emphasis, or focus, so-to-speak.

Example: In our continuing example the core will be the software which we are to develop.

The components will be the computers(s), the mechanical, electro-mechanical, etc. devices needed to heat the liquid: a gas-burner consisting of gas pipes, valves, blower, ignition device, flame detector, etc. The blower usually consists of several separately sensable and controllable sub-components: fan, motor, manual start/stop toggle switch, electronically sensable and controllable on/off relay, etc.

If our focal point had been that of blower designer it, with its sub-parts, would be the core, and the software and the 'other' components mentioned before would be the (new) components, and the environment would (we assume) be the same. •

Interfaces: The interfaces are here, at an abstract level, considered as being the properties that express relations between the environment, components and core.

The interfaces are the quantities that can be sensed or actuated and which (in this way) "connect" components to the environment, components to the core, and the core to the environment.

Example: In our continuing example the interface sensors and actuators are such things as thermometers, switches/relays, hygrometer, etc. •

Given a particular decomposition into environment, components, core and interfaces, we can now, for "small" aggregations of one or more of: components, interfaces and parts of the core establish formal 'aggregate relations' which serve to validate the choice of components and interfaces. Validation here means showing that the chosen components implement part of the control-theoretic model. By suitably combining aggregate relations we can verify correctness of the system model wrt. control-theoretic model — under the asumptions that the environment, the components and the core satisfy their interfaces.

Figure 1 informally indicates the variety of entities involved in a system.

Operations: As part of the system decomposition into core, components, environment and interfaces we find the careful determination of all those 'points' where human intervention may be required for the sake of system operations.

For each of these human/system interfaces, including the human/computer interfaces (HCI), careful assumptions and expectations must be established.

Safety Analysis Certain assumptions were made in the system model. Due to the likelihood of component + environment + environment failures

Figure 1: System Conceptualisation

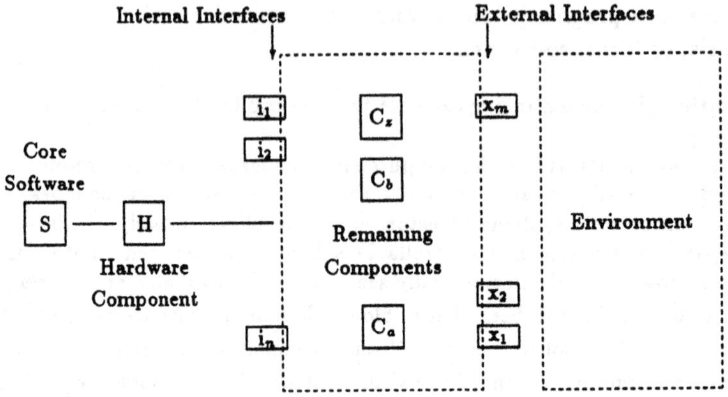

Internal Interfaces   External Interfaces

Core
Software
S — H ————
Hardware
Component

i_1
i_2

i_n

C_x

C_b

Remaining
Components

C_a

x_m

x_2
x_1

Environment

we are faced with the problem of safety criticality. Recall that we assume the core to be failure free!

A safety analysis is a study of all the things that can go wrong and all the things that must still go right — such that if nothing goes wrong then the system will satisfy the problem domain and control requirements.

A safety analysis leads to an enrichment of the requirements. These requirements now additionally express what erroneous situations (component + environment failures) the system is expected to respond to — not how.

Example: In our continuing example the safety analysis will express such things as: 'the valves must not be open and the flame off for more than a summed total of 1 second per any contiguous 20 second period', and 'the leak of gas must otherwise (ie. through leaky valves) must not exceed x volume units per y time units', etcetera.
●

The safety analysis typically captures so-called real-time requirements. These usually first enter our concern at this stage of development. The safety analysis usually is expressed in some modal logic and/or using a duration calculus like in [56].

Examples of informal and formal safety requirements are given in [39, 17, 20, 18, 35, 54].

Dependability Analysis: the safety model gives rise to a dependability analysis. Using for example Markov model techniques one can predict a facet of the system dependability given probabilities of single failures of any component — [33, 34, 52, 53, 15].

Operability: Given the system decomposition and its identification of human/system, incl. computer, interfaces, one is now capable of establishing formal or rigorous models of those human interfaces.

Performance Requirements As a final stage of requirements capture, definition and analysis stages one establishes performance requirements. These have to do with the specifics of core interfaces to other components. Examples of components are: operating system, possibly through it input/output, incl. the human/computer intergace (CHI), sensors and actuators, and the computer hardware. Examples of performance requirements are: assumptions about system table sizes and usage, input/output response times, cognitive facets of for example visual display usage, linguistic facets of textual interfaces, core storage consumption, etc. Some performance requirements, such as time criticality, will have already been dealt with under safety analysis.

Summary of the Requirements Stages Four sets of mathematics based models emanate from the requirements part of systems development. Each set exposes different facets of the evolving system. Together the models allow an analysis of the requirements put on the system now to be synthesized.

Requirements definition expresses properties, speaks about the core aspects of the system in extension: about what the core must offer, rather than how it achieves its functionality.

Example: In our continuing example the sum total of the requirements are requirements put to the software to be developed. •

The next sections shall only deal with such development aspects which are relevant for the case of the core being software.

Reports and publication [38, 47, 45, 46, 49, 42, 43] cover several stages of the requirements part of development.

Prototyping: Prototyping enters our concern for various reasons. The customer might wish to get an early "feel' for certain facets of the human/system interfaces. Or the producer might wish to capture a contract by demonstrating crucial new design concepts to potential clients. Or there might be facets of the system whose capture is made difficult because of vagueness on the part of either the consumer or the developer — and it is then hoped that an experimental prototype can help sharpen their conceptions. The above prototype cases all build on (otherwise) sharp conceptualisations, and they all exhibit but their particular "corner" of the system/core eventually to be developed.

Prototyping never enters our own world as a means to develop a first crude version of the core, a version from which final versions are later built. Thus prototyping is never a means to convince ourselves of the viablity of our plans. The whole sequence of formal requirements document as well as the functional specification serves that purpose. As means to convince us we have the intellectual, formal documents that are subjected to a human scrutinisation, a socialisation process that far better, we think, than often inadequate breadboard prototype models, give us insight into desired properties.

Systems Engineering Systems engineering is the larger context in which development includes the development of each component of our system individually treated as a core — and the overall co-ordination of such development.

Thus systems engineering involves many methods.

A First Evaluation Thus the product qualities of fitness for purpose: solving the problem, operability, and comprehensibility, are thoroughly dealt with, we think, by the first three stages of the requirements development: the mathematical model of the problem domain, the control theoretic model, and the system delineation and decomposition.

The product qualities of conformability are partly taken care of by our insistance on formal models, and thus by a clear understanding of what has been formally expressed and can hence be verified, and what has been only informally expressed and hence has to be validated. The software development stages will address remaining conformability expectations wrt. the core only.

The product qualities of reliability, fault tolerance and security is the very reason why we perform the safety and performance analysis stages — but must otherwise be secured by the core, ie. the software development process.

Finally the product qualities of adaptability, perfectability and portability must be secured by the software development process, and will be so by its insistance on homomorphic transformations from functional specification through decreasingly abstract, increasingly concrete designs to code.

The project qualities are likewise secured by the above and below fine grained meta-meta and meta-models of requirements and software development, by their insistance on using precise techniques, etc.

4.3 Programming Systems Development

We see programming systems development as consisting of several stages of transformation: from abstract specification which emphasize what the programs are to offer, via stages of from abstract to concrete design, to coding which finally prescribes how programs will provide their services.

Functional Specification The prerequisite for this stage is the control--theoretic model, the core interfaces, and the safety analysis. Even taken together they only describe requirements. They do not present a 'whole'.

The purpose of a functional specification is now to tie all the various facets together into an architectural specification of what the programs will offer.

Taken one-by-one the various requirements shall then be shown to be satisfied by the functional specification.

In addition to the above the specified programming system will offer functionalities not explicitly required, but made either necessary or made possible as a result of the need to put together, in the functional specification, a coherent whole.

Example: The functional specification for the liquid heating system is expressed in terms of traces of events observable and desirable across interfaces and pre-/post-conditions on implied actions — [40, 21, 19, 32, 50]. •

The functional specification stage either is not capable of formalising all requirements, and then it will typically be the performance requirements, or it is not necessary to deal with these at the early abstract functionality stages.

It is therefore the task of subsequent design stages to dispose of such requirements.

Abstract Design The abstract design proceeds from the functional specification and expresses the first decisive design decisions: a decomposition of the functional specification into separately implementable parts.

Properties of these parts are abstract specified as are interfaces between parts.

Usual techniques of correctness preserving transformations (etc.) and correctness theorem proofs apply — verifying this stage wrt. to the functional specification.

Example: In our continuing example the abstract design introduces an abstract notion of parallel processes; their basic series, interleaved parallel and guarded composition; synchronizing and value-passing channel communications (implementing traces of events); and expresses, in response to communication event, state changes of, or in, individual processes. •

Requirements emanating from the safety and performance stages may now be dispensed: either by formalizing them, or by showing that the proposed design will satisfy earlier stated requirements.

Concrete Design The concrete design now transforms and refines the design abstractions: 'realizes' pre-/post- specified operations in terms of explictly defined function; and 'reifies' abstract data types in terms of concrete data structures.

The abstract to concrete design stages usually imply more than 2 stages. Again these stages are verified wrt. preceding stages.

Example: In the case of the liquid heating system our transformations are guided by application of a design calculus, a set of laws that permit transformation of specification expressions into design expressions. These laws have been proven correct, once and for all, and hence correctness is guaranteed. •

Requirements emanating from the safety and performance stages may again be dispensed with: either by formalizing them, or by showing that the concretized design will satisfy earlier stated requirements.

Coding At a certain stage of concrete design it is possible to make the final development step into executable code.

Example: This executable code, in our example, is occam-2. An example is given in [44]. •

4.4 Software Installation, Use and Maintenance

The proper CASE shall also cater for these facets — but we will omit any further analysis etc. of why, what and how.

5 Rôle of Developers

CASEs are to be used by people. Hence we need examine the various professional disciplines that characterizes the entire development staff.

In section 4 we have sketched a rather disciplined set of stages without mentioning the requirements to be put on the staff who carries out the implied tasks.

This section will now review these qualifications.

5.1 Requirements Capturers, Definers and Analyzers

The group carrying out the requirements stages, see subsection 4.2, involve diverse skills:

- Problem domain specialists and mathematicians for domain modelling (subsection 4.2).

  The problem domain specialists are interviewed by the mathematicians.

  One outcome of this stage is a mathematical model, produced by the mathematicians, representing the knowledge of — and hence buddy checked by — the problem domain specialists.

  The mathematicians treat the problem domain model as a set of formal objects, and creates theories about these.

  Another outcome of this stage is a set of — more or less formally expressed — technology constraints.

The problem domain specialists treat the problem domain as a set of physical objects, and plans experiments with, test and uses of these objects.

- Control-theoreticians for control-theoretic modelling (subsection 4.2).

  The control theoreticians treat the problem, partly as a formal mathematical object, partly, as engineers, as a physical object with which they experiment.

- Automatic control, component, computer, software and human/system interface engineers for system modelling (subsection 4.2).

  The system engineers treat the problem as a physical object. Usually they do not state formal theories about the interface composition of components, the core and the environment. But we see an increasing need for this, especially wrt. to the human/system interfaces.

- Safety engineers and programmers for safety analysis (subsection 4.2).

  The safety engineers must be well-versed in the problem domain, and view it as engineers, that is: as a disciplined composition of physical components. The programmers are there to help express, formally, the safety requirements informally expressed by the safety engineers.

  We shall find that system and safety engineers of the future shall design their systems compositionally, that is: such that certain (homomorphism) compositionality properties emerge, properties that facilitate reasoning (ie. analysis), including safety and correctness arguments.

- Performance engineers (subsection 4.2).

  Performance engineers view the system as a physical objects prone to erroneous operation.

  They establish and use statistical and operations research models of the system. These models are not implemented, but are classical models that help understand and predict system behaviour.

5.2 Programmers

Programmers create safety definitions, functional specifications, design specifications, both abstract and concrete, and derive program code.

Programmers are concerned with the correctness of the development stages alluded to in the previous paragraph: from requirements models to software code.

Programmers create theories. They treat definitions, specifications and programs as formal, mathematical objects. They reason about these and their development, that is: about relations between them, logically. For each stage programmers build up supporting theoretical insight which helps secure adherence to all product quality facets (subsection 2).

Programmers base their work on theoretical computer science and computing science: programming methodology.

5.3 Software Engineers

Software engineers treat definitions, specifications, programs and code as physical objects (documents).

Software engineers create versions and revisions, and on the basis of these they perform configuration management; they track requirements and design decisions; they generate test cases to validate against mistakes in proofs of correctness and for functionalities that were or cannot be formally treated; they monitor and control change requests; and they build documentation.

Software engineers base their work on laws of physical sciences and laws of engineering.

5.4 Resident Computer Scientists

In any development there will be places where attempts are made to apply a formal technique for which an underlying theory has yet to be established. The resident computer scientist helps secure the validity of such approaches for the individual example instances.

The scientist focuses on the mathematics underlying the development.

The scientists base their work on mathematics, physics, chemistry, etc.

5.5 Project Managers

Project managers treat development as a sociological object.

Project managers plan the development approach, establish financing, allocates resources (people, tools, time, money), schedule their consumption, monitor and control their eventual deployment and plans, etc., remedial reaction in case of deviation from plans etc.

Project managers treat human resources both as human and as formal objects, and all other resources as formal objects.

Project managers base their work on laws of sociology (incl. economics).

5.6 Management: Meta-Planning

At the meta-level: before actual requirements and software development, etc. is commenced it is management's rôle to plan the project. In a subsequent subsection we shall see more to the meaning of this (7.3).

6 State and Rôle of Formal Techniques

6.1 Maturity of Formal Methods

Programmers: The requirements definition and analysis, the function specification, the abstract towards concrete design specifications, and the final transition to programs — all this is based on stepwise transformations, design calculi, proofs of properties, incl. correctness, and is especially amenable to formal support.

The various languages used have formal mathematical semantics', have corresponding consistent, but not necessarily complete, proof systems, and usually have design calculi, ie. laws for transforming abstract specifications into concrete ones.

Software Engineers: The rules for forming versions and revisions, and for configuring products are only beginning to be formalised. The rules for tracing requirements and design decisions are similarly embryonic. The applied science behind test generation and validation is well established. The rules for propagating changes are basically not understood. Etcetera.

Thus software engineering is largely informal. Much work need be done to R&D, to assess the utility of and to understand such laws.

Managers: Management rules of planning, allocating and scheduling — in connection with software development — presents a rather "complete void". There are basically no rules available today of any methodological nature, let alone based on comforting theories, for the meta-planning aspects.

One problem is that the three main players in software development: programmers, engineers and managers, each have their totally differently founded conception of the software development process.

There are a lot of so-called tools, rules etc. But when you examine the rôle of management vis-a-vis the very specific rôles of mathematicians, control theoreticians, operations analysts, safety and performance engineers, programmers and software engineers, then you will soon realise that, as they are rapidly becoming increasingly competent in their areas, usual managers are becoming the intellectual proletariate of development, distrusted and dispiced by the staff they are supposed to lead!

As is also carefully concluded in [10], we find that formal methods have far from covered the ground in systems development. Claims are being made wrt. usefulness of formal methods — claims that are just that: not substantiated.

6.2 A Rationale for Process Models

The prime objective of a software development process model, if it exists, is to normalize the interfaces between programmers, engineers, scientists, and managers. To introduce a vocabulary generally agreed upon, and normative rules for its use.

A secondary objective for a process model is to see whether a CASE system can meaningfully support the clerical, burdensome tasks of the individuals while securing the interfaces between co-workers from all four software development areas.

This requires far more independent research. This research must necessarily take it departure point in what available formal methods have to offer.

7   Software Development Support

We have outlined a great number of the facets which form essential parts of the requirements background for what is to be the essence of this paper: the mechanical (CASE) support for software development. This support is to help achieve quality (see subsections 2–2),

7.1   Software Development Process Models

Figure 2 (page 15) illustrates the "waterfall" life cycle ([12, 51, 13, 37]) of the systems development outlined in section 4. If anything is new then it is our insistance on formalising all the shown stages of requirements and software development.

This insistance is not dogmatically motivated — we would like to believe — but is based on the joy and excitement development staff have had using formal methods, and the impressive quality improvements their use have brought about.
The free dangling arrows going into requirements boxes shall indicate that additional requirements are heaped upon the development as the requirements are slowly unfolding.

The similarly free dangling arows leaving requirements boxes shall indicate that some requirements are not "disposed" off till early or late software development boxes — into which we hence see similarly dangling arrows.

This bewilderment of "dangling references" require that there be a rather solid requirements and design decision tracking system, for example in the form of some HyperText linkage support system!

7.2   Requirements to Process Models and CASESs

A CASE then is a co-ordinated collection of individual programs. The co-ordination reflects some process model, and the individual program packages support specific management, programming, software engineering, or other tasks.

The co-ordination somehow is intended to support the developer in following procedures for selecting and applying according to certain principles — whereas the individual programs are intended to reflect the techniques and notations.

Figure 2: A Waterfall Life Cycle Graph

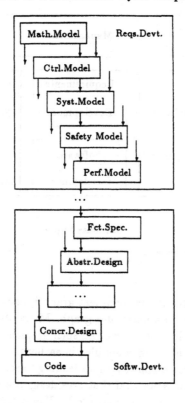

For us the process model reflected by the software development graph shown earlier gathers the four developer rôles: managers, software engineers, programmers and resident computer scientists.

That simplified water-fall diagram was far too simplistic — as everyone agrees. In the next subsection — after an introductory ("superficial") graph, we show an instance of a more detailed, problem domain specific graph.

7.3 A Process and CASE Reference Model

The "waterfall life cycle" diagram of figure 4 is far from satisfactory. In figure 3 we embed the two development boxes (requirements and software) in the larger context of a-priori planning, temporal monitoring and control, tool integration and selection, and data base support:

Within the two development boxes the above diagrams are almost meaningless anyway. What we need is a far more detailed view. We call it a Software Development Graph view.

The problem domain specific graph to be illustrated only reflects software development. That is: it does not cover the requirements development "half" of systems development.

Figure 3:

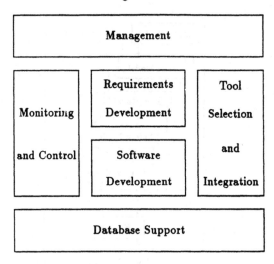

An example software development graph is shown in figure 4 (page 17). It is just a snapshot of a particular graph. Many others exist. We are going to describe and define the class of all such graphs.

The below graph has been detailed in earlier papers [2, 3, 4, 5]. The basic facts are that nodes designate actions leading to requirements, specification, design or code documents, and that arcs designate development transitions and their verification (validation, etc.). The more detailed facts are that these nodes and arcs designate clearly delineated tasks for all of: managers, software engineers, programmers, etc.

We first explain this graph as prototypical of all these graphs, then we tighten up the description in preparation for a formal definition of the Domain SDG of all graphs.

A software development graph consists of uniquely named nodes. In figure 4 the nodes are suitably subscripted r's, s's, d's and c's (for requirements, specification, design and code nodes). Unnamed ars (directed edges) lead from some nodes to other nodes. With nodes we associated 0, 1 or more (but a finite number of) uniquely named documents. With node d_3 we show this association. (There may be other node-document associations, not illustrated.) Here we have n distinctly identified id_i (for $1 \leq i \leq n$) documents δ_i. With arcs we associate 0, or 1 document. With the arc leading from node d_8 to node c_4 we have exemplified the document α. (There may be other arc-document associations not shown.)

We model the node-arc structure basically in terms of a map from nodes to sets of immediate successor nodes:

1.0 $SDG' = K_{\overline{m}} K\text{-}\underline{set}$

Figure 4: A Software Development Graph

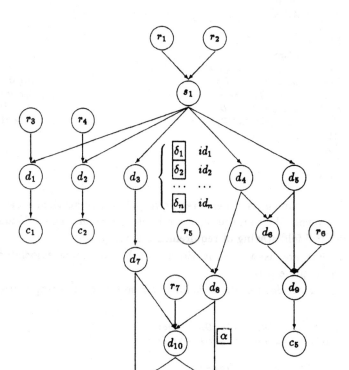

With each node we associate node information KI, so we revise (1):

2.0 $SDG'' = K_{\overline{m}}(KI \times K\text{-set})$

With each arc, ie. with each node in the set of immediate successor nodes, we associate arc information AI, so we revise (2):

3.0 $SDG''' = K_{\overline{m}}(KI \times (AI \times K)\text{-set})$

Now we are prepared to give the full formal definition:

4.0	SDG	$= K_{\vec{m}}(KI \times (A_{\vec{m}}(AI \times K)))$
5.0	K	$= \text{TOKEN}$
6.0	A	$= \text{TOKEN}$
7.0	AI	$= ADoc$
8.0	$ADoc$	$= \ldots$
9.0	KI	$= Aid_{\vec{m}}ATTR$
10.0	Aid	$= \text{TOKEN}$
11.0	$ATTR$	$= REQ|SPE|DES|COD$

12.0	REQ	$:: Rid_{\vec{m}}(RTxt \times RDoc)$	*Requirements*
13.0	SPE	$:: Sid_{\vec{m}}(STxt \times SDoc)$	*Specifications*
14.0	DES	$:: Did_{\vec{m}}(DTxt \times DDoc)$	*Designs*
15.0	COD	$:: Cid_{\vec{m}}(CTxt \times CDoc)$	*Code Modules*
16.0	$RDoc$	$= \ldots$	
17.0	$SDoc$	$= \ldots$	
18.0	$DDoc$	$= \ldots$	
19.0	$CDoc$	$= \ldots$	

An attribute document is either a requirements, a specification, a design or a code document. We could further subdivide the requirements documents to reflect our 5 fold staging of requirements development.

Documents are likewise subdivided. Each have some associated formalised, descriptive text.

We can model documents as being the result of configuring versions of such:

20.0	DOC	$= RDoc|SDoc|DDoc|CDoc$	or:
21.0	$d{:}DOC$	$= Doc \times (V_{\vec{m}}DOC \times VerFct)$	
22.0	Doc	$= \ldots$	
23.0	$f{:}VerFct$	$= (Doc \times Doc) \longrightarrow Doc$	

The version functions f apply to a document d and a version v document d_v to yield an update document: $f(d, d_v)$. A document consists of the root document updated with all the version document along a path of the recursively defined document hierarchy formalised, in (21.0), above.

Similar models can be given for change request propagation control, test generation and validation, etc.

The above models only abstracted the data structures, not the (more interesting) operations.

The very extensive internal report collections: [31, 26, 30] establish, as their individual titles indicate, several formal models for programming, graph development, software engineering and management, and for underlying database support.

Process Models and HyperText The above model is but one of several possible. To properly keep track of change request control, requirements and design decisions, etc., it is suggested that a dynamically changeable HyperText data structure be super-imposable upon the shown graphs. In fact, one may claim that the basic graph structure is nothing but a base HyperText structure imposed on the related documents.

We maintain the usefulness of making the distinction: a reasonably static software development graph being part of the a-priori common agreement with which all developers are intimately familiar, and the dynamically changing (ie. growing) hypertext links which are created, on-the-fly, spur-of-the-moment, and which can later be examined, and hopefully understood, by other than their creators.

We refer to [24, 25] in which formal models of HyperText are presented. These publications also sketches process model implications.

Meta-Planning: — Software Development, Project and Product Graphs: Like we can establish detailed, extensively annotated software development graphs, so we can establish similarly annotated requirements development graphs — either before, or during developments!

To establish such graphs, to tie resource estimation (budgetting), allocation and scheduling to such graphs, to instantiate such graphs to specific projects, and, within projects, to instantiate project graphs to product versions, all with their more detailed annotations wrt. the 5–6 categories of requirements developers and 3 categories of software developers (programmers, engineers and scientists), is part of meta-planning.

This meta-planning also involves decisions as to detail of graphing versus reliance on HyperText, planning of granularity of database object support, tool selection, instrumentation and integration, and the monitoring and control procedures to be maintained during development.

Graph-Iteration vs. "Spirals" The Spiral Life-Cycle Model is arrived at by an interpretation of the ordinary life-cycle model, and can likewise be imposed on the graph models just outlined. Consider a project graph, that is: an instantiation of a software development graph. Consider a specific project to have arrived at a state where activities are taking place along a "wave-front" which stretches clear across a project graph — intersecting nodes and arcs such that there are no two such on the wave-front which are also along a path in the graph from in-degree 0 node to an out-degree 0 node, and such that the wave-front otherwise disects the graph in to parts. If in such a state a need arises to "roll back" development to "redo" activities of earlier states, then we consider the project graph to be the same, but its history, the project history graph, to be an un-rolling of the project graph.

That is: the semantics of a project graph is that it denotes all its indefinite un-rollings!

The morale of this viewpoint is that the various process models proposed for software developments can usually be seen as different, or additional, complementary semantics of certain syntactic, usually graphic renditions!

7.4 Areas of Experimental R&D

We find the following areas of interest for further R&D:

- Abstract data type formulations of Version Control and Configuration Management — as superficially hinted at above.

- Similar models for Change Request Control (of propagation).

- Similar models for Test Generation and Validation — merged with the by-now fairly well established models for Implementation Relations, Correctness Theorems and their Proofs.

- Once all the above software engineering data models are well understood, as are already today the data models for all requirements development and all the software development programming documents, then we can meaningfully R&D possible data models for the entire development.

- And once the document etc. data models are well understood we can likewise R&D possible hypertext models.

- Now we can consolidate the Software Development Graph and the Hypertext notions of Process Models.

- Finally we R&D meta-models for the planning process part of process models.

  We find that each well concluded project was a success because a considerable effort was spent on meta-planning: on finding how, exactly, to conduct the project — before committing large development, tooling and support resources.

  It is easy, now, after [36], to plan the next large compiler development project — but it is not so straightforward to plan the development of a software component with whose problem domain one has no experience, that is: to develop a first-time product! And most interesting projects seem to be first-timers!

For each of the above models we seek Algebras: Laws of Behaviour.

7.5 Some Critical Remarks

We find that all the currently proposed, let alone the existing commercial software engineering supports for the above, are far too complicated. We believe that there must be established simple, transparent rules, amounting to laws, that govern relations between versions and configurations; and between, on one hand change requests and original objects and, on the other hand, their changed results, etc., etc.

As it is now, in industry, there is no "law-and-order", there is anarchy, in the most basic software engineering facets of software development. This lawlessness must be seen on the background of ever increasing law-and-order within the programming disciplines. Both programming and software engineering are needed, both reflect crucial facets; one must not become the orphaned stepchild of the other!

We also find that most industry R&D projects which study, prototype, and even product develop CASEs, do so top-down, from some vague beliefs in the software process. We believe that one here has to work bottom-up: from well established, confirmed basic techniques to unfold higher and higher CASE requirements and CASE products.

8 The RAISE and LaCoS Projects

8.1 Introduction

Rigorous Approach to Software Engineering: RAISE stands for Rigorous Approach to Industrial Software Engineering. RAISE is a formal method whose method and tools encompass both programming and software engineering. RAISE builds on VDM and permits from systematic, via rigorous to fully formal use of the method and RSL.

The RAISE Project: The RAISE project (1985–1990) developed the RAISE method, tools and specification language RSL. This was done in cooperation between CRI, Nordic Brown Boveri, ICL, and STC.

LaCoS: Large-scale Correct Systems: LaCoS stands for: 'Large-scale Correct Systems using formal methods'.

In LaCoS, RAISE is applied primarily to embedded, real-time, safety critical systems development: train control, tethered satellite control, marine engine control, real-time satellite borne worldwide transaction processing system, etc. A large number of industry staff is here applying a formal method for the first time.

The LaCoS Project: The LaCoS project takes place in the period 1990–1995.

The LaCoS RAISE users: Bull (F), Inisel Espacio (E), Lloyd's Register (GB), Matra Transportation (F), Space Software Italia (SSI) (I), and TechniSystems (H), are thus using RAISE in carefully evaluated real-life projects. The leader of the LaCoS project is CRI.

Among many aims of the project is the technology transfer of a formal method into industry, maturing the method, languages and tools, and possibly standardisation. [29] surveys conformance of RAISE to the ESA Life Cycle.

8.2 The RAISE Tool Set

Overview: The RAISE tools are a collection of tools for manipulating a variety of entities that are relevant during a development process: modules, relations between modules, etc. Individual tools for manipulating such entities are centered around the RAISE Library, which is a specialised database system.

The environment provided by the RAISE Tools provides facilities for tracking and documenting complete developments of software systems. The environment supports the maintenance and evolution of software systems throughout their lifetime. The RAISE method defines concepts such that tangible milestones in the form of specification, design and code documents can be set up in order to manage and monitor the development process; the RAISE Tools implements them.

The environment is intended to be used in organisations concerned with the development of industrial, large-scale complex software systems, involving many designers and programmers. The environment is currently based on Unix and X with underlying database support provided by Oracle, and is operating on Sun[5] and DEC workstations; it is expected to be ported to other systems, including the PS/2 AD/Cycle environment and IBM 6000 workstations, DEC, HP and Sony workstations.

Library Entities: The RAISE Library holds a number of kinds of entities, each of which play a particular rôle in the RAISE Method. The Library, which implements configuration and version control, is built on top of the Oracle relational database management system, in order to be able to sustain the load from large development projects. The version control scheme is non-destructive in that stored entities cannot be revised: rather, new versions may be added [6]. The library comes with a set of functions for change propagation, purging and pruning in order to avoid "version-explosions".

The following entity kinds are supported:

Modules: These are individual RSL modules, stored together with version-specific information about references to other modules.

Development relations: These record relations among pairs of modules, such as the formal implementation relation, or some relation (stipulation) formulated by a user.

Theories: These are collections of predicates, written in RSL, that are purportedly true of one or more modules.

Developments: These are basically sequences of development steps, describing a particular development process. Development entities may be composed, in order to describe even very complex projects.

Justifications: These are arguments why certain conditions are believed to be fulfilled. Justifications may be informal statements (like "obvious") at the one extreme, and completely formal proofs at the other extreme.

---

[5] SunView may be used as an alternative to X.
[6] Versions are stored using a space-saving delta mechanism.

In general, proofs and informal statements may be mixed, such that a justification may be in part formal, in part informal. Justifications may relate to development relations, theories, or confidence conditions within modules.

Configuration specifications: These are entities specifying a strategy for building a complete RSL document (a configuration) out of the library contents. A configuration specification allows users to specify strategies such as using particular versions of particular modules, the currently newest version, substituting the fastest implementation for a specification module, etc.

Configurations: These are RSL documents (i.e.: collections of modules) built according to a configuration specification.

Hints: These are entities which contain informal text, and which may refer to any number of library entities. Hints may be used for informal comments, or perhaps for information to be interpreted by tools added to the RAISE Tools[7].

Individual RAISE Tools

The Module Editor The module editor is the primary work-horse, used for creating (new versions of) modules. The module editor is in part a syntax directed editor, in which the user selects and refines syntax categories (using mouse and keys), and in part a normal text editor, in which the user may type in and edit RSL text. The module editor ensures syntactic correctness and furthermore continuously checks for static conditions (typing rules, visibility rules) and displays relevant error messages at the points of error.

In the module editor, references to other modules are made via "contexts", that specify particular versions of such other modules (defaulting to the currently newest). A (small) module with a context could look like

```
24.0    context: STACK;23, WORD;1
  .1     object WORDSTACK:
  .2     STACK(WORD{ Word for Element})
```

The module browser is a read-only variant of the module editor. The module browser may be used to inspect a module.

Other Entity Editors Based on the same underlying editing technology as for the module editor, there are editors and browsers for: development re-

---

[7]Several entity kinds have, similarly, room for such information. This is the general mechanism to be used to build for example project management tools on top of the RAISE Tools.

lations, developments, justifications, configuration specifications, hints, and theories.

List and Query Editors Again based on the combined syntax and text oriented editing technology, the list and query editors are used to formulate and execute library queries. Lists are by entity kind and name (using wildcards); queries may be formed concerning library contents, status of modules, pending justifications, etc.

Change Propagation The RAISE library implements version control; contexts are specific versions of library entities. If, for example, a user wants to make a minor change to a module on which a number of others depend then it would be tedious to change them all (in the right order) by hand. The change propagator does this automatically. It propagates the change as far as it can until errors are caused. It then (in interactive mode) invites the user to edit the new entity further or (in batch mode) reports on the error.

Justification Tools The justifications tools are a collection of tools provided to help the user in generating conditions to be justified, and in developing the justifications themselves:

Implementation condition generator: Whenever the formal relation of implementation has been claimed among two modules, this tool may be used to generate the detailed conditions under which this relation will actually hold. These conditions may then later be discharged by the simplifier or by justifications.

Confidence condition generator: This tool may be used to generate confidence conditions within a single module. Confidence conditions are extensions of the normal static conditions (such as type checking), pin-pointing troublesome constructs like potential division by zero. Confidence conditions may later be discharged by the simplifier or by justifications.

Animator: The animator is a symbolic execution engine that may manipulate a subset of RSL. The animator may be used for symbolic evaluation of RSL terms, and thus serve as an interpreter or prototyping aid.

Simplifier: The simplifier is a specialised variant of the animator, that will attempt to prove conditions (i.e. reduce them to **true**). The simplifier is used automatically whenever conditions are generated, in order to reduce the number of conditions the user may have to consider, and is available for tackling sub-conditions within the justification editor.

Justification editor: The justification editor is used to develop coherent justifications. Whenever a subpart of a justification is a (fragment of

a) formal proof, the justification editor will enable the user to develop such proofs in a formally valid manner. The justification editor is built using the same technology as for other RAISE editors.

Transformer: The transformer may be used to apply meaning-preserving transformations to fragments (terms) of RSL. The transformer is an essential part of the justification editor (for applying RSL proof rules), rather than a general development tool available for users.

Translators The translators are used to generate programming language code from low-level designs expressed in RSL. There are translators for the following languages: Ada and

Usually, a manual transcription from low-level design into code is in principle quite simple; however, in practice it is extremely error-prone. Moreover, producing final code manually tends to cause maintenance to be restricted to the code level. By providing automatic translation in the final transcription step a large number of errors can be avoided, and maintenance at the specification and design levels made much more attractive.

Pragmatic Tools The tools described above all relate to RSL or concepts defined as part of the RAISE method. In addition to those tools, some facilities are offered for supporting more pragmatic activities.

Cross reference handler: The cross reference handler is generally avialable from within RAISE editors, for bringing up (in a browser) the definition of some entity. For example, in a module editor this facility may be used to show non-local definitions.

Help facility: The help facility is generally available from within RAISE editors, and may be used to bring up the text from the manual describing a RAISE concept. For example, in a module editor the help facility may be used to bring up relevant sections of the RSL Reference Manual.

Document formatter: For the purpose of producing hard-copy documents, such as reports, containing informal text and RSL modules, the document formatter may be used to extract RSL modules in a form appropriate for formatting. Currently, the LaTeX formatting system is supported.

Summary

The RAISE tools are an environment and collection of individual tools in which users can create and manipulate RAISE entities. The philosophy behind the architecture of this environment and the interplay between the tools is to allow for a variety of working styles and organisations of projects, rather than enforcing a particular discipline.

9 Conclusion

When a formal method, like VDM or RAISE, is introduced in a "classical" software life-cycle "milieu", its conceptual picture of its traditional life-cycle changes. Initially smoothly — eventually radically.

One can indeed introduce a formal method into an existing classical, traditional, imprecise life-cycle model. But gradually such an introduction implies a precise semantics to the various stages of the previously imprecise model — some of these eventually will become more meaningful. Eventually developers find that several sub-stages that were previously pursued in a bureaucratic manner: producing masses of cross-referenced documents which did not explictly contribute to the constructive design stages, that these sub-stages can be simply omitted. They are now subsumed by, and/or indirectly results from applying some of the constructive formal techniques, or they are becoming considered superfluous.

We have shown a bit of formalism ourselves in this paper to suggest that we can and should, in a meta-sense, also be formal about our process models and CASEs. The internal reports: [28, 31, 26, 30, 27] as well as publications [24, 25] amply demonstrate the benefits from establishing such formal models.

We have carefully examined most of the very many facets that enter software development in order to sketch implications for CASE architectures. We claim that most CASE efforts today do not take the implications of formal techniques and tools seriously enough. We believe that the notion of process models must be viewed from the ground up in the light primarily of formal techniques. We believe that lasting CASE architectures must be formally based — and that when so developed will become radically different from current CASEs.

The critical opinions expressed in this position paper are those of the main author.

Postscript

The CEC is supporting formal methods through *Formal Methods Europe*. FME is an 'organisation' devoted to propagating formal methods in industry and will advice the CEC and industry on such matters as industrial support for, acceptance of and experience with formal methods, need for R&D wrt. formal methods and their tools, international standardisation, etc.

10 Acknowledgements

We acknowledge the support given through the CEC ESPRIT I + II projects RAISE and LaCoS, the CEC BRA project ProCoS, and the Danish Technical Research Foundation RapID project.

We also acknowledge the support of our colleagues and students in these projects: (CRI:) Peter Michael Bruun, Bendt Dandanell, Kirsten E. Eriksen, Chris W. George, Peter L. Haff, Peter Haastrup, Jens Langeland Knudsen, and Jan Storbank Pedersen, and (DTH:) Kirsten Mark Jensen, Bo Bichel Nørbæk, Danny B. Lange, Steen Lynenskjold, Ole Frost Mikkellsen, Jens Nordahl, Anders P. Ravn, Hans Rischel, and Erling V. Sørensen.

11 Bibliography

Every development project should start by establishing its terminology, and, over this terminology, a taxonomy. Every project must adhere to this terminoloy/taxonomy, including maintaining it.

In this paper we have introduced many terms, but have neither indexed these, nor taxonomised them.

Every development project must likewise establish its intellectual base — typically manifested through a bibliography. We have made references. Now we list these:

References

[1] D. Bjørner, , C.A.R. Hoare, and H. Langmaack, editors. *VDM & Z — Formal Methods in Software Development, Proc. of VDM-Europe Symposium '90*, volume 428 of *Lectures Notes in Computer Science*. Springer-Verlag, Heidelberg, Germany, 1990.

[2] D. Bjørner. Project graphs and meta-programs: Towards a theory of software development. In N. Habermann and U. Montanari, editors, *Proc. Capri '86 Conf. on Innovative Software Factories and Ada, Lecture Notes on Computer Science*. Springer-Verlag, Heidelberg, Germany, May 1986.

[3] D. Bjørner. Software development graphs - a unifying concept for software development? In K.V. Nori, editor, *Vol. 241 of Lecture Notes in Computer Science: Foundations of Software Technology and Theoretical Computer Science*, pages 1-9. Springer-Verlag, Heidelberg, Germany, Dec. 1986.

[4] D. Bjørner. On the use of formal methods in software development. In *Proc. of 9th International Conf. on Software Engineering, Monterey, California*. IEEE, April 1987.

[5] D. Bjørner. The stepwise development of software development graphs - meta-programming VDM developments. In *[11]*, pages 77-96. Springer-Verlag, Heidelberg, Germany, 1987.

[6] D. Bjørner. A procos project description. General Information Version 3, Dept. of Computer Science, Technical University of Denmark, October 1989.

[7] D. Bjørner. Interim deliverable: Procos — esprit bra 3104 provably correct systems. Report Version 5, Dept. of Computer Science, Technical University of Denmark, June 30 1990.

[8] D. Bjørner. *Software Architectures and Programming Systems Design; volume I: Specification Principles — the VDM Approach*. Addison-Wesley/ACM Press, 1991.

[9] D. Bjørner. *Software Architectures and Programming Systems Design; volume II: Implementation Principles — the VDM Approach*. Addison-Wesley/ACM Press, 1991.

[10] D. Bjørner and L.M. Druffel. Industrial experience in using formal methods. In *Intl. Coonf. on Software Engineering*. ACM and IEEE, 1990.

[11] D. Bjørner, M. Mac an Airchinnigh, E. Neuhold, and C.B. Jones, editors. *VDM - A Formal Method at Work, Proc. of VDM-Europe Symposium '87*. Lectures Notes in Computer Science. Springer-Verlag, Heidelberg, Germany, 1987.

[12] B.W. Boehm. *Software Engineering Economics*. Prentice-Hall, Englewood Cliffs, NJ., USA, 1981.

[13] ESA Publications Division. ESA Software Engineering Standards. Technical report, European Space Agency (SA), ESA Technology Center (ESTEC), Nordwijk, The Ntherlands, 1987.

[14] The RAISE Language Group. *The RAISE Specification Language*. ACM Press. Addison-Wesley Publishing Company, 1991.

[15] N.H. Hansen and E.V. Sørensen. On risk prediction for repairable safety-critical systems, a theoretical foundation. Technical report Version 0, Dept. of Computer Science, Technical University of Denmark, November 30 1990.

[16] J.F. He and E.-R. Olderog, editors. *ProCoS: Provably Correct Systems, vol.2 — Language Interfaces for Concurrent Systems*. tbd, November 1991.

[17] K.M. Jensen. Requirements for a cruise control system. Note Version 1, Dept. of Computer Science, Technical University of Denmark, August 13 1990.

[18] K.M. Jensen. Requirements for a lift control system. Report Version 2, Dept. of Computer Science, Technical University of Denmark, 11 December 1990.

[19] K.M. Jensen. Specification of a lift control system. Report Version 1, Dept. of Computer Science, Technical University of Denmark, November 6 1990.

[20] K.M. Jensen. Specification of a gas-burner. Report Version 2, Dept. of Computer Science, Technical University of Denmark, 25 January 1991.

[21] K.M. Jensen and H. Rischel. Specification of a taximeter 1. Note Version 0.1, Dept. of Computer Science, Technical University of Denmark, March 16 1990.

[22] C.B. Jones. *Systematic Software Development — Using VDM, 2nd Edition*. Prentice-Hall International, 1989.

[23] C.B. Jones and R.C. Shaw. *Case Studies in Systematic Sotware Development*. Prentice-Hall International, 1990.

[24] D.B. Lange. A formal approach to hypertext using post-prototype formal specification. In Bjørner et al., editor, *see [1]*, pages 99–121. Springer-Verlag, Heidelberg, Germany, 1990.

[25] D.B. Lange. A formal model of hypertext. Technical Report ID-TR: 1990–69, ISSN 0902–2821, Dept. of Comp. Sci., Techn. Univ. of Denmark, 1990.

[26] S. Lynenskjold. The DiProGS Project. Software Enginering and Management. Technical Report Vol. 3, Dept. of Comp. Sci., Techn. Univ. of Denmark, 1987.

[27] S. Lynenskjold, O. Frost Mikkelsen, and B. Bichel Nørbæk. The DiProGS Project. LaTeX Tools. Technical Report Vol. 5, Dept. of Comp. Sci., Techn. Univ. of Denmark, 1987.

[28] S. Lynenskjold, O. Frost Mikkelsen, and B. Bichel Nørbæk. The DiProGS Project. Status and Perspectives. Technical Report Vol. 1, Dept. of Comp. Sci., Techn. Univ. of Denmark, 1987.

[29] E. Manero. RAISE Life-Cycle vs. ESA Software Engineering Standards Life-Cycle. Technical Report LaCoS Project Report, CEC ESPRIT II, Inisel Espacio, Barcelona, Spain, 1991.

[30] O. Frost Mikkelsen. The DiProGS project. Object-Oriented Databases. Technical Report Vol. 4, Dept. of Comp. Sci., Techn. Univ. of Denmark, 1987.

[31] B. Bichel Nørbæk. The DiProGS Project. Programming and Graph Development. Technical Report Vol. 2, Dept. of Comp. Sci., Techn. Univ. of Denmark, 1987.

[32] J. Nordahl. A real-time temporal logic specification of a safety critial system. Note Version 1, Dept. of Computer Science, Technical University of Denmark, October 25 1989.

[33] J. Nordahl. Dependability in a process algebraic framework. Note Version 0.2, Dept. of Computer Science, Technical University of Denmark, June 25 1990.

[34] J. Nordahl. Design for dependability. Note Version 1, Dept. of Computer Science, Technical University of Denmark, November 29 1990.

[35] J. Nordahl. Requirements specification for a railway level crossing. Note Version 0, Dept. of Computer Science, Technical University of Denmark, February 27 1990.

[36] O. Oest. VDM from research to practice. In H.-J. Kugler, editor, *Information Processing '86*, pages 527–533. International Federation for Information Processing, World Congress Proceedings, North-Holland Publ. Co., Amsterdam, The Netherlands, 1986.

[37] R.S. Pressman. *Software Engineering: A Practitioner's Approach.* McGraw-Hill, 1989.

[38] A. P. Ravn and V. Stavridou. Criteria for specification and programming language for engineering safety-critical software. Technical Report Version 0.1, Dept. of Computer Science, Technical University of Denmark, October 24 1989.

[39] A.P. Ravn. Control program for an autopilot: Requirements procos case study 0. Note Version 1.1, Dept. of Computer Science, Technical University of Denmark, November 16 1989.

[40] A.P. Ravn. Control program for an auto pilot: Specification and development. Unreleased notes, Dept. of Computer Science, Technical University of Denmark, 1990.

[41] A.P. Ravn, editor. *ProCoS: Provably Correct Systems, vol.1 — Development of Embedded, Real-Time Computing Systems.* tbd, November 1991.

[42] A.P. Ravn and H. Rischel. Requirements capture for embedded real-time systems. Conference Paper Version 1, Dept. of Computer Science, Technical University of Denmark, February 1991.

[43] A.P. Ravn and H. Rischel. Requirements capture for embedded real-time systems. In P. Borne, editor, *IMACS-IFAC Symposium MCTS, Villeneuve d'Ascq, France, May 1991.* IMACS Transaction Series, 1991.

[44] A.P. Ravn, H. Rischel, and E.V. Sørensen. Control program for a gas burner: Requirements, procos case study 0. Note Version 1.1, Dept. of Computer Science, Technical University of Denmark, October 16 1989.

[45] A.P. Ravn, H. Rischel, and V. Stavridou. Development of safety critical software, a procos position statement. Note Version 1.2, Dept. of Computer Science, Technical University of Denmark, April 2 1990.

[46] A.P. Ravn, H. Rischel, and V. Stavridou. Provably correct safety critical software. Technical Report Version 1, Dept. of Computer Science, Technical University of Denmark, June 1990.

[47] A.P. Ravn and V. Stavridou. Specification and development of safety-critical software: An assesment of mod draft standard 00-55. Note Version 1, Dept. of Computer Science, Technical University of Denmark, April 2 1990.

[48] H. Rischel, editor. *ProCoS: Provably Correct Systems, vol.4 Selected Papers.* tbd, November 1991.

[49] H. Rischel and A.P. Ravn. Requirements capture for computer based systems. Report Version 2, Dept. of Computer Science, Technical University of Denmark, October 10 1990.

[50] S. Schneider. A timed csp specification of the gas burner control system and its verification,. Unreleased notes, Programming Research Group, Oxford University Computing Laboratory, England, April 1990.

[51] I. Sommerville. *Software Engineering.* Addison-Wesley, 1982.

[52] E.V. Sørensen. Brief tutorial on dependability concepts. Unpublished Note Pre-Draft, Dept. of Computer Science, Technical University of Denmark, April 1 1990.

[53] E.V. Sørensen. On dependability prediction of safety critical systems. Unpublished Note Pre-Draft, Dept. of Computer Science, Technical University of Denmark, April 20 1990.

[54] E.V. Sørensen, A.P. Ravn, and H. Rischel. Control program for a gas burner: Part 1: Informal requirements, procos case study 1. Technical Report Version 1, Dept. of Computer Science, Technical University of Denmark, March 22 1990.

[55] B. von Karger and H.H. Løvengreen, editors. *ProCoS: Provably Correct Systems, vol.3 — Base Systems Development: Compilers and Kernels.* tbd, November 1991.

[56] C.C. Zhou, C.A.R. Hoare, and A.P. Ravn. A calculus of durations. Technical Report ProCoS ID/DTH (+ OU/PRG) ZCC/3/1, Dept. of Comp. Sci., Techn. Univ. of Denmark and Programming Research Group, Oxford Univ., Feb. 1991.

Modeling of Software Architectures: Importance, Notions, Experiences

Manfred Nagl
Lehrstuhl f. Informatik III
Aachen University of Technology
Ahornstr. 55, 5100 Aachen, Germany

Abstract

This article is a strong pleading for the importance of architecture modeling, i.e. for a careful development and maintenance of software systems in order to solve the actual software problems, namely maintenance, quality improvement and reuse. This is due to the fact that a software architecture is the "essential" structure of a software system and that most of the software documents are directly or indirectly dependent on this structure.

For denoting software architectures we suggest two different languages: a graphical language for denoting an overview of an architecture (architecture diagram) and a textual language for discribing the details of components as well as relations between components identified in the architecture diagram. This paper sketches the syntax, as well as the application, of these languages to typical situations within architectures and to complete architectures. Furthermore, the mapping of these languages to relevant programming languages is discussed. Finally, we present some open problems of architecture modeling.

1. Introduction and Motivation

The *software crisis* is *still alive* in the industrial practice! We know from figures from the seventies that about 80% of the total effort of DP applications (hardware and software) go into software construction and maintenance /Bo 76/ and we assume that this portion has not been reduced. Software systems nowadays often consist of thousands or tens of thousands of source text pages where the inherent structure of the system is not explicitly documented. Instead, it is hidden in this huge amount of detailed information, namely the source code. Especially, the relations between different parts of a software system can hardly be detected. In most cases, software is constructed from scratch, it is completely hardwired, and it is full of errors.

Therefore, in our opinion the *current major problems* of software engineering in research as well as in practice are (1) managing the problems of software maintenance, taking about 60% of software costs /Bo 76/, (2) avoiding to start from scratch and, therefore, increasing productivity by reusing knowledge, components (more general , software documents), or the proceeding of previous developments, and (3) improving the quality of all involved software documents. All these problems require (a) accumulating knowledge about software systems, (b) developing suitable notions and methods to express this knowledge, and (c) developing tools which give support to denote, evaluate, and reuse software documents.

A prerequisite for a solution to all three problems is to think about, to design, to careful-ly denote the "essential" *structure* of a *software system*, and to be able to talk and write about this structure. We call this structure the *architecture* of a software system. The architecture denotation has to contain a survey representation giving an overview of the structure (introducing the components and showing which ones are related to each other) but also a detailed description of all of its components (detailed corresponding export, import). In any case, the description has to remain on the programming-in-the-large level, therefore factorizing out all the details which have to do with the implementation of components' bodies or the underlying programming language.

Assuming such a representation of the essential structure of a software system we have a chance to *tackle* the above *problems*. We can identify which parts of a software system are directly or indirectly changed in maintenance, we can speak about the struc-ture of a software system and, therefore, about quality properties such as flexibility, and we can identify reusable structures and components. We can do this without getting lost in the details of source code, i.e. the details of programming-in-the-small and the corres-ponding programming language.

This *article* is intended to give a *summary* of a book /Na 90/. Therefore, it can only motivate and sketch the importance, problems, notions, experiences, and tools of archi-tecture modeling. For details the reader is referred to this book and its rich bibliography. The underlying ideas underwent different stages of development (/Al 78/, /Ga 83/, /Na 82/, /LN 85/, /Le 88/). Similar books which, however, are not directly devoted to software architecture modeling are /Bu 84/, /Bo 87/, and /Me 88/.

The *contents* of this paper are as follows: In the next section we give some figures about the importance of architecture modeling, explain the logical level on which architec-ture modeling has to take place, and show evident errors to be made by a purely function-al decomposition. In the next section we introduce two languages for architecture model-ing, a graphical one for overview architecture diagrams and a textual one for the detailed description of its components. These languages assume that modules and module rela-tions are either of certain sorts. In the next section we apply these languages and, there-by, introduce further concepts like subsystems, genericity and object-orientedness. The following section shows how the architecture languages can be mapped onto program-ming languages. Finally, in the last two sections we introduce some strategies for soft-ware design which improve adaptability and reuse, and list some open problems of archi-tecture modeling we are still facing.

2. Modeling of Software Architectures: Level, Importance, and Evident Errors

The result of the design phase is the design specification. This design specification consists of the software architecture, together with the semantical description of the in-volved modules. The realization of the components identified in the architecture is due to the implementation phase. Fig. 1 indicates this situation. The same holds true for mainte-nance which yields changes on the architecture level and, in the sequel, on the imple-mentation level. The software architecture contains all logical levels of a software system (layers), enumerates all components (modules), and shows their interrelation. Thereby, we do not program the module bodies. Let us call this characterization of the development/maintenance process the *architecture paradigm*. Therefore, we assume a discrete paradigm of the development and maintenance process, namely activities on the architecture level called programming–in–the–large and on the module body level, called programming–in–the–small. An architecture is an abstraction, where the details of module bodies are factorized out from a complete software system . This abstraction should not be intermixed with an abstraction due to a certain layer of a software system.

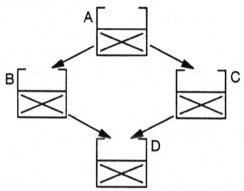

Fig.1: The architecture paradigm: Modeling a software system without programming the module bodies

Of course, this *view* of software development/maintenance is *idealized* /SB 82/: It is hard to think about all levels of a software system and to develop a complete architecture if we do not implement the module bodies. Therefore, in architecture modeling we often forget modules, which are detected later during the implementation of a module body as necessary resources and introduce superfluous modules, which are better realized within the bodies of other modules. Following the architecture paradigm, we have to think (in advance) about module implementations and we shall often backtrack later from implementation to design.

However, this idealization *cannot be avoided:* In software systems of relevant size we have a division of labour for different persons with different roles (designer, implementor, quality assurance engineer etc.). Gluing design and implementation together would bear the risk that no architecture is developed at all, or that both levels design and implementation are permanently intermixed. Detection of similarities and commonalities is only possible if the design is in the hands of designers and not programmers. Verification of an architecture before realizing the module bodies is only possible if the architecture is developed first.

We know from literature /Ze 79/ that the activities in early phases of software development/maintenance, such as those performed on requirements and on design level are carried out with minor effort. In industrial practice this is often the case even nowadays. We furthermore know /Ra 84/ that many mistakes are made in these working areas. We also know from /Bo 84/ that errors within software, which is already working in the field, are extremely expensive to repair. As many errors are made on the requirements engineering or on the programming–in–the–large level we can also find a lot of them amongst these expensive errors. So, we can conclude that modeling on the *requirements engineering* and on the *programming–in–the–large–level* has to be carried out with *more care* and more *resources*.

Comparing requirements engineering and programming–in–the–large the latter one is even more important (see Fig. 2.). One reason is that, to a certain degree, requirements errors can be compensated on the programming–in–the–large level. The second and even more important reason is that *programming–in–the–large* is the *center* of most *activities* of software development and maintenance. Most software documents are directly, and to a great portion, dependent on the structure of the architecture of a software system. Furthermore, we should take into account that the greatest portion of labour in software development and maintenance is done after design or redesign. So, the software architecture is not only the master document in that it is the essence of a software system, its structure also masters the structure of most of the other documents. Let us make this clear by taking only one example: The technical documentation describes the overall structure of a software system and its design decisions. This is directly dependent on the overall structure of the architecture which we denote as the architecture diagram in the following text. Furthermore, a technical documentation gives a detailed description of the components of a software system (modules and subsystems). These descriptions are directly dependent on the detailed descriptions of software components of the software architecture. Therefore, a bad architecture induces bad dependent software documents or, saying it the other way round, design errors are the most expensive ones.

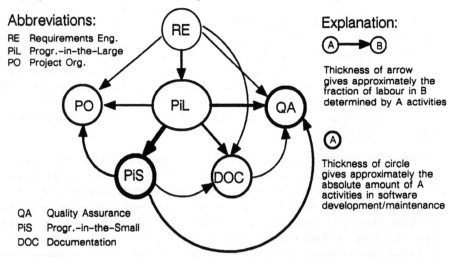

Abbreviations:

RE   Requirements Eng.
PiL Progr.–in–the–Large
PO   Project Org.

Explanation:

Thickness of arrow gives approximately the fraction of labour in B determined by A activities

Thickness of circle gives approximately the absolute amount of A activities in software development/maintenance

QA   Quality Assurance
PiS Progr.–in–the–Small
DOC Documentation

Fig. 2: Architecture modeling in the center of software development and maintenance

Before starting to introduce our architecture language, let us recall the situation how *architectures* are often *modeled* nowadays in *industrial practice*. We do this by introducing a simple example, namely a small interactive system for boxes of record cards which can be accessed by keys. Such a system can be used for storing addresses of persons, bibliographies, or anything else. There are user commands on boxes as Show-AllBoxes, CreateANewBox, DeleteABox etc., operations on a certain box as ShowACertainCard, CreateACardAndFillItOut, DeleteACard etc., and operations on a set of cards of a box as SearchForAKey, which is partially determined etc. Without going into the details of this example (c.f. /Na 90/), the reader will get a rough idea by looking at the architecture of Fig. 3, which in this shape or in a similar shape will result if designed by people not familiar with modern architecture concepts and notions.

If we try to *characterize* this *architecture* we can immediately make the following statements: (a) Only functional modules which realize exactly one function of the program system are used, (b) edges which are used have the semantics that a module delegates a task to another module and waits for the completion of this task. (c) The overall structure is a tree. This is the result of the top–down development on the one side and of the fact that on the other side we did not detect similarities and commonalities. (d) The tree is partially ordered so that it reflects the order of activations in the father modules. (In our example, ordering is not relevant because the control modules consist mostly of case statements). (e) The structure of the architecture is nearly 1–1 identical to the requirements definition. (f) The given architecture is based on resources which do not appear in Fig. 3 as, for example, a namelist for boxes or a list of all cards of a box because we assume we have a suitable file system on which we directly implement these lists. (g) Global data are handled, for example, the information of the current card. (h) Handling global data leads to data flow between the corresponding modules.

By developing an architecture in this way we will definitely *miss* the *overall goals* of *architecture modeling* given in section 1. Architectures of the form shown in Fig. 3 are easy to develop, but they are hard to maintain. This is because (i) they directly reflect the functionality of the requirements and often also the shape of the user interface, which both are likely to change when a system is developing. (ii) Global data and corresponding data flows yield a very close connection between different modules, which is neither necessary from the given task nor which is made explicit. (iii) The architecture is directly and strongly dependent on the underlying basic machine (file system, I/O device), which is also likely to change. (iv) Commonalities such as basic components for storing the relevant objects are not detected as well as (v) similarities like preparing menus and processing commands which are implemented twice (see Fig. 3). Because the system was developed from the scratch, there was no discussion about the overall structure of interactive systems in general, the errors which should be avoided by designing an interactive system, or standard components which should be found in interactive systems.

Before introducing suitable languages for architecture modeling let us clearly state that the *term architecture* has another meaning in this paper than in many other papers in the literature (for example the IMS–Architecture in /So 88/). By components (modules) we do not mean blocks of a certain undefined complexity which can lay outside of a system to be modeled (such as the user). Instead, modules have a clearly defined export interface, i.e. an interface they provide for other components. Furthermore, edges introduced in an architecture diagram here do not vaguely mean that components have something to do with each other (data flow, dependence, call relation, channel for both, etc.). They clearly define the import interface of a module by enumerating all resources of another component necessary to define or implement this component, or they define underlying structure relations. Therefore, the difference between both meanings of the term architecture is (a) that in our architectures we have a much finer granularity, and (b) that the components as

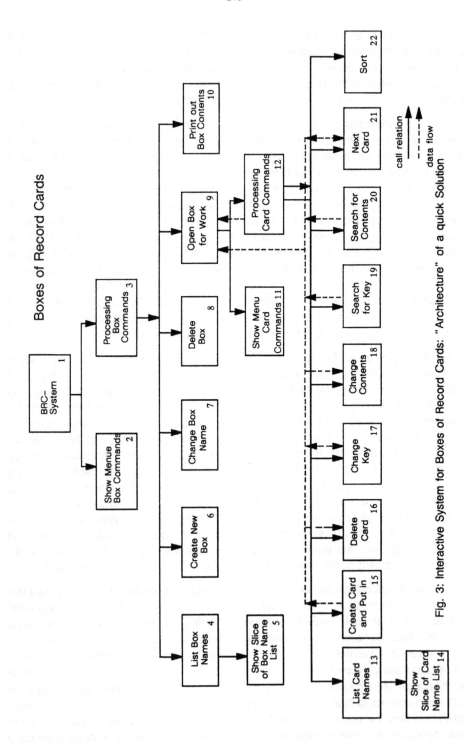

Fig. 3: Interactive System for Boxes of Record Cards: "Architecture" of a quick Solution

well as the relations between them are clearly defined.

3. How to Denote Software Architectures

A *software architecture* should be denoted on two *different levels*: (1) Graphical architecture diagrams that identify all components (modules, later also subsystems) and all relations between components (see Fig. 4). (2) A *detailed* textual *description* of all architecture components contains their export and import interface (see Fig. 5 for the module AbstractCard). The detailed description of modules contains all information; the architecture diagram is an extract of this information. For example, the edges which indicate certain types of imports are contained as import clauses of a certain type in the textual description of the importing module. Architecture diagrams are especially important for discussions about architectures because, besides all details, we firstly need an overall impression of a software system. Experienced designers can do most of the design on this graphical level, adding the details of the modules in later steps.

In order to understand an architecture two further documents should be available (see Fig. 6 for a fraction of both): (1) A *design rationale* should clearly state the design decisions for introduced modules, for introduced relations between modules, for certain layers of components, as well as for certain quality properties (as adaptability, portability) and, finally, for maintenance and reuse considerations, and how they are achieved. This design rationale is a part of the technical documentation of a system. (2) Furthermore, for any module of a software system, a specification of its body should be available in the form of a few lines of pseudocode. We call this the module body's *minispec*. This is no contradiction to the architecture paradigm of section 2. There, we claimed that we do not implement the bodies on programming-in-the-large level, but we have to think roughly about what's going on within these bodies. Minispecs are important (a) because, to a certain degree, they prevent the introduction of trivial modules later deleted in a design backtracking step. Analogously, working out a minispec decreases the danger that we introduce "huge" modules which in a later design backtracking step have to be broken down into different modules. Because the design rationale belongs to the technical documentation and the minispecs are steps in the direction of programming-in-the-small, both are not further discussed in this paper, which is devoted to architecture modeling.

If we look on the architecture diagram in Fig. 4 we see that three *different sorts* of *modules* are introduced in the architecture languages to be discussed now. There are functional modules (abbreviated by f) having an input/output or transformational behavior like AdmBoxesAndCards. Functional modules serve for functional abstractions within software systems. Such modules do not have an internal state: Whenever their functions are invoked with the same parameters, they yield the same result.

For supporting the data abstraction principle there are two further different sorts of modules: (1) There are abstract data object modules (abbr. ado), which represent one abstract data object like AbstractCard. In the case that we do need more than one abstract data object (2) we use data type modules (abbr. adt, as arbCard in Fig. 4). Those modules are templates for abstract data objects. Here, we distinguish between adt modules exporting a type (and access operations) or a creation operation (together with access operations. The first sort of adt modules create abstract data objects with vari-

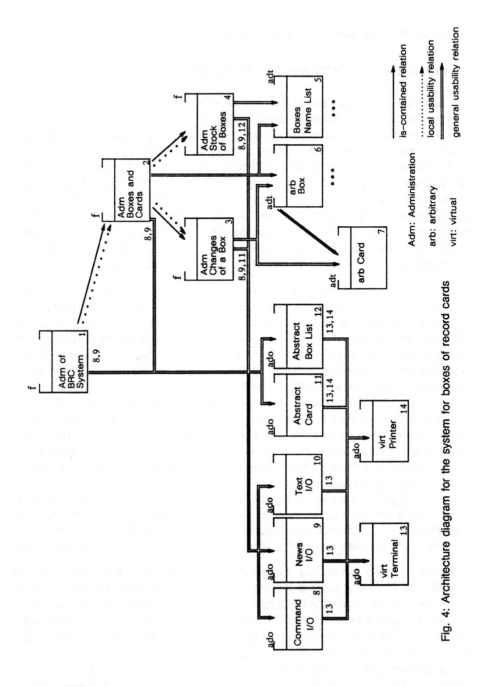

Fig. 4: Architecture diagram for the system for boxes of record cards

```
abstract data object module AbstractCard is -- ********************************
    -- The module offers all necessary operations on an abstract card for input   --
    -- and output. Abstract card here means that we abstract from all details of   --
    -- layout representation. The set operations are done by the system. The read--
    -- operations assume that the user has put in corresponding components         --
    -- before they are read.                                                        --
    -- The semantics of the access operations is the following: ...                 --
    -- general import from BRCTypes using KEY_T, COMP1_T, ...;
    procedure InitializeCardIO;
    procedure DeleteCardContents;
    procedure SetKey (KEY: in KEY_T);
    function ReadKey return KEY_T;
    procedure SetComp1 (C1: in COMP1_T);
    function ReadComp1 return COMP1_T;
    ...
    -- A read and write operation for each component of the abstract card inclu-  --
    -- ding the key.                                                               --
end A bstractCard;-- **************************************************************
```

Fig. 5: Detailed description for the export interface of module AbstractCard

a) 3. Layer for Abstract Input and Output

This layer consists of two parts. One part contains the modules commandIO,
NewsIO and TextIO which serve for abstract input and output of commands,
news and texts, respectively. All layout representation details for CommandIO,
NewsIO and TextIO (how commands are represented and selected, how news are
represented and confirmed, how texts are represented (e.g. for parameter input))
are encapsulated here. The other modules AbstractCard and AbstractBoxList
abstract from layout details corresponding to the input/output of a single card
and the output of the list of box names.

3.1 CommandIO

...

3.4 AbstractCard

This module encapsulates the layout form of a mask for handling the input and
output on a card. Therefore, it is called AbstractCard. The rest of the
architecture is free from these details. The abstraction holds true for output,
i.e. all access output operations do not reflect how the mask is built up and
how the parameters are represented within the mask. Conversely, input access
operations, which assume that the user has put in the corresponding components
and which are used within the system for processing and storing the contents of
a mask, are also abstract in this sense. So, a global decision of this module
is to restrict changes of layout representation of cards to the body of this
module. As at any time only one card can be seen on the screen an abstract data
object module suffices.

3.5 Abstract BoxList

...

b) ...

AbstractCard - Minispec:

InitializeCardIO builds up the card mask if not already on the screen; DeleteCard-
Contents erases the value of a card's components which, before, have been set either
by the user or by the system; SetKey outputs a key on a certain area of the screen;
ReadKey opens user input on a certain area of the screen and returns the value
the user put in; ...

Fig. 6: (a) Cutout of the design rationale, (b) minispec of AbstractCard module body able, the latter one with pointer semantics.) In /Na 90/ a lot of rules and hints are given for formulating the export interface of data abstraction modules.

Corresponding to *module relations* we also distinguish between *different sorts*. Before explaining them we should point out, that these relations are on usability level and not on the use level (see Fig. 7). Usability means that some rights for use (some imports) are conceded. Usability level is the only level which, according to the architecture paradigm, is important for architecture modeling.

There, we distinguish between local usability and general usability. *Local* usability (dotted arrows in Fig. 4) is bound to occur within trees, which are spanned by the is–contained relation (solid arrows), usually expressed by nesting in programming languages. It is furthermore bound to scope/visibility rules. The difference to those rules in our language is that use is not automatically allowed within the whole visibility region (eventually a big portion of an architecture). The designer explicitly has to state by local usability in which modules the use shall be allowed. By the "is–contained" relation, modules are fixed within a software architecture.These modules only have a special and local importance, i.e. they are used in only one context. This allows information hiding on the architecture level, because for understanding the functionality of a "is–contained" tree from outside we only have to understand the functionality of its root. In Fig. 4 we see that the functional modules below the main module only have local importance.

By the *general* usability relation we include modules into software architectures which have some general importance. In general, therefore, they are made usable in different modules. By the general usability relation, arbitrary hierarchies are built up. As to be seen from the example of Fig. 4, general usability relations are often directed to data abstraction modules.

In the textual representation the "is–contained" relation is expressed by a clause contained in the specification of the contained module (target of the corresponding arrow). Local usability is expressed by a local–import clause in the importing module as well as general usability by a general–import clause.

For an architecture denoted in the above two languages, a lot of *consistency conditions* (context sensitive syntax relations) hold true. They can be classified according to Fig. 7 into (1) whether they can be detected on architecture diagram level ((a) in Fig. 7), (2) whether they belong to the conformity between export interface and import of two modules (A(b) and B(c) in Fig. 7) and, therefore, belong to the textual language for modules. Furthermore, because in our architecture language only certain sorts of modules are allowed (3) we can state conditions how the export interface of such a module has to be built up (A(b)), or (4) how this interface plays together with the corresponding import clause (again A(b) and B(c)). Finally, now leaving the programming–in–the–large level and pointing to programming–in–the–small (5) some rules state relations between module bodies and export interfaces or import clauses, respectively. An example for (1) is that the "is–contained" relation of a software system has to be a forest, an example for (2) is that nothing can be imported which is not exported. An example for (3) is that for any state changing operation of a data abstraction module there should be a value reading operation, by which the user is able to get information about dangerous situations which might occur (such as a full stack), an example for (4) is that importing from a data type module only makes sense if the type (or creation operation) is imported, too.

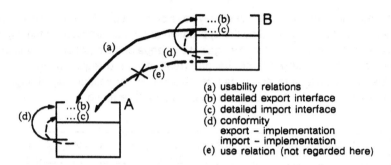

(a) usability relations
(b) detailed export interface
(c) detailed import interface
(d) conformity
   export – implementation
   import – implementation
(e) use relation (not regarded here)

Fig. 7: Different levels for consistency conditions

4. Lessons Learned, and Further Concepts

In Fig. 8 we list the *main applications* of *functional* abstraction and of *data abstraction*. Let us take *some examples* and let us make clear from which details we abstract. If a functional module is used for control or coordination, this means that all the realization details of this control or coordination are made local to the body of this module, or to a part of the architecture below this module. If we use an adt module for handling and storing complex entries, we factorize out all the representation details of this entry (how single components are represented, how the access to a certain component is realized, whether there are further components for internal reasons and alike). An ado module for a collection of entries hides how the underlying set is realized, where it is stored, how the order is realized, and how the corresponding access mode (such as FIFO) is implemented. Furthermore, an ado module for an I/O device (virtual device) factorizes out all the details of this device and, finally, an adt module for handling abstract output supresses all the details which might occur in the layout of a certain printed list.

We can find these applications of functional and data *abstraction* in our *example* in Fig. 4. The upper modules are responsible for coordinating the user dialogues. In arbCard we find an adt module for handling and storing complex entries, in arbBox and in Boxes-NameList two adt modules for collections. All ado modules in the left side of Fig. 4 and on the second row from the bottom have to factorize out layout details, the two ado modules below this layer abstract from details of physical devices.

Therefore, the main message of Fig. 4 (and one of the main messages of the book /Na 90/) is the importance of the *data abstraction principle* for *software engineering* especially for getting a clean architecture, for adaptability, portability, and reuse. If we compare both solutions (see Fig. 3 and 4) we see that the new architecture is no longer a tree, but mostly prefers generally usable modules, and that most of them are data abstraction modules. All *realization decisions* which are likely to change are encapsulated (details for realizing entries, collections, details of devices, details of layout, details of user interface elements (like command names, which we also subsume under abstract input/output). Furthermore, consequent application of data abstraction also has an indirect consequence: Processing of user interface commands is no longer scattered over the whole architecture as in Fig. 3. Instead, processing is grouped semantically in one module each, according to the abstract data object they have an effect on. So, the functional part of an architecture is also influenced by the application of data abstraction. Summing up, the new architecture is much more stable against a *change* of the *functionality* and *user interface* of the system. Both kinds of changes (realization and requirements) can be applied to the new architecture and it can be shown that corresponding changes of architecture remain local. In /Na 90/ some examples can be found.

Type of Module	functional module	abstract data object module	abstract data type module
appli-ca-tion situa-tion	• control or coordination • transformation • complex evaluation utility above one or more ado modules (funct. layer between data abstraction layers	single, complex entry (record) • collection of entries with certain access operations • I/O device • abstract input/output	• handling complex entries • handling collections of entries • handling I/O devices • handling abstract inputs/outputs

• means especially important and often occuring

Fig. 8: Main application of functional or data abstraction

How can we find all these *situations* where *data abstraction* should be applied? A practical and promising procedure is to arrange two *brainstorming* sessions: one in the preparation of the requirements definition and the other one during building up the architecture. The question for both sessions is: "What can be changed or what is likely to change?". The first session mostly delivers enhancements of the functionality/user interface, or changes of the context (underlying machine) to be kept in mind during the design process. The second yields realization changes. Watching the results of both discussions almost automatically leads to all situations where data abstraction should be applied.

The following *rules* of *experiences* in architecture modeling which do not strictly apply can be found (see Fig. 4 for an example): functional modules more often occur in the upper layers of a software architecture; data abstraction modules in the lower layers. Also, local usability is more likely in the upper and general usability in the lower levels. Top–down design prefers functional decompostion and local usability, bottom–up design layers of data abstraction modules connected by the general usability relation. Therefore, as one can see from Fig. 3, top–down design is more dangerous.

A consequent application of the data abstraction principle has some further consequences: (1) Data abstraction could and should be used to *localize dangerous* and diffi-cult to survey *situations*, like handling with pointers. (2) Data abstraction guarantees a *loose coupling* of modules, namely a coupling reduced to the semantically necessary kernel. This argument is nothing else than another formulation of the adaptability argu-ment from above. (3) In architectures, where in all possible situations data abstraction is applied, there is *no* longer a *distinction* between *programs* and *data*, where the com-plexity of both determines the complexity of the total system. Each complex data object is represented on the architecture level as a data abstraction module. Therefore, the archi-tecture documents contain the whole complexity of a software system.

Applying the above *concepts* and *languages* to architecture modeling some *standard questions* arise in handling specific and local situations: One is the question: "What is a functional and what is a data abstraction, especially ado, module?". To answer that question, one has to concentrate on the export interface of a module. Either looking into the body or regarding the context in which the module is embedded, may lead to a wrong answer. Another question is: "Where we can find the memory of data abstraction modules in order to keep internal states?". Further questions are: "How do functional and data abstraction modules cooperate? How the design of the architecture below a data abstraction module is made? How layers of data abstraction are modelled?" and, finally: "How are situations of entries of collections handled, where data abstraction has to be applied on entry as well as on collection level?". There is not space available here to discuss the situations and the range of possible answers.

In modeling software architectures with the languages of section 3, the necessity arises to *extend* the above *architecture languages* in order to handle some standard situations of parts of an architecture more conveniently. In the rest of this section we will sketch these extensions.

The first extension is related to *subsystems*. A subsystem is a "logical" collection of modules to build up a new component. Some of them are usable outside. Therefore, those resources of the export interfaces of these modules needed outside build up the export interface of the subsystem. All the modules are in the body of the subsystem. Fig. 9. gives the graphical representation of a subsystem, the textual representation is not included. The designer of the subsystem uses the representation of Fig. 9.a., i.e. an architecture diagram inside the body and a module symbol around this architecture diagram with the additional information, which of the modules comprise the subsystem's export interface. For the use of a subsystem the subsytems internals, i.e. the corresponding architecture diagram, are not interesting (see Fig. 9.b.) Of course subsystems can be contained in subsystems and so forth. However in most cases, a two–level design approach will suffice even in larger projects. On a global level the overall architecture of a software system is developed consisting of modules and subsystems. Subsystems are then developed by different groups of designers. The reader should notice that the problems discussed in section 2 in connection with the architecture paradigm are even greater but, again, unavoidable. To understand an architecture it is important to see what is a subsystem and what is a module. Within subsystems and between subsystems and other components the above module relations can take place. So, module relations also extend to subsytems. However, some additional consistency conditions have to be watched which we do not explain here. Subsystems have something to do with building up portions of a complete system to be developed independently, also on an architecture level. Therefore, subsystems are natural candidates for subprojects.

The next idea to be introduced on architecture level is *genericity*. Genericity is used to introduce templates for architecture components (modules, subsystems). By genericity we implement a set of components leaving some (generic) parameters open. Typical generic parameters are types, procedures but also simple objects as constants, for example to fix the number of entries in a collection. Corresponding to which constructs are available in the underlying programming language there are different views on generic components. If generic components are macro expanded at compile time (such as in

Ada) a generic component is not an architectural component, but a template from which we can get architectural components (by generic instantiations). If, on the other hand, the underlying programming language has type and procedure parameters to be handled at runtime, then a generic component is a usual architecture component. Because most relevant programming languages of practice do not have this feature, we regard genericity as belonging to the first alternative. Genericity, of course, should not be restricted to modules. For example, the entry-collection situation in Fig. 9 could be generic inasmuch as the key type of entries is a generic topic (together with operations to compare keys, see Fig. 10).

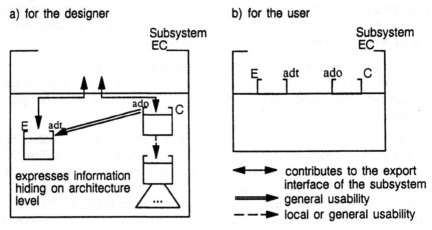

a) for the designer b) for the user

Fig. 9: Graphical representation of a subsystem

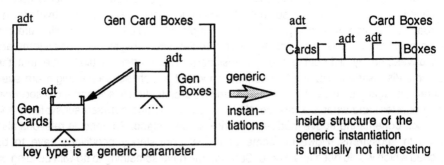

Fig. 10: A generic subsystem

The last concept to be introduced here, again only on architecture diagram level, is *object-orientedness* (see Fig. 11). Classes (adt modules) are connected by the structure relation specialization (dashed arrows). Specialization means inheritance of all properties of (export interfaces) of superclasses. We represent inheritance hierarchies upside-down in order to adopt them to the usual top-bottom abstraction framework. In order to avoid not regulated message passing potentially possible between all classes of a hierarchy we introduce a further sort of import relations within such an inheritance hierarchy. This inheritance usability can be regarded as installing channels through which message passing must occur. In the example these import relations are always directed from a class to its ancestor. Therefore, they are omitted.

Object–oriented architecture modeling essentially means to enrich a predefined inheritance hierarchy by subhierarchies, thereby enlarging the set of predefined classes. This is an advantage (reuse) but also a danger (getting lost in the huge amount of predefined classes). Generalization (the inverse of specialization) is semantically different from general usability: Here, a module can only be used if it is not only an arbitrary suitable means for realization. In addition, it encapsulates the common behavior of all of its subclasses. As object–orientedness is a natural continuation of data abstraction, it can be used for all applications of the data abstraction principle (see Fig. 8, last column) where similarities can be expressed. A good example for the collection application is the hierarchy of predefined collection classes in the Smalltalk system /GR 83/.

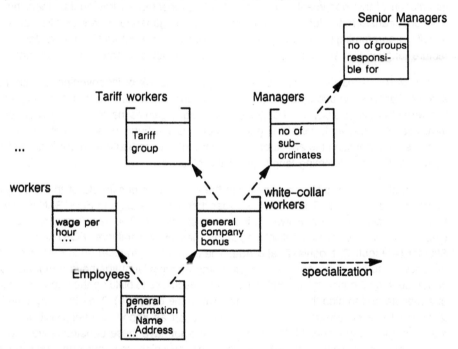

Fig. 11: A simple inheritance hierarchy

For software architectures built up with the two (enhanced) architecture languages some *rules* for *methodological applications* can be found. Let us give only a few examples: (a) "is–contained" trees should not be too deep. One should always think about whether a module/subsystem has a more general importance and, therefore, is to be connected to an architecture by a general usability edge. (b) If a module has many incoming general usability edges we should be careful, especially if these edges originate from very different abstraction levels (layers) of the architecture. It might be true that in this case some modules in higher levels (some abstractions) have been forgotten. (c) In an inheritance hierarchy one should be careful with inheritance usability to classes of the same hierarchy level. It is probable that it was forgotten to formulate the commonalities between those classes by introducing another suitable class.

5. Mapping on Programming Languages for Implementation

Mapping our language on programming languages can be fully and automatically *done by tools*. This transformation is sometimes called coding-in-the-large as it generates text frames for architectural components. The development of such a tool is especially easy if there is an integrated set of tools for progarmming-in-the-large, i.e. a software architecture modeling environment. Tools of this working area should be part of a more comprehensive software development environment. This paper does not discuss integrated software development environments. But having such an environment at hand which, for any software document to be modelled by the user, contains all structural information of this document (so-called structure-oriented environments), then, by an additional transformator tool, called unparser, we can generate source text frames for a specific programming language. In /Le 88/ such an environment which supports the architecture language of section 3 and its mapping on Modula-2 and C is discussed.

Transforming manually, besides the evident drawback of inconvenience, also has some *advantages* in understanding the architectural concepts introduced in this paper: We carefully have to study our architecture language again as the source of an automatic translation process and, therefore, get a deeper insight. Furthermore, we realize the logical distance between the architecture language of section 3 and 4 on one side and the corresponding programming language on the other.

The problems of translation depend on the richness of constructs of the underlying programming language. Therefore, it is clear that the translation to FORTRAN is harder than the translation to Ada. However, it is never impossible. The transformation was studied for a series of programming languages, namely Assemblers, FORTRAN, Cobol, Standard-Pascal, C, Modula-2, and Ada. The *difficulty* of *translation* is determined by the answers to two questions: (a) Does the programming language have a *module construct*, such as a construct to combine different resources to build up the export interface of a module and to hide the implementation within the body? (b) Does the programming language have *constructs* on *usability level*, such as import clauses, visibility rules across module boundaries? If the language does not have these constructs we have to build them in mind, we have to textually group units by which the above constructs can be simulated, we have to use comments in order to make this mental constructs clear, and we have to use some discipline in order to avoid the violation of the consistency constraints mentioned above.

The *programming languages* of practical importance listed above (and others) can be devided into *three classes*: (a) programming languages with independent program units which can be compiled apart from others (Assemblers, FORTRAN, Basic, Cobol, C, etc.), (b) block-structured programming languages without a module construct (Algol 60, Algol 68, Standard-Pascal, etc.), and (c) classical modern programming languages with modules (Ada, Pascal dialects, Modula-2, etc.). In the following we restrict our considerations on class (a), taking FORTRAN as a representative. For the mapping of our architecture languages to other classes the reader is referred to /Na 90/.

227

```
C      ****************************************************
C      *                                                 *
C      * abstract data object module INTEGER_STACK is    *
C      *   procedure PUSH(X: in INTEGER);                *
C      *   procedure POP;                                *
C      *   function READ_TOP return INTEGER;  --RDTOP    *
C      *   function IS_EMPTY return BOOLEAN;  --ISEMTY   *
C      *   function IS_FULL return BOOLEAN;   --ISFULL   *
C      *   ...                                           *
C      *   Angabe der Bedeutung der Operationen:         *
C      *   ...                                           *
C      * end INTEGER_STACK;----------------------------------*
C
C         local import from INTEGER_LIST using all;
C      * module body INTEGER_STACK is ----------------------------
C
       SUBROUTINE PUSH(ELEMNT)
          INTEGER STACK(100), POINTR, ELEMNT
          COMMON /STDATA/ STACK, POINTR
          ...
          RETURN
       END
C
       SUBROUTINE POP
          INTEGER STACK(100), POINTR
          COMMON /STDATA/ STACK, POINTR
          ...
          RETURN
       END
C
       INTEGER FUNCTION RDTOP
          INTEGER STACK(100), POINTR
          COMMON /STDATA/ STACK, POINTR
          ...
          RETURN
       END
C
       ...
       BLOCKDATA
          INTEGER STACK(100), POINTR
          COMMON /STDATA/ STACK, POINTR
          ...
       END
C      * end INTEGER_STACK;                               *
C      ****************************************************
```

Fig. 12: Abstract data object module in FORTRAN

Because no module construct is available in *FORTRAN*, the interface as well as the body of a module have to be built up by comments. In the case of functional modules the body consists of subroutines corresponding to the functions of the export interface. In the case of an abstract data object module (c.f. Fig. 12 for a simple example) a named COMMON is used to realize the abstract data object. The access operations are subroutines working on this COMMON. In the case of abstract data type modules, is clear that only abstract data type modules of the second reuse (a creation operation for generating abstract data objects) is possible as no type declaration is available in FORTRAN. The is–contained relation is mapped on a corresponding clause represented as comment in the interface of a contained module. The local usability as well as the general usability is · mapped on a corresponding clause in the importing module (c.f. Fig. 12). For subsystems a two–step simulation has to take place. The interface and the body of a subsystem are built up in very much the same way as for modules. Genericity in FORTRAN is only possible by a macro extension tool, generating instantiated modules or subsystems. Object–orientedness is hard to map on FORTRAN as no dynamic mechanisms are available. Therefore, only very special cases can be simulated.

If we ask which *consistency conditions* for the FORTRAN source code have to be preserved by discipline, regardless whether the source is manually or automatically transformed, we can give the following answer: Of course, all conditions which are contained in the architecture languages must hold as none of these architecture language constructs is available in FORTRAN. Furthermore, as no module construct is available the designer/programmer is responsible that only modules of the above sorts are used and that the internals of a body are not used outside of this body or are used to get knowledge in order to directly change encapsulated objects (abstract data object in case of an abstract data type module).

The transformation into *Standard–Pascal* is even harder than into FORTRAN. Nesting of Pascal cannot be used because nesting is not available for modules (because there are no modules in Pascal). Therefore, a Pascal program structure resulting from a mapping is quite different from the usual program structures (usually deep trees). It is a flat collection of "modules" in the outermost block, quite similar to the situation we find in FORTRAN. The translation into *Ada* is, of course, much simpler because modules are available which only have to be used by discipline, nesting is possible for modules and conveniently usable by subunits, and as the with–clause can directly be used for general usability. However, answering the question: "Which consistency conditions are checked by the Ada compiler?". We see, that 2/3 of these conditions are still due to discipline. Therefore, our (textual) architecture language can be seen as a methodical use of Ada for specification purposes. As already indicated, there is however a significant difference between the logical level of the architecture language and Ada, even without regarding object–orientedness.

6. Strategies for Adaptability and Reuse

Looking into an *architecture* a lot of *questions* can be *answered* about a software system (see Fig. 13). In most cases these questions can be answered even by regarding only the architecture diagram. We now have a well–founded discussion about maintenance, structural aspects, quality evaluation, and reuse considerations of a software system. One corresponding question for each of these topics is given in Fig. 13. This means that we do get a considerable improvement by carefully modeling on architecture level. This however, does not mean that an architecture is easy to build. A good architecture may be the result of months or years of work. In contrast, bad and dirty architectures are easily bolted together as seen from the architecture in Fig. 3 which, in a seminar, is the outcome of an one hour discussion. So, good architecture modeling is a long term investment.

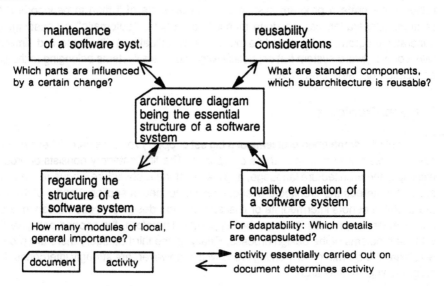

Fig. 13: The role of architecture diagrams

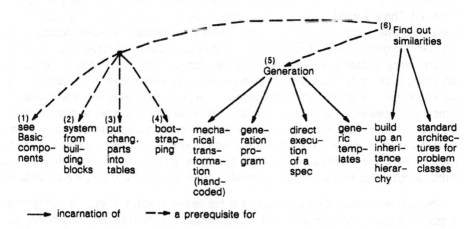

Fig. 14: Summary of strategies for adaptability and reuse

There are some *strategies* for *quality software* which we can only cite here without giving examples which prove their value. The implication of these strategies on reuse and maintainability as well as the discussion which of the architectural concepts of above are usable for these strategies are left as exercises to the reader. The list is as follows: (1) Try to get basic components or, if the architecture of a certain class of systems is made clear, standard components. (2) Try to build up a software system from building blocks such that you can get stripped or enhanced versions by adding or deleting these building blocks. (3) Put parts of a software system, which are likely to change, into data structures (for examples tables) and do not hardwire them. (4) Use bootstrapping (development of concepts, methods, languages and rules applicable for their own realization). (5) Try rather to generate a program system or essential parts of it than to handcode it from scratch. (Generation can be done manually by a fixed "automatic" proceeding, by a generator program, or by directly executing a specification.) (6) Try to find similarities within one software system but especially within software systems belonging to the same application or "structural" class.

7. Open Problems

We only list some open problems of a big set of *open problems* here. These problems can be classified to belong to *three categories*. The first category consists of problems existing in the architecture language, application of the architecture language, and its tool support. Whereas the architecture languages introduced in section 3 and 4 of this paper are useful to denote intermediate or final states of the design process we can in addition ask whether the process itself can be supported. Therefore, the second category deals with the problems of the design process. Finally, in the third category there are problems which have to do with other working areas which, however, are strongly interconnected to programming–in–the–large.

In the problem category *architecture modeling* one problem is to integrate object-orientedness, genericity, and subsystems with the architecture language concepts of section 3. There are still some open problems. Especially, the question: "In which situation should which concept be used in order to get a good result?" is open. Another deep problem is to get even more experience in handling situations occuring as partial architectures in many software systems. Furthermore, classes of systems have to be studied according to the application area (office automation systems, commercial systems, software for engineers etc.) or structural aspects (transformation problems, interactive systems, rule based systems etc.) in order to get standard architectures so that the knowledge about such a class need not be reinvented in building a specific system. For concurrent and/ or distributed systems the question is whether further concepts have to be integrated into our architectural language in order to discribe those systems. Finally, a formal architecture metric should be useful in order to evaluate different architectures.

The second problem category belongs to the design *process*. Here, we look for concepts, languages, and tools to support this process. A special questions is whether certain strategies (top–down, bottom–up etc.) can be supported in order to minimize the drawbacks related to each strategy. Furthermore, the question is how the reuse of concepts, tools, and solutions is to be supported. Structural changes of software systems (for example the transformation of a recursive descent parser into a table–driven one in order to improve flexibility and to reduce the effort of writing a parser) can be described as an architecture transformation. How does a complete set of such transformations look? Finally, the question is how the strategies for getting quality software of the last section can be supported by tools.

The last problem category handles with the *connection* of programming-in-the-large to *other problem areas*. As argued in section 2, requirements engineering is also very important in solving the actual software problems. However, the requirements specification and the architecture of a software system are different with respect to the logical level (view from outside, inside view on the level which forgets module bodies) and granularity. From these arguments we see that the connection between both documents cannot be automated. On the other hand both documents have very much to do with each other. How then does the connection and its support by tools look /Ja 90/? Similar questions arise for the other problem areas (programming-in-the-small, documentation support, quality assurance, project organization). In project organization an area of special importance and strong connection to programming-in-the-large is version, variant, and configuration control /We 90/. Finally, in mixed hardware/software systems special problems arise because software design is embedded in system design. The document against which a software architecture has to be compared is rather the architecture of the total system than a requirements definition.

Acknowledgements

The author is indebted to Drs. W. Altmann, R. Gall and C. Lewerentz, who contributed to the architectural concepts of this paper. Furthermore, we thankfully remember many stimulating discussions with J. Börstler, Dr. G. Engels, Th. Janning, A. Schürr and others. Finally, J. Börstler took the load of carefully reading the paper and Mrs. A. Fleck and M. Hirsch prepared its perfect layout appearance.

References

/AI 78/   W. Altmann: Description of Program Modules for the Design of Reliable Software, Ph. D. Thesis, University of Erlangen, Techn. Report IMMD 11-16 (1978).

/Bo 84/   B. W. Boehm: Software Lifecycle Factors, in Vick/Ramamoorthy (Eds.): Handbook on Software Engineering, 494-518, New York: van Nostrand Reinhold (1984).

/Bo 87/   G. Booch: Software Components with Ada, Menlo Park: Benjamin Cummings (1987).

/Bu 84/   R.J.A. Buhr: System Design with Ada, Englewood Cliffs: Prentice Hall (1984).

/Co 86/   B. Cox: Object-oriented Programming – An Evolutionary Approach, Reading: Addison Wesley (1986).

/DoD 83/   Department of Defense (USA): Reference Manual for the Ada Programming Language, ANSI-MIL-STD 1815 A.

/ENS 86/   G. Engels/M. Nagl/W. Schäfer: On the Structure of Structure-Oriented Editors for Different Applications, in P. Henderson (Ed.), Proc. 2nd ACM Symp. on Pract. Softw. Dev. Env., ACM SIGPLAN Notices 23, 1, 190-198 (1987).

/ES 89/   G. Engels/W. Schäfer: Program Support Environments, Concepts and Realization (in German), Stuttgart: Teubner-Verlag (1989).

/EW 86/   H. Ehrig/H. Weber: Specification of Modular Systems, IEEE Trans. on Softw. Eng. SE-12, 7, 784-789 (1986).

/Ga 83/   R. Gall: Formal Description of Programming-in-the-Large by Graph Grammars (in German), Ph. D. Thesis, University of Erlangen, Techn. Report IMMD 16-1 (1983).

/GHW 85/   J.V. Guttag/J.J. Horning/J.M. Wing: The Larch Family of Specification Languages, IEEE Software 2,5, 24-36 (1985).

/GR 83/   A. Goldberg/D. Robbson: Smalltalk-80: The Language and its Implementation, Reading: Addison Wesley (1983).

/HO 89/   HOOD Working Group: HOOD Reference Manual, European Space Agency WME 89-173/JB.

/HP 80/   H.N. Habermann/D. Perry: Well-formed System Compositions, Technical Report CMU-CS-80-117, Carnegie-Mellon University (1980).

/Ja 90/   Th. Janning: Ph.D. Thesis forthcoming, RWTH Aachen.

/KG 87/   G. Kaiser/D. Garlan: Melding Software Systems from Reusable Building Blocks, IEEE Software, July 87, 17-24.

/Le 88/   C. Lewerentz: Interactive Design of Large Program Systems - Concepts and Tools (in German), Ph. D. Thesis RWTH Aachen, Informatik-Fachberichte 194, Berlin:Springer-Verlag (1988).

/LN 85/   C. Lewerentz/M. Nagl: Incremental Programming-in-the-Large: Syntax-aided Specification Editing, Integration and Maintenance, Proc. 18th Hawaii Int. Conf. on System Sciences, 638-649 (1985).

/Me 86/   B. Meyer: Genericity versus Inheritance, Proc. OOPSLA '86, ACM SIGPLAN Notices 21, 11, 391-405 (1986).

/Me 88/   B. Meyer: Object-oriented Software Construction, New York: Prentice Hall (1988).

/Mü 86/   A.H. Müller: Rigi - A Model for Software System Construction, Integration, and Evolution based on Module Interface Specifications, Ph. D. Thesis, Rice University, Techn. Report COMP.TR 86-36, Houston (1986).

/Na 82, 88/   M. Nagl: Introduction to the Programming Language Ada (in German) first and second edition, Braunschweig: Vieweg-Verlag (1982, 1988).

/Na 90/   M. Nagl: Software Engineering: Methodological Programming-in-the-Large (in German), Berlin: Springer-Verlag (1990).

/OOPSLA/   Proceedings of the Conferences on Object-oriented Programming Systems, Languages and Applications, OOPSLA '86 - '89, ACM SIGPLAN Notices.

/Pa 72/   D.L. Parnas: On the Criteria To Be Used in Decomposing Systems into Modules, Comm. ACM 15, 12, 1053-1058 (1972).

/Ra 84/   C.V. Ramamoorthy et al.: Software Engineering - Problems and Perspectives, Computer 10/84, 191-209 (1984).

/SB 82/   W. Swartout/R. Balzer: On the Inevitable Intertwining of Specification and Implementation, Comm. ACM 25, 7, 438-440 (1982).

/St 88/   B. Stroustrup: What is Object-oriented Programming, IEEE Software, May 88, 10-20.

/So 88/   I. Somerville: Interacting with an Active, Integrated Environment, in P. Henderson (Ed.): Proc. 3rd ACM Symp. on Pract. Softw. Dev. Env., ACM Software Eng. Notes 13, 5, 76-84 (1988).

/We 87/   P. Wegner: The object-oriented Classification Paradigm, in P. Wegner/B. Shriver: Research Directions in Object-oriented Programming Cambridge: MIT Press, 479-550 (1987).

/We 90/   B. Westfechtel: Revision Control in an Integrated Development Environment, PH.D. Thesis forthcoming, RWTH Aachen (1990).

/Ze 79/   M. Zelkowitz et al.: Principles of Software Engineering and Design, Englewood Cliffs: Prentice Hall (1979).

A Configurable Framework for Method and Tool Integration

Jeff Kramer and Anthony Finkelstein

Department of Computing,

Imperial College of Science, Technology and Medicine,

180 Queen's Gate, London SW7 2BZ, UK.

jk@doc.ic.ac.uk , *acwf @doc.ic.ac.uk*

ABSTRACT

There is an urgent need to provide a sound generic framework for method and tool integration, where many differing notations are used, software development is distributed and management support for the software development process is provided. This paper argues that there is much to be learnt from proven practical techniques for software construction, particularly those that support distributed software integration, heterogeneity and software management. *Configuration Programming* is one such approach which advocates the use of a separate, declarative configuration language for the description of system structure. It has been used in the Conic Environment for the development of distributable software, and is being extended for the configuration of heterogeneous components programmed in different programming languages. A number of software tools exist for the development, construction and management of Conic systems. This paper shows how an analogous set of the principles, practice and tools from configuration programming can be combined with recent work on ViewPoints[1] to provide a configurable framework for method and tool integration.

1. INTRODUCTION

The process of software production involves many stages, from requirements elicitation and specification through to system construction and maintenance. A large number of methods can be used during this process, each covering different stages of the process. Each method generally consists of one or more representation schemes (notations) together with a set of recommended procedures and heuristics as to how to complete each representation and guidance on how to move to the next representation. These methods may overlap or be disjoint. It is left

---

[1] The work on ViewPoints [6] has been conducted in close collaboration with Michael Goedicke of the University of Dortmund, but the obsession with configurations presented in this paper is that of the authors.

to the project team to try to convert information to a suitable form for the next stage, to ensure consistency and to try to bridge the gaps between methods and notations by some *ad hoc* means. In addition, even at a single stage in the process, it is necessary to represent different aspects of the application, not only in terms of a partitioning of the application domain but also to provide different views (such as functional, performance, fault tolerance, safety and others). There is no doubt that different companies and project personnel will also wish to tailor individual methods and the overall software process according to their experience and the particular application domain.

Thus there is a need for multiple methods and their notations, together with the ability to modify and integrate them. The vision is of a framework for method integration, which supports distributed development by teams of personnel and provides tool support. How can methods be "glued" together? How can information transfer and consistency checks between notations be supported? How can advice and tool support for the use of each notation and between notations be provided?

The ViewPoints Approach

This paper addresses these issues and proposes a configurable framework for method and tool integration. The approach is based on decomposition of the application domain, the notations and the method steps. The basic entities which are configured in this framework are ViewPoints [6]. Each ViewPoint (fig.1) describes a part of the application *domain* using a single *style* (representation notation or formalism). A *workplan* provides the rules and heuristics for use of the notation together with relations or mappings to other ViewPoints to express information transfer and consistency checks. The result is a ViewPoint *specification* of a particular part of the application in a particular notation, together with its *workrecord* which records the current status of the specification elaboration.

Style : definition of representation notation
Domain : selected part of the application
Specification in the style for the particular domain
Work Plan : style use and interaction rules and heuristics
Work Record : specification status and history

Figure 1.   A ViewPoint

Loosely speaking, a method is described as a configuration of "interacting" ViewPoint types (templates). Method use involves ViewPoint instantiation to provide the specifications in each notation. Method integration is at the ViewPoint level, by configuration to form a software process. Each ViewPoint can be elaborated separately subject to interaction constraints. Tool support can be provided for each type of ViewPoint and for configuration and interaction.

Why is it that we believe that configuring ViewPoints provides a sound generic framework for method and tool integration? In this paper we argue that there is much to be learnt from proven practical techniques for software construction, particularly those that support distributed software integration and interaction, heterogeneity and software management.

Learning from Software Configuration

Practical experience in software engineering has taught us that complex systems can be built and managed provided we adhere to sound principles. Software modularity is essential to encapsulate functionality behind clearly defined interfaces through which components can interact with their environment. Descriptions of the constituent software components and their interconnection patterns provide a clear and concise level at which to specify and design systems, and can be used directly by construction tools to generate the system itself. This approach has been variously referred to as "programming-in-the-large" [3], component-based system building using module interconnection languages [9,20], and "configuration programming" [15, 18]. Furthermore, evolution of the system can be achieved by making extensions or changes to the system configuration by the addition or replacement of components [16].

Configuration programming [18] advocates the use of the interconnected-component model for software design and construction through to evolution. The description of system structure (configuration), as a set of components and their interconnections, is separated from the functional description of individual component behaviour. This general approach has been successfully used in the Conic Environment for the development of distributable software. Graphical and textual software tools are provided to construct, manage and evolve software systems so that they correspond to their declarative configuration descriptions. Complex components can be composed as interconnected instances of simpler component types. The approach is considered "constructive" since it emphasises the satisfaction of system requirements by composition of components. Provided that components adhere to interface standards, the configuration framework can also be used to construct systems from heterogeneous components ie. components written in different languages. Although the configuration descriptions vary from one system to another, many of the basic component types pertaining to an application domain tend to be the same. System variation is directed mainly at the configuration level, with some variation being embedded in particular components. Thus the opportunities for the employment of reusable components within an application domain are excellent, with the configuration language providing the means to select and tailor their use to the particular task at hand (cf. program families from information hiding modules [28]).

The analogy to configurations of ViewPoints and their interactions is obvious. We see ViewPoints as the means for encapsulating each aspect and notation, and configurations as the means for gluing them together. The description of method and process structure as a configuration is separate from the description of a primitive ViewPoint. In order to provide for the description of methods at different levels of abstraction, complex ViewPoints can also be defined as compositions of simpler ones. We believe that the configuration level provides a convenient level of abstraction at which to view and manage methods and software projects. In addition, its declarative structural form makes it independent of the procedural aspects, thereby implicitly supporting distributed (concurrent) development except where explicitly constrained by dependencies.

In this paper we describe the principles which underlie the configuration programming approach and briefly illustrate their usefulness by examples of some of the features of the Conic environment. The vision of the configuration framework for method integration using ViewPoints is then presented, based on analogous principles.

2. CONFIGURATION PROGRAMMING

2.1 Basic Principles

The basic principles of the configuration programming approach can be summarised as follows:

1. *The configuration language used for structural description should be separate from the programming language used for basic component programming.*
   This separation of concerns facilitates the description, comprehension and manipulation, both by man and machine, of the system in terms of its structure. This is achieved by abstracting away from the component programming concerns. The structural nature of the configuration specification makes it amenable to both textual and graphical description. System construction can be performed by translation of the structural configuration description by component creation and interconnection. Furthermore, the configuration language should be *declarative*, describing what the structure is, not how it is to be constructed. Declarative descriptions tend to be more concise and amenable to analysis, interpretation, and manipulation than their imperative equivalents.

2. *Components should be defined as context independent types with well-defined interfaces.*
   Context independence [12] means that the component makes no direct reference to any non-local entities, but can be integrated into any compatible context without redefining or recompiling it. We therefore require that components access only local data and use

indirect naming (such as local ports) to refer to connected components. Definition as a type permits instantiation and reuse in different contexts. The component interface should describe the interaction points with other components and permits validation of interconnections at configuration time.

3. *Using the configuration language, complex components should be definable as a composition of instances of component types.*

Hierarchies are a natural and convenient means for the support of subcomponent encapsulation and information hiding. Interconnected instances of more basic component types can be composed to form more complex components (ie. an *instance* hierarchy). These composite components should themselves be component types, available for use in further definitions. Such an approach also permits the definition and construction of recursive structures.

4. *Change should be expressed at the configuration level, as changes of the component instances and/or their interconnections.*

This follows from the first principle. Given that it is beneficial to utilise a structural description to comprehend and manipulate the system, then change can also be beneficially expressed as structural change. Changes can be made to component instances, which are then of a new and different type.

2.2 An Exemplar of Configuration Programming: Conic Environment

The Conic environment [12, 22], developed by the Distributed Computing Group at Imperial College, provides support for configuration programming for distributed and concurrent programs based on the above principles. The environment provides support for two languages, one for programming individual components (processes) with explicitly defined interfaces, and one for the configuration of programs from groups of components. The Conic configuration language includes facilities for hierarchic definition of composite components, for parametrisation of components, for conditional configurations with evaluation of guards at component instantiation, and even for recursive definition of components [4]. In addition, the environment provides support for dynamic configuration using on-line management tools which permit dynamic creation, control and modification of application programs.

We now briefly illustrate some of the features of the Conic use of configuration programming for describing, constructing, monitoring and changing distributable systems. In order to provide a feel for the approach, we use a simple example: a patient monitoring system [24]. The intensive care ward in a hospital consists of a number of beds. Patients in each bed are continuously monitored for a number of factors, such as pulse, temperature and blood pressure. For each patient the current readings can be displayed both at the bedside and at the nurse unit.

If any of the factor readings of a patient are outside of preset limits, then an alarm is sent to the central nurse station.

Component Types: - Provision of context-independent components (principle 2).

The patient monitoring system is constructed from the two context independent component types (referred to as *modules* in Conic) defined both graphically and textually below in Figure 2. The interface to a component is defined by typed exit- and entryports. Messages are sent out via **exitports** and received from **entryports**. The type definitions for messages and ports are imported from definition modules by the **use** clause

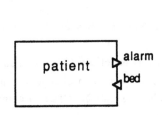

group module patient;

    use monmsg: bedtype, alarmstype;
    exitport
        alarm:alarmstype;
    entryport
        bed:signaltype **reply** bedtype;

    Periodically reads patient sensors.
    Readings outside range cause alarm
    messages to be sent to *alarm.*
    Request message received on *bed*
    returns current readings and ranges.
end.

group module nurse (maxbed:integer=5);

    use monmsg: bedtype, alarmstype;
    entryport
        alarm[1..maxbed]:alarmstype;
    exitport
        bed[1..maxbed]:signaltype **reply** bedtype;

    Displays alarms received from *alarm[]*

    Requests particular patient data via *bed[]*

end.

Figure 2. The Patient and Nurse Component Types

Component Hierarchies: - Composition of component instances (principle 3).

In the above, we have described the main component types to be used to construct the patient monitoring system. In fact, each of the two component types used are themselves configurations of components. For example, the internal structure of the patient component is depicted in Figure 3. It is defined by instantiating an instance of each of a scanner and monitor component types and interconnecting their exit- and entryports. The links between exitports and entryports allow components to communicate by message passing. The Conic environment permits only ports of the same type to be connected.

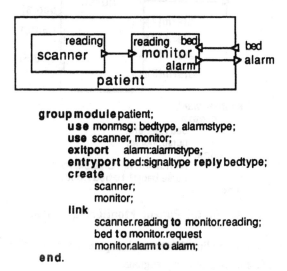

```
group module patient;
     use monmsg: bedtype, alarmstype;
     use scanner, monitor;
     exitport     alarm:alarmstype;
     entryport bed:signaltype reply bedtype;
     create
          scanner;
          monitor;
     link
          scanner.reading to monitor.reading;
          bed to monitor.request
          monitor.alarm to alarm;
end.
```

Figure 3.   Internal structure of Patient Module

A system in Conic is thus an hierarchic structure of component instances. The components at the bottom of the hierarchy are sequential tasks, implemented in a programming language. In Conic, the internal programming language is Pascal extended to support message passing for the distributed environment. Instances of these task modules execute concurrently.

Constructing Systems in Conic: - *Component instantiation and interconnection using a separate configuration language (principle 1).*

We can construct an initial patient monitoring system consisting of one nurse and one patient by instantiating one instance of each of the above component types and interconnecting their exit- and entryports. Again, the Conic environment permits only ports of the same type to be connected. The configuration description for this initial system is again shown both textually and graphically in Figure 4.

The system is created by submitting the configuration description to a configuration manager tool which downloads and interconnects component code. The configuration management tool and its supporting environment is described in [22]. In addition to instance creation and linking (interconnection), the configuration description can include component location (omitted here) and parameters. For example the nurse has a default parameter setting to the value 5 (Figure 2) however this could have been changed when the instance was specified, eg. **create** nurse: nurse(3).

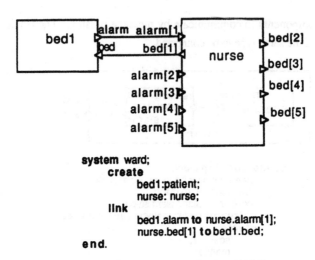

```
system ward;
        create
                bed1:patient;
                nurse: nurse;
        link
                bed1.alarm to nurse.alarm[1];
                nurse.bed[1] to bed1.bed;
end.
```

Figure 4. Initial Patient Monitoring System

REX, an ESPRIT II project, is extending the approach to permit configuration of heterogeneous components written in different programming languages.

Note that the use of a declarative configuration language enables the actual order in which configuration operations are performed to be left to the underlying support system. It can then exploit the inherent parallelism of the underlying architecture where appropriate. If the configuration statements were embedded in a procedural language, the current state of the system configuration would depend on the state of the configuration program (as in [19]). This would complicate the provision of support for dynamic configuration and the user/management view of the system, both of which are discussed below.

```
change ward;
        create
                bed2:patient;
        link
                bed2.alarm to nurse.alarm[2];
                nurse.bed[2] to bed2.bed;
end
```

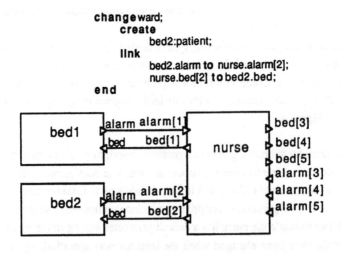

Figure 5 - Extended Patient Monitoring System

Dynamic Configuration for System Evolution:- (principle 4).

In addition to programming initial configurations, the Conic toolkit permits dynamic configuration: changes to running systems. For example, extending the above system to include an additional patient unit can be performed by submitting the configuration change of the system 'ward' (figure 5) to a configuration manager. The change can be thought of as an edit, in configuration terms, of the configuration specification *and* the system itself. It results in both a new specification and a correspondingly changed system. Thus the system itself can evolve rather than necessarily regenerating the system *ab initio*. Recent work on change management [16] has provided a sound basis for controlling change while preserving consistency and without disrupting the unaffected components.

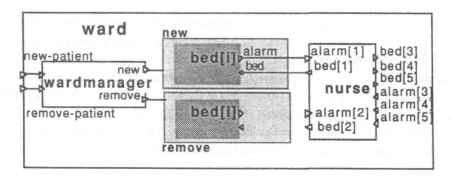

```
component ward (N:integer=5);

        entryport new-patient, remove-patient;
        use        patient, nurse, manager;

        create
            wardmanager:manager ;
            nurse: nurse(N) ;
        link
            wardmanager.new-patient        to new-patient;
            wardmanager. remove-patient to remove-patient;
            wardmanager.new        to new;
            wardmanager.remove to remove;

        change new (i:1..N);
            create bed[i]:patient;
            link   bed[i].alarm to nurse.alarm[i];
            link   nurse.bed[i]} to bed[i].bed;
        end;

        change remove (i:1..N);
            remove bed[i];
        end;

    end.
```

Figure 6. Patient Monitoring System with Programmed Changes

The REX project is again extending this work to permit the definition of programmed reconfiguration changes to a composite component at the same level (and scope) as the definition of the component. What changes are permissible are defined in the configuration language; components determine when the changes should occur by invoking them. For instance, figure 6 shows a possible description of a ward component in which a wardmanager can invoke changes to create or remove patients, either under some internally specified condition or as a result of a request initiated from outside the ward (ie. by a request to new-patient). There is a general need to serialise the changes to a component to prevent interference between concurrent changes.

Tool Support: Graphical Configuration Monitoring and Management

In addition to language compilers, runtime environments and communications support, the Conic environment has provided software tools for monitoring system structure and component status, for dynamic configuration and even for "spying" on the message contents of a particular connection. We concentrate here on a graphics tool, ConicDraw, which can be used to display and manage system configurations. As depicted in figure 7, ConicDraw maintains a graphic representation of executing Conic systems in terms of the component instances which exist in the system, their interconnections and their execution state. It gathers this information directly from the executing system by communicating with a configuration manager.

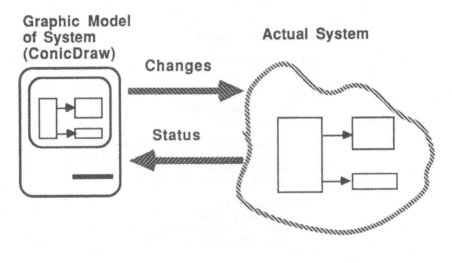

Figure 7. Interaction between ConicDraw and an Operational System.

Changes to the system are reported to ConicDraw by configuration management to enable it to maintain an uptodate view of the system. In addition, ConicDraw can itself instigate changes to the system as a result of edits to the graphic representation.

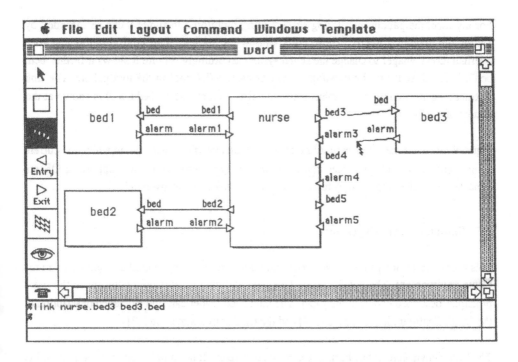

Figure 8. System Structure Monitoring and Linking via ConicDraw.

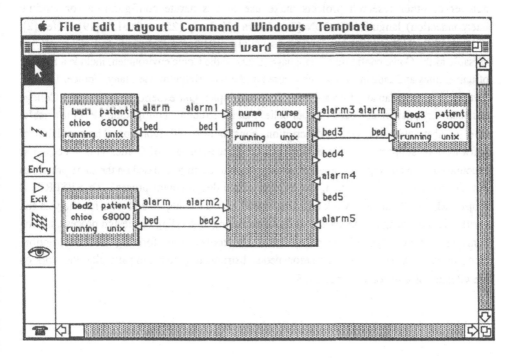

Figure 9. System Status Monitoring via ConicDraw.

For instance, the patient monitoring system being monitored in figure 8 can be extended by editing the diagram directly. These edits caused the tool to send configuration text to a configuration manager to change the actual system accordingly. Figure 8 shows a further bed, bed3, being linked into the existing system using the *link* tool in the tool palette. The link instruction generated by this graphic operation (**link** nurse.bed3 **to** bed3.bed) is shown at the bottom of the figure.

Figure 9 illustrates the status monitoring facilities available via ConicDraw, in which the current component name and type, machine location and type, and status and supporting OS are indicated for each component. A full description of ConicDraw is given in [15].

2.3 Summary and Experience

This section has briefly outlined how configuration programming is used and supported in the Conic environment. The configuration language and components both conform to the basic principles described earlier in the paper. The interested reader can find a detailed description of the Conic Configuration language in [4] and the Conic environment in [22].

The Conic environment has been in use for over 5 years. It has amply demonstrated the utility of configuration level programming and the need for the separate configuration perspective. A number of other research projects make use of a separate configuration (or module interconnection) language (DICON [21], Durra [1], Lady [25], NETSLA [19], RNet [2], Polylith [29], STILE [32]) but few are as widely distributed and used, and as simple yet versatile as the Conic configuration language. Users of the Conic environment include a number of universities and industrial research centres in the UK, Belgium, Germany, France, Greece, Sweden, Finland, Canada, Korea, Hong Kong and Japan. Our experience at Imperial College has been very positive and confirms our belief that the structural configuration level is a useful level of abstraction for system description, construction and evolution. The provision of software tool support has been essential in the successful use of Conic. This success has encouraged us to embark on a broader and more ambitious project, based on the same principles but incorporating many more of the aspects of the development process. This ESPRIT II project, REX [30], includes work on formal specification techniques and tools for analysis and verification, on design methods and tools for recording and aiding the design process, and on configuration and dynamic reconfiguration and tools for performing the construction, reconfiguration and extension of heterogeneous distributed systems. In particular, the work on ViewPoints has also been adopted for REX.

3. VIEWPOINTS

The concept of a ViewPoint is a synthesis of the concepts of "view" and "viewpoint" in earlier work. The requirements analysis method CORE [23, 31] is based round the notion of viewpoints which is characterised as "something that does things" in the domain under consideration, akin to an agent or role. Thus the CORE viewpoint can be seen to be the particular source for *domain* decomposition. The notion of views as partial specifications and as the principal basis for incremental construction of specifications was developed in the PEACOCK [7, 8] and PRISMA [26] projects. These projects have convinced us of the importance of selecting the *representation* to suit the particular ViewPoint specification task, and of subsequently combining representations. The notion of forming "configurations" of ViewPoints is suggested by the need to provide an explicit structure for describing ViewPoint relations, and the interesting analogy between the configuration of ViewPoints used in the software process and the resulting software structure [17].

This section provides a general characterisation of ViewPoints and elaborates on the analogy with the principles, techniques and tools offered in Conic for configuration programming.

3.1 ViewPoint Definition and Characterisation

A ViewPoint is a loosely coupled, locally managed object which encapsulates partial knowledge about the application domain, specified in a particular, suitable formal representation, and partial knowledge of the process of software development.

A ViewPoint (figure 1) is thus a combination of the following parts which we refer to as slots:

a style, the representation scheme in which the ViewPoint expresses what it can see (examples of styles are data flow analysis, entity-relationship-attribute modelling, Petri nets, equational logic, and so on);

a domain defines which part of the "world" delineated in the style (given that the style defines a structured representation) can be seen by the ViewPoint (for example, a lift-control system would include domains such as user, lift and controller);

a specification, the statements expressed in the ViewPoint's style describing particular domains;

a work plan, how and in what circumstances the contents of the specification are elaborated and changed;

a work record, an account of the current state of the development.

As can be seen, the ViewPoint encapsulates knowledge in the form of various slots e.g. a *style* and a *specification*. The slots style and work plan represent general knowledge, in the sense that it can be applied to a wide range of problems. In contrast to this the knowledge encapsulated in the slots *domain*, *specification* and *work record* of a ViewPoint represent specific knowledge related to one particular problem. The *specification* is given in a single consistent style and describes an identified *domain* of the problem area. The *work record* describes the current state of the specification with respect to the development activities and concerns of the ViewPoint. This would include interaction between viewpoints to transfer information and perform activities such as consistency checks. For instance, if a particular ViewPoint is required to use data flow diagrams in its specification slot for a particular domain, the other slots would employ appropriate languages to specify the DFD representation, its workplan and workrecord.

ViewPoints are organised in *configurations* which are collections of related ViewPoints. In the descriptions which follow, we will show how a *method* in this setting can be viewed is a set of ViewPoint templates (types), and their relationships, together with actions governing their construction and consistency. A *specification* is viewed a configuration of ViewPoint instances.

3.2   Applying Configuration Programming Principles to ViewPoints

1. *The configuration language used for structural description should be separate from the language used for ViewPoint descriptions.*
   As before we separate the languages used for structural description from that used for the slots in primitive ViewPoints. This structural view is useful for description, comprehension and manipulation of the ViewPoints. The configuration language is *declarative*, describing what the structure is, not how it is to be constructed; that is part of the role of the workplan slot.

2. *ViewPoints should be defined as context independent types with well-defined interfaces.*
   We refer to these as *templates* (eg. figure 10). A *ViewPoint template* consists of a ViewPoint in which only the style and the work plan have been defined. Context independence means that the workplan makes no direct reference to any non-local entities ie. those mappings to other ViewPoints are indirect to permit its ready use with different ViewPoints. A ViewPoint interface describes the interaction points with other ViewPoints.

3. *Using the configuration language, complex ViewPoints should be definable as a composition of instances of ViewPoint templates.*
   The style slot of a complex ViewPoint permits the use of the configuration language to specify it as a configuration.

4. *Change should be expressed at the configuration level, as changes of the ViewPoint*

instances and/or their interconnections.

Modifications to the method and specification (at a large grain level) are reflected as changes to the configuration.

In order to illustrate the use of these principles and their relation to configuration programming, we now overview the configuration of ViewPoints approach, following the same structure of the description of Conic and its facilities and tools given in the previous section. The illustration is made more concrete by using the framework to overview part of the JSD Method (Jackson System Design [10]). We concentrate on the first three steps which produce an initial model of the required system and its environment:

1. Entity-Action step: identify each real world entity (object) of interest, and list the actions performed or suffered by it, and the data attributes for each action.

2. Entity-Structure step: impose an ordering on the actions of each entity (like a process) using a diagrammatic notation (as in JSP) and text.

3. Initial Model step: identify the relation between the real world entities (processes) and the system processes in a process model with connections, called an initial System Specification Diagram (SSD).

The descriptions of our framework are rough and informal so as to convey the general approach. Detailed examples are available elsewhere [6, 27].

3.3 An Analogous Configuration Framework for ViewPoints

ViewPoint Templates:- context independent ViewPoint types (principle 2)

As mentioned, a ViewPoint *template* elaborates only the style and workplan slots. These aspects are closely related as the work plan describes the basic actions which need to be performed in order to provide a specification in the given style. As such, these actions are general, and can be used to guide the specification of any specific, selected portion of the application domain. Such a specification is termed a ViewPoint *instance* since it refers to a specific instantiation of the template, and would include identification of the selected domain and elaboration of the specification and its state of development, given as the work record.

A *method* is defined as a form of configuration of a selected set of ViewPoint templates which together describe the styles and work plans to be used in the method. The mappings and checks between templates should also be specified. The dynamics of the method are described by permitting one ViewPoint to create (or spawn) another as the method unfolds. Information in a "parent" ViewPoint which is relevant to "child" ViewPoint can be transferred using the mappings. Method *use* is thus represented as a dynamically evolving configuration of ViewPoints.

The method designers are thus responsible for the definition of ViewPoint templates, while the method users are responsible for following the workplans in ViewPoint instances and for elaborating the specification in the given style.

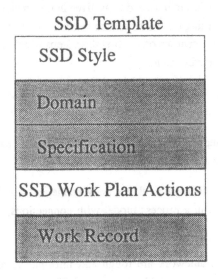

Figure 10. ViewPoint Template for System Specification Diagrams in JSD

An example of a template for the initial model step of JSD is given in figure 10. This models the real world in a style called the System Specification Diagram (fig. 11). This description provides the syntax and constraints for a "well-formed" diagram in the style. The description of the workplan actions describe how to construct a specification in SSD, together with any desired constraints on the ordering of workplan actions (eg. using pre- and post-conditions), heuristics and mappings to other ViewPoints. Other templates required for JSD include the entity-action and entity-structure templates (fig. 12). Since the structure template provides an ordering for the actions specified in the action list, we indicate this mapping by an arc. The mapping can be interpreted at the recipient in either of two manners:

1. *Either* the information received by the structure ViewPoint is used as the source of the actions to be ordered,

2. *or* the information is used by the structure ViewPoint to check consistency and completness of the actions with those of the action ViewPoint.

This dual interpretation is generally useful in that it permits the completion of the ViewPoint specifications to be performed sequentially (in which case the former interpretation may be preferable) or concurrently (in which case the latter consistency check may be desirable). In this case, the sequential order is the most likely, but one need not enforce that constraint unless it is specifically required.

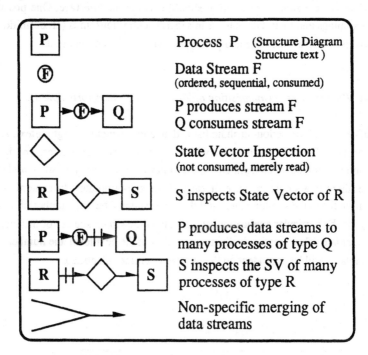

Figure 11. Outline Style for System Specification Diagrams in JSD

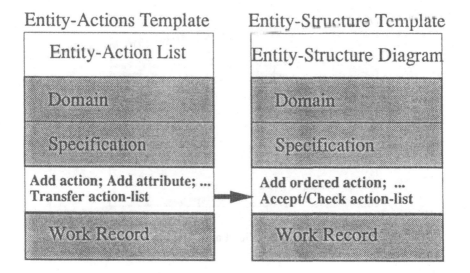

Figure 12. ViewPoint Templates for Entity-Actions and Entity-Structure

Although the principle of context independence requires that a template interface be defined, irrespective of the actual connection to other ViewPoints, we have not yet found a suitable means for the definition of template interfaces. The intention is that that part of the workplan which produces or consumes information should become the interface. One possibility is to define the mappings and their data content in separate definitions units (cf. definitions modules in Conic which can define message and port types) which are then imported.

ViewPoint Hierarchies*: - Composition of ViewPoint instances (principle 3).*

In JSD, each entity has an action-attribute list and an entity structure diagram/text. A composite template can be defined for each entity which combines these templates, and indicates the transfer of information between them and to the "interface" of the composite template (fig. 13). In this case, there is a single instance of each of the sub-templates. In general, a composite template will indicate the sub-templates and their interactions, but the number of instances may well depend on the particular application, and hence on the circumstances of instantiation of the composite template. This situation is illustrated in that, at the next level, the number of instances of entity templates will be dependent on the number of entities identified.

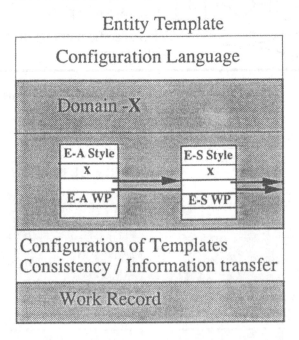

Figure 13. Composite ViewPoint Template for an Entity

Initial Model

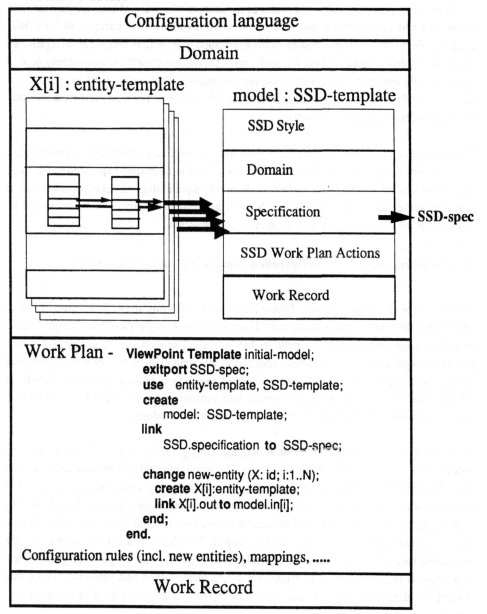

Figure 14. Initial Model Specification for JSD using ViewPoints

Constructing Specifications: - ViewPoint instantiation and interconnection using a separate configuration language (principle 1), including dynamic configuration (principle 4).

A *system specification* is a configuration of (consistent) specifications given in selected ViewPoint instances describing those parts of the domain which are of interest. As described above, method use is represented as a dynamically evolving configuration of ViewPoint instances. For instance, the partitioning of the application domain (into entities in JSD) provides a variable dimension to the method. For each part of the domain (entity) the method may need to create a configuration of ViewPoints as the method unfolds. This is illustrated in figure 14 for the initial model steps of JSD, together with a possible outline of the configuration description which would form part of the workplan.

We believe that the configuration and its dynamics are well described using a configuration language with the permissible changes (usually restricted to extensions) specified in the same declarative structural language. As with configuration programming, the decision as to *when* to perform configuration changes, such as ViewPoint creation and interconnection, would be described in the general workplan rather than the configuration.

Tool Support: Graphical Configuration Monitoring and Management

A particular benefit which seems to follow from the identification and encapsulation of a style (representation) and its workplan (specification method) in a single ViewPoint Template is the opportunity for tool support. We believe that individual support can be designed for each template in a particular method, thereby simplifying the complexity of the tool in much the same way as one expects to simplify the steps and expression of that particular ViewPoint specification. We can then envisage method tool support as comprising a configuration of template support tools, configured to suit the particular method adopted.

In addition to individual ViewPoint tools, the configuration view of the method and specifications seems to offer the promise of practical monitoring and management tools. As with ConicDraw for configuration programming, one can envisage a graphical management tool to support monitoring the current configuration structure of an ongoing project. In addition, the status of each individual ViewPoint (reflected in its workrecord) could be monitored in order to gain insight into the current status of the project. This form of status monitoring of the partitioned parts of a method were successfully prototyped in the TARA project [13,14] for the requirements method CORE (see figure 15, which marked each part asfollows: blank- not needed for elaboration, shaded- not started, ?- started but not completed or consistent, √- completed).

Finally, the configuration management approach also offers the possibility of performing external, evolutionary adjustments and modifications to the method and development structure dynamically, while in use. Although the opportunity and facilities to perform such arbitrary adjustments does seem to be desirable, they should obviously be performed in a careful and controlled manner. The kind of change management approach adopted for configuration programming [16] may also provide some guidance as to how to control dynamic change.

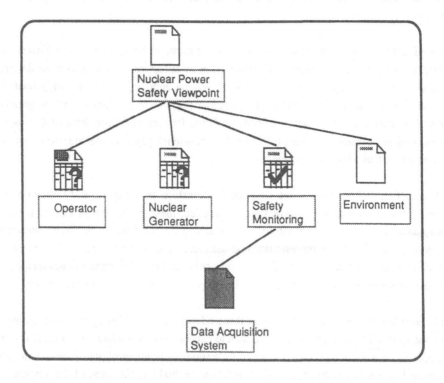

Figure 15. Status Monitoring for parts of a CORE Specification in TARA

4. CONCLUSIONS

Configuration programming, with its use of a separate configuration language, provides an excellent means for expressing system structure rather than the embedding of structural decisions in the software components themselves. The approach produces systems which are comprehensible, maintainable and amenable to change and has facilitated the provision of software tools to support system construction and management. The Conic environment for distributed programming is an exemplar for configuration programming. In this paper, we have argued that a configurable framework, analogous to that in configuration programming, can be combined with the notion of ViewPoints to provide similar benefits to the problem of method and tool integration. A vision of this configurable framework has been proposed.

The ViewPoint approach to software development advocates the use of multiple ViewPoints to partition the domain information, the development method and the formal representations used to express software specifications. System specifications and methods are described as configurations of related ViewPoints. The partitioning of knowledge exemplified in the ViewPoints approach facilitates distributed development and the use of multiple representation schemes.

Since all method steps are expressed in this common form, we believe that ViewPoints are also particularly useful in the description of integrated or mixed approaches such as those described as "multiparadigm programming" [33]. The ViewPoint approach is also strongly related to Jackson's recent work on views and implementations [11] in which he describes "complexity in terms of separation and composition of concerns", and focuses on the problems of coping with the relationships between concerns (cf. ViewPoint relationships). As expected, the major issue is the expression of ViewPoint interaction.

Although the number of different kinds of relationships between arbitrary ViewPoints is theoretically enormous, we believe that, in practice, these relationships can be kept to a manageable number. ViewPoints are not selected arbitrarily: the domains obviously interact and are closely related, and the representation styles can and should be selected so as to express different aspects yet permit reasonable mappings between them. It is certainly advantageous to describe the same domain using different styles to specify different aspects of behaviour.

We believe that the explicit expression of these relationships is aided by the need to consider only one formalism (style) at a time, and then to express its relationship with others. The style slot provides the required representation information while the workplan provides the place where such relations can be expressed. In addition the dual interpretation of the relationships, as information transfer or consistency check, is useful. Expressing relationships as a ViewPoint interface still requires further investigation.

An additional benefit which seems to follow from the identification and encapsulation of style (representation) and workplan (specification method) in a single ViewPoint Template is the opportunity for tool support. Individual support could be designed for each template in a particular method, thereby simplifying the complexity of the tool in much the same way as one expects to simplify the steps and expression of that particular ViewPoint specification. We can then envisage method tool support as comprising a configuration of template support tools, configured to suit the particular method adopted.

An interesting suggestion considering ViewPoints as active agents has been proposed by the notion of a "software development participant" in the IC~DC project [5]. There it is an active, autonomous and loosely coupled agent - in the distributed artificial intelligence style.

Current work is being conducted within the REX and SEED (Software Engineering - Engineering Design) projects. A design tool, RexDesigner, is under construction using a restricted form of ViewPoints for CDA (Constructive Design Approach [17] for distributed programming). Other work using ViewPoints is examining methods associated with PrtNets, an extended form of Petri Nets, and CSP, and a general framework is being prototyped in Smalltalk.

Acknowledgements

Acknowledgement is made to my colleagues at Imperial College, Naranker Dulay, Anthony Finkelstein, Jeff Magee, Keng Ng, Morris Sloman and Kevin Twidle for their contribution to the configuration programming work described in this paper. Anthony Finkelstein, Michael Goedicke and Bashar Nuseibeh have contributed much to the work on ViewPoints. Finally I gratefully acknowledge the SERC under grant GE/F/04605 and the CEC in the REX Project (2080) for their financial support.

REFERENCES

[1]   M.R.Barbacci, C.B.Weinstock, and J.M.Wing, "Programming at the Processor - Memory - Switch Level", Proc. of 10th IEEE Int. Conf. on Software Engineering, Singapore, April 1988.

[2]   M. Coulas, G. MacEwen, G. Marquis, "RNet: A Hard Real-Time Distributed Programming System", IEEE Transactions on Computers, C-36 (8), August 1987.

[3]   F. DeRemer, H.H.Kron. "Programming-in-the-large Versus Programming-in-the-small, IEEE Trans. Software Engineering", Vol. SE-2, 2, June 1976.

[4]   N. Dulay, "A Configuration Language for Distributed Programming", Ph.D. Thesis, Imperial College, London University, 1990.

[5]   A.Finkelstein and H.Fuks, "Multi-Party Specification"; Proc 5th International Workshop on Software Specification & Design; pp 185-196, IEEE CS Press.

[6]   A. Finkelstein , J. Kramer, and M. Goedicke. " ViewPoint Oriented Software Development", Proc. of 3rd International Workshop on Software Engineering and its Applications, Toulouse, France, December 1990.

[7]   M.Goedicke, W.Ditt, H.Schippers, "The ∏-Language Reference Manual", Research Report No 295 1989, Department of Computer Science, University of Dortmund.

[8]   M.Goedicke, "Paradigms of Modular Software Development" Mitchell R.J. (Ed); Managing Complexity in Software Engineering; Peter Peregrinus, 1990, England.

[9]   J.A.Goguen. "Reusing and Interconnecting Software Components", IEEE Computer, (Designing for Adaptability), Vol. 19, 2, February 1986.

[10] M.A.Jackson, "System Development", Prentice Hall 1983.

[11] M.A.Jackson, "Some Complexities in Computer-Based Systems and their implications for System Development", Proc. of IEEE Int. Conf. on Computer Systems and Software Engineering (CompEuro 90), Tel-Aviv, Israel, May 1990, 344-351.

[12] J.Kramer, J.Magee, "Dynamic Configuration for Distributed Systems", IEEE Transactions on Software Engineering, SE-11 (4), April 1985, pp. 424-436.

[13] Kramer J., Finkelstein A., Ng K., Potts C. & Whitehead K. (1987);"Tool Assisted

Requirements Analysis: TARA final report"; Imperial College, Dept. of Computing, Technical Report 87/18.

[14] J. Kramer, K. Ng, C. Potts, K. Whitehead, "Tool Support for Requirements Analysis", IEE Software Engineering Journal, Vol. 3,3, May 1988.

[15] J. Kramer, J. Magee, K. Ng, "Graphical Configuration Programming", IEEE Computer, 22(10), October 1989, 53-65.

[16] J. Kramer, J. Magee, "The Evolving Philosophers Problem: Dynamic Change Management", to appear in IEEE Trans. on Software Eng., November 1990.

[17] J. Kramer, J. Magee, A. Finkelstein, "A Constructive Approach to the Design of Distributed Systems", to be presented at the 10th Int. Conf. on Distributed Computing Systems, May 1990.

[18] J. Kramer, "Configuration Programming - A Framework fo the Development of Distributable Systems", Proc. of IEEE Int. Conf. on Computer Systems and Software Engineering (CompEuro 90), Israel, May 1990.

[19] R.J. Leblanc and A.B. MacCabe, "The Design of a Programming Language based on a Connectivity Network", Proc. 3rd Int. Conf. On Distributed Computing Systems, 1982.

[20] T. LeBlanc and S. Friedberg. "HPC: A model of structure and change in distributed systems". IEEE Trans. on Computers, Vol. C-34, 12, December 1985.

[21] I. Lee, N. Prywes, B. Szymanski, "Partitioning of Massive/Real-Time Programs for Parallel Processing", in Advances in Computers, ed. M.C. Yovits, Vol.25, Academic Press 1986.

[22] J.Magee, J.Kramer, and M.Sloman, "Constructing Distributed Systems in Conic" IEEE Transactions on Software Engineering, SE-15 (6), June 1989.

[23] G.Mullery, "Acquisition - Environment"; (In) Paul, M. & Siegert, H. "Distributed Systems: Methods and Tools for Specification"; Springer Verlag LNCS 190, 1985.

[24] W.P. Myers, G.F. Myers and L.C. Constantine. "Structured design", IBM Syst. J., vol. 13, no. 2, pp. 115-139, 1974.

[25] J. Nehmer, D. Haban, F. Mattern, D. Wybranietz, D. Rombach, "Key Concepts of the INCAS Multicomputer Project", IEEE Transactions on Software Engineering, SE-13 (8), August 1987.

[26] C.Niskier, T.Maibaum, D.Schwabe, "A Look Through PRISMA: towards knowledge-based environments for software specification"; Proc 5th International Workshop on Software Specification & Design; pp 128-136, IEEE CS Press.

[27] B. Nuseibeh, "ViewPoint Oriented Systems Engineering: an Interim Report and Case Study", Internal Report, Department of Computing, Imperial College, March 1991.

[28] D.L. Parnas, "On the Design and Development of Program Families", IEEE Transactions on Software Engineering, SE-2 (1), March 1976, pp. 1-9.

[29] J. Purtilo, "A Software Interconnection Technology", Computer Science Dept., University of Maryland, TR-2139, 1988.

[30] REX Technical Annexe, ESPRIT Project 2080, European Economic Commission, March 1989.

[31] M.Stephens, K.Whitehead, "The Analyst — A Workstation for Analysis and Design"; Proc 8th ICSE; IEEE CS Press.

[32] M. Stovsky, B. Weide, "STILE: A Graphical Design and Development Environment", Digest Compcon Spring 87, CS Press, California.

[33] P.Zave, "An Operational Approach to Requirements Specification for Embedded Systems", IEEE Trans. on Software Engineering, SE-8 (3), 1982.

RECENT FINDINGS IN SOFTWARE PROCESS MATURITY

Watts S. Humphrey
Software Engineering Institute
Carnegie Mellon University
Pittsburgh, PA 15213 USA

Abstract

After several years of using the Software Engineering Institute (SEI) software process maturity framework, preliminary data is now available. This paper provides an overview of the SEI methods, summarizes the current data, and discusses the trends and implications of this work. The paper opens with a brief summary of the importance of software to modern society. It then discusses the software process and software process maturity. The principles of software process assessments are next described along with the various assessment types introduced by the SEI. The general state of software practice is then covered, including data on U.S. and Japanese software organizations. The paper concludes with some observations on the state of software practice and comments on the rates of organizational improvement.

Keywords: assessment, improvement, management, process maturity, productivity, quality, software, state of practice

1. Introduction

Software is now crucial to business success. Many organizations understand that their software capability affects their profitability and their long-term competitive survival. Managers in manufacturing industries generally recognize that the best products have the best functions and that software often provides the only way to economically implement the most sophisticated product functions. For service industries, customer responsiveness and service quality are critical and increasingly, software is the element that provides these capabilities. Software today is the limiting factor for the growth and well-being of just about every business.

In spite of software's increasing importance, the performance of many software development groups has not materially improved in the last 20 years. When ranked on a maturity scale of one to five (with five being best), a sample of some 200 U.S. software respondents showed over 80% of these organizations at the lowest level, with most of the rest at level two. One would expect that software's key problems would be highly technical, but based on studies of many software development organizations, their major problems are managerial instead [HUM89b]. The critical needs of most software organizations are for improved project management. This is not a new problem and it has been previously addressed in other fields.

This paper briefly describes the work of the Software Engineering Institute (SEI) at Carnegie Mellon University to address the need for improving software capability. Section 2 briefly outlines the motivation and general approach of software process management and Section 3 presents the SEI software process maturity framework. This framework provides the foundation for the process assessments described in section 4 and the process maturity data in section 5. The paper then concludes with some recent observations on improvement trends and their implications for the software industry.

2. Software Process Background

The SEI was established by the U.S. Government to focus on improving the state of U.S. software development. In pursuing this charter, the SEI approach has emphasized the following:

1. Developing and validating a software process framework and evaluation methodology for identifying capable organizations.

2. Transitioning the evaluation methodology to U.S. Government software acquisition agencies and their prime contractors.

3. Developing and refining an associated assessment methodology for use by the software contracting community for assessing their software engineering capabilities and determining improvement needs.

4. Characterizing and reporting on the state of software engineering practice.

5. Facilitating software process improvement in U.S. industry.

Since early 1987, the SEI Software Process Program has focused on software process as a means of improving the ability of software organizations to produce software products according to plan. This focus on software process is based on the premises that 1) the process of producing and evolving software products can be defined, managed, measured, and progressively improved and 2) the quality of a software product is largely governed by the quality of the process used to create and maintain it.

The software process is the set of activities, methods, and practices that guide people in the production of software. An effective process must consider the relationships of the required tasks, the tools and methods, and the developers' skills, training, and motivation.

Software process management is the application of process engineering concepts, techniques, and practices to explicitly monitor, control, and improve the software process [OLS89]. It is only one of several activities that must be effectively performed for software-producing organizations to be consistently successful. Capable and motivated technical people are critical; knowledge of the ultimate application environment is needed, as is detailed understanding of the end user's needs [CUR88]. Even with all these capabilities, however, inattention to the software management problems will likely result in disappointing organizational performance.

This view of process and process management has led to the development of a process maturity model, a related software process maturity questionnaire, and a software process assessment methodology. These form the key elements of SEI's methods for assessing and improving software organizations. Section 3 briefly discusses these elements and the methods for applying them to software process improvement.

3. The SEI Software Process Maturity Model

The software engineering capability of an organization can be characterized with the aid of the software process maturity model shown in Figure 1 [HUM89a]. This model provides five maturity levels, identifies the key improvements required at each level, and establishes a priority order for moving to higher levels of process maturity.

Level	Characteristic	Key Challenges	Result
5 Optimizing	Improvement feedback into process	Still human intensive process Maintain organization at optimizing level	Productivity & Quality
4 Managed	(Quantitative) Measured process	Changing technology Problem analysis Problem prevention	
3 Defined	(Qualitative) Process defined and institutionalized	Process measurement Process analysis Quantitative quality plans	Risk
2 Repeatable	(Intuitive) Process dependent on individuals	Training Process focus Technical practices • standards, • reviews, testing process groups	
1 Initial	(Ad hoc / chaotic)	Project management Project planning Configuration management Software quality assurance	

Figure 1. SEI Software Process Maturity Model

At the initial level (level 1), an organization can be characterized as having an ad hoc, or possibly chaotic, process. Typically, the organization operates without formalized procedures, cost estimates, and project plans. Even if formal project control procedures exist, there are no management mechanisms to ensure that they are followed. Tools are neither well integrated with the process, nor uniformly applied. In addition, change control is lax and senior management is not exposed to or does not understand the key software problems and issues. When projects do succeed, it is generally because of the heroic efforts of a dedicated team rather than the capability of the organization.

An organization at the repeatable level (level 2) has established basic project controls: project management, management oversight, product assurance, and change control. The strength of the organization stems from its experience at doing similar work, but it faces major risks when presented with new challenges. The organization has frequent quality problems and lacks an orderly framework for improvement.

At the defined level (level 3), the organization has laid the foundation for examining the process and deciding how to improve it. A Software Engineering Process Group (SEPG) has been established to focus and lead the process improvement efforts, to keep management informed on the status of these efforts, and to facilitate the introduction of a family of software engineering methods and technologies.

The managed level (level 4) builds on the foundation established at the defined level. When the process is defined, it can be examined and improved but there is little data to indicate effectiveness. Thus, to advance to the managed level, an organization should establish a minimum set of measurements for the quality and productivity parameters of each key task. The organization should also establish a process database with resources to manage and maintain it, to analyze the data, and to advise project members on its meaning and use.

Two requirements are fundamental to advance from the managed to the optimizing level (level 5). Data gathering should be automated, and management should redirect its focus from the product to process analysis and improvement. At the optimizing level, the organization has the means to identify the weakest process elements and strengthen them, data are available to justify applying technology to various critical tasks, and numerical evidence is available on the effectiveness with which the process has been applied. The key additional activity at the optimizing level is rigorous defect cause analysis and defect prevention.

These maturity levels have been selected because they do the following.

- Reasonably represent the historical phases of evolutionary improvement of actual software organizations.
- Represent a measure of improvement that is reasonable to achieve from the prior level.
- Suggest interim improvement goals and progress measures.

- Make obvious a set of immediate improvement priorities, once an organization's status in this framework is known.

While there are many aspects to the transition from one maturity level to another, the basic objective is to achieve a controlled and measured process as the foundation for continuous improvement.

It has been SEI's experience (based on 16 SEI-assisted assessments conducted from 1987 through 1990) that when software organizations are assessed against this maturity framework, the assessment method enables reasonably accurate placement of them on the maturity scale and helps to identify key improvement needs. Generally, when management focuses on the few highest priority items, their organizations rapidly improve their capability to produce quality software products on time and within budget. While the use of tools and technology can enhance software engineering capability, investments in advanced technology are generally of limited value for organizations with low-maturity software processes.

Based on this maturity framework, a questionnaire has been developed to help organizations identify their status [HUM87].

4. Assessing Software Organizations

To assist organizations in improving their software capability, the SEI has developed several aids and methods:

- SEI-assisted assessments
- assessment tutorials
- self-assessments
- SEI-licensed vendor assessments
- capability evaluations

The data in this report was obtained from SEI-assisted assessments and assessment tutorials as well as other SEI studies and reports [HUM89b, HUM91b]. The observations and trends, however, are drawn from all the assessment work done to date.

The goal of an SEI-assisted assessment is to facilitate improvement of the organization's software process. Typically, the assessment team is composed of four to six SEI professionals and one to three professionals from the organization being assessed. This team initially receives training in the methodology. During the actual assessment, they identify the most important software process issues currently facing the organization and develop recommendations to deal with them. These assessments are conducted in accordance with an assessment agreement which provides for senior .management involvement, organizational representation on the assessment team, confidentiality of results, and follow-up actions.

At assessment tutorials, process management concepts, assessment techniques, and the SEI assessment methodology are presented. The attendees supply demographic data on themselves and their organizations as well as on a project for which they complete an assessment questionnaire. Assessment tutorials are typically conducted at software conferences and symposia.

Self-assessments are similar to SEI-assisted assessments, with the primary difference being assessment team composition. Self-assessment teams are composed primarily of software professionals from the organization being assessed with possibly one or two SEI software professionals present. The objectives and method are the same as for SEI-assisted assessments.

Vendor-assisted assessments are SEI assessments conducted under the guidance of commercial vendors who have been trained and licensed to do so by the SEI. The assessment team is trained by the vendor and consists of software professionals from the organization being assessed plus at least one vendor professional who has been qualified by the SEI. Licensing commercial vendors to offer these assessment services makes SEI software process assessments available to a wider audience than the SEI would otherwise be capable of supporting.

Capability evaluations, like SEI-assisted assessments and self-assessments, are appraisals of an organization's current software process; however, the context, purpose, and assessment team composition are different. Capability evaluations are done as part of an acquisition process, and their purpose is to provide the acquisition agency with an evaluation of the organization's software engineering capabilities. This information is then used in the source selection decision. Here, validation of maturity questionnaire responses is a major consideration.

5. Process Maturity Status

After using these methods for several years, the SEI has gathered a substantial amount of data. This material was first published in a state-of-the-practice report in 1989 [HUM89b]. While considerable data has been gathered since that time, it is not yet sufficient to warrant a new state-of-the-practice report. This paper summarizes the 1989 findings, a more recent study of Japanese software organizations, and some general observations from the most recent assessment findings [HUM89b, HUM91b].

For the U.S., Figure 2 shows the software process maturity distributions for assessment tutorials and Figure 3 shows the data for SEI-assisted assessments.

For both these figures, the vertical axis represents the percentage of data points in the population; the horizontal axis represents the software process maturity scale. In producing these figures, a data point is one set of yes-no responses to the software process assessment instrument; the scope of these responses is a specific software project. Each data point's location in the maturity level distribution was determined by the number of additional affirmative responses needed to rate the project at the next higher process maturity level. The range of these values was then divided into four "buckets" or quartiles. The quartiles are identified in the charts using the notation x - Qy, where x is the level (1-5), and y is the quartile (1-4). In Figure 3, for example, 2 - Q4 refers to the fourth (and last) quartile for level 2 and contains approximately 13% of the sample. It should be noted that these quartiles are used solely for the purpose of providing low-maturity organizations with a more precise way to evaluate their improvement progress. Thus a level 1 organization in any quartile would be of level 1 and would still generally experience serious schedule, cost, and quality problems. Because of the limited data at levels 4 and 5, only the lowest 12 of the

20 quartiles are shown [HUM91b].

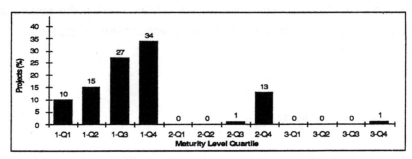

Figure 2. **U.S. Assessment Tutorial Maturity Level Distribution**
(113 Data Points)

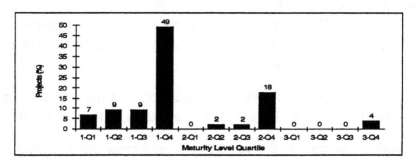

Figure 3. **U.S. SEI Assisted Assessment Maturity Level Distribution**
(55 Data Points)

The assessment tutorial results shown in Figure 2 indicate that the majority of the respondents reported projects at the initial level of maturity. With minimal improvement, a large percentage of these projects could be classified as level 2. Fourteen percent of all the tutorial respondents reported projects at the repeatable level (level 2), and only 1% of those respondents described projects at level 3, the defined level. No tutorial respondents reported projects at either the managed level (level 4) or the optimizing level (level 5) of software process maturity.

The maturity level distribution for projects reviewed by SEI-assisted assessments, shown in Figure 3, is similar to that for the tutorial data. Here, however, the population is skewed slightly towards higher levels of process maturity. As can be seen, the many projects in quartile 4 of maturity levels 1, 2, and 3 are close to achieving the next higher maturity level.

An SEI team also gathered data on some Japanese software organizations during a trip in October and November 1990. The maturity distribution for the Japanese responses is shown in Figure 4.

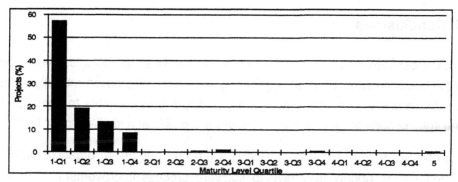

Figure 4. Software Process Maturity Level Distribution Japanese Assessment Tutorial Data (196 Data Points)

As can be seen, almost all Japanese responses were at level 1. One response, however, was obtained at level 5 and one at level 2. The level 5 response was for an operating system development group in a large computer company (data was obtained on only one such group). Several hours of discussions were held with this level 5 group and it was concluded that their practices were clearly at level 5 and were equivalent to anything found so far in the U.S.

In comparing U.S. and Japanese data, one bias was noted that could be responsible for much of the reported difference between the U.S. and Japanese software maturity levels. In the U.S., most of the SEI maturity data has been obtained from software contractors. While the largest portion of these respondents are clustered near the top of level 1, some are at level 2 and above. The limited SEI data on those U.S. commercial groups who develop business applications show these projects all cluster at the bottom of level 1 with no project at level 2. The bulk of the Japanese software projects surveyed are in this category. While there is not sufficient data on U.S. business application programming groups to make a definitive comparison, this factor could partially explain the lower maturity level of the Japanese groups. Other potential sources of bias concern the limited data from Japanese computer manufacturers and language translation issues. These points are discussed in more detail in [HUM91b].

6. Conclusions

It is clear from these studies that the state of software practice, at least in those organizations reviewed, is at a generally poor level of process maturity. Based on the consistency of these results it also appears reasonable to conclude that the state of software practice throughout the world is at a similarly poor level.

Since SEI started this work in 1987, a growing number of organizations have increased the priority they give to software process improvement. Of the 10 largest U.S. Department of Defense contractors, all are working with the Software Engineering Institute to apply these methods. Many U.S. companies have started major software process improvement programs, including DEC, Hughes Aircraft, Hewlett Packard, IBM, Raytheon, Texas Instruments, TRW, Unisys, and many others. Several acquisition groups in the U.S. Department of Defense are also using these methods to help them select capable software contractors.

These efforts are having an effect. While there are few cases of organizations which have been assessed more than once, a growing number are reporting significant benefits from these efforts. For example, organizations are moving from level 1 to level 2 in two to three years, and from level 2 to level 3 in one or two. There is not yet evidence on how long it takes to progress from level 3 to level 4 or level 4 to level 5, but each transition will probably take about one or two years. While such improvement rates have been achieved by several software organizations, the most successful groups recognize that software process improvement is a long-term effort.

These software improvement methods are demonstrably effective. Hughes

Aircraft, for example, reports annual profit benefits of ten times software process improvement costs [HUM91a]. IBM was an early proponent of software process improvement, and its experience with the NASA shuttle has been remarkable [KOL88]. Raytheon, in an 18 month period, obtained cost savings of $5.3 million. This was over a three to one return on their investment in software process improvement [DIO89]. Cusumano, has described the effectiveness of a consistent process focus for several leading Japanese firms [CUS89]. Hitachi doubled software productivity in one year, reduced late projects from 72% to 12%, and reduced bugs by eight times. Toshiba better than doubled software productivity and reduced bugs by up to seven times. NEC improved productivity by between 26% to 91% and reduced bugs by one third. Fujitsu reduced bugs by 19 times in eight years and improved productivity by two thirds. While this data is uniquely Japanese, Cusumano points out that these same methods are also being used successfully in the U.S., but to a limited degree.

There are now several cases where U.S. software organizations have achieved level 3 and level 4, and even a few have achieved level 5. While these cases are limited, the numbers are increasing and impressive progress is being made. There are now reported to be level 3 projects in Israel, Japan, and Sweden, and, as noted above, the SEI has reviewed the work of one level 5 Japanese software development laboratory of 2000 people.

The capability of software organizations is of growing international importance. It is clear from SEI's work that major efforts are needed to improve the process maturity of most software organizations. Early evidence indicates that these methods are effective in supporting such improvement efforts and in improving the overall business performance of these organizations.

Acknowledgments

The material in this paper was gathered through the efforts of many people in the SEI Software Process Program. In particular, Dave Kitson and Julia Gale participated in the study of the Japanese software industry. In addition, Tim

Kasse, Steve Masters, Mary Merrill, George Pandelious, Jeff Perdue, and many others contributed to the U.S. maturity level studies. Several people gave their time to review and comment on this paper. I particularly thank Mary Beth Chrissis, Julia Gale, and Dave Kitson. Dorothy Josephson has also provided invaluable help in producing the manuscript.

References

[1] [CUR88] Curtis, B., H. Krasner, N. Iscoe, "A Field Study of the Software Design Process for Large Systems," Communications of the ACM, 31 (11), November 1988, pp. 1268-1287.

[2] [CUS89] Cusumano, M., "The Software Factory: A Historical Interpretation," IEEE Software, March 1989, pp. 23-30.

[3] [DIO89] Dion, R., "Qualifying the Benefit of Software Process Improvement," Proceedings, 1989 SEPG Workshop, Software Engineering Institute, Carnegie Mellon University.

[4] [HUM87] Humphrey, W. S., W. Sweet, et al., A Method for Assessing the Software Engineering Capability of Contractors, Software Engineering Institute, CMU/SEI-87-TR-23, ADA187230, September 1987.

[5] [HUM89a] Humphrey, W. S., Managing the Software Process, Addison-Wesley, Reading, MA, 1989.

[6] [HUM89b] Humphrey, W. S., D. H. Kitson, T. K. Kasse, The State of Software Engineering Practice: A Preliminary Report, Technical Report CMU/SEI-89-TR-1, Software Engineering Institute, Carnegie Mellon University, February 1989.

[7] [HUM91a] Humphrey, W. S., T. Snyder, and R. Willis, "Software Process Improvement at Hughes Aircraft Company," IEEE Software, in press, 1991.

[8] [HUM91b] Humphrey, W. S., D. H. Kitson, and J. L. Gale, "A Comparison of U.S. and Japanese Software Process Maturity," Proceedings 13th International Conference on Software Engineering, Austin, TX, May 1991.

[9] [KOL] Kolkhorst, B. G. and A. J. Macinea, "Developing Error-Free Software, Proceedings of Computer Assurance Congress '88, IEEE Washington Section on System Safety, 27 June 1-July 1988, pp. 99-107.

[10] [OLS89] Olson, T. G., W. S. Humphrey, and D. H. Kitson, Conducting SEI-Assisted Software Process Assessments, Technical Report CMU/SEI-89-TR-7, Software Engineering Institute, Carnegie Mellon University, February 1989.

Validation and Verification of Software Process Models

Volker Gruhn

Computer Science, Software Technology

University of Dortmund

P.O. Box 500 500

D-4600 Dortmund 50

e-mail: gruhn@udo.informatik.uni-dortmund.de

Abstract

We introduce a software process modeling language - called **FUNSOFT nets** - which has a formally defined semantics in terms of Predicate/Transition nets. For this language we have implemented various analysis facilities. We point out which benefits can be gained from a thorough software process model analysis. We explain how software process models can be validated and how software process model properties can be verified. The proposed software process model validation is based on software process simulation, the proposed verification of software process model properties is based on well-known Petri net algorithms and on the notion of quantity restricted coverability trees. Finally, we explain how the proposed analysis facilities are implemented in the analysis tool ANAMEL, which is embedded into the software process management environment MELMAC.

1 Introduction

Software process modeling aims at software process models that can be used for governing software processes. Using a software process model for governing a software process, means to detect deviations of an actual software process from its model automatically. Thus, executable software process models contribute to the increase of software development productivity and of software quality.

Quite a number of research projects have recognized the necessity of including a process model into a software development environment as a means to improve the industrial-like production of software (e.g. ESF [SW88] , ALF [BBCD89], ARCADIA [TBC+88], ATMOSPHERE [BOSV89]).

We distinguish several phases of managing software processes. These phases are:

- the *modeling* of software processes, i.e. the building of process models which specify a class of software processes,

- the *instantiation* of software process models, i.e. the attachement of tools, initial objects, humans and other resources to the respective process model entities,

- the *analysis* of software process models, i.e. the detection of errors and insufficiencies in a process model,

- the *execution* of software process models, i.e. the conduction of software processes resulting in assistance of software developers within their work,

- the *animation* of software processes, i.e. the visualization of project states, and

- the *adaptation* of software process models, i.e. the change of software process models because of evolving software processes.

In contrast to various purely management-oriented plans for software development (such as Gantt diagrams and PERT charts), software process models do not only express ideas about how to carry out software processes, but they are used for governing software processes. Therefore, software process model analysis is a promising subject, since one can be sure that problems detected in a software process model would eventually affect software processes. Analogously, one can be sure that, if a software process model M is proved to have a certain property (e.g. absence of deadlocks, bounded number of objects of certain object types), then all software processes $S_1, \ldots, S_n$ governed by that model (we write $S_1, \ldots, S_n \in SP(M)$) have that property as well. Thus, the analysis of software process models contributes to avoid the execution of erroneous software process models. Thereby, software process model analysis contributes to saving resources, manpower as well as hardware resources.

The organization of this paper is as follows: In section 2 we introduce the software process modeling language FUNSOFT nets briefly. Section 3 discusses how software process models can be validated by software process simulation. Section 4 focuses on the verification of FUNSOFT net properties which are interesting from a software process management point of view. Section 5 discusses the architecture of the analysis tool for FUNSOFT nets. Finally, section 6 concludes this paper, pointing out what are the directions of our future research on software process management.

2 FUNSOFT Nets

Regarding the aim of software process model validation and verification, we developed a software process modeling language that fulfills the requirements for analysis-supporting software process modeling language. This language - called FUNSOFT nets - is introduced in [Gru91b].

FUNSOFT nets are a software process modeling language that can be used as basis of executing software process models just as well as for analyzing software process models. FUNSOFT nets are a high level type of Petri nets whose semantics is defined in terms of Predicate/Transition nets (Pr/T nets) extended by multi-sets [Gen87].

A FUNSOFT net consists of

- a Petri net structure $(S; T, F)$ [Rei86, Pet81] (the S-elements are called channels, the T-elements are called agencies, the F-elements are called edges).

- a set of jobs J. A job represents a software development activity, such as *editing of a module*, *compile a module, meeting with the software development team*. The function T_J attaches jobs to agencies. A job is formally specified by a Pr/T net that specifies the input/output behavior of the activity. The *editing of a module*, for example, accesses a *module* and delivers a *module*, a *meeting with the software development team* reads a *list of agenda items* and produces a *list of tasks* that are forwarded to certain persons. A job is implemented by an executable piece of software, e.g. a program, a shell script or an envelope around a tool. The executable part of a job j is executed whenever an agency t with $T_J(t) = j$ is fired.

- a set of object type definitions O. The function S_T attaches object types to channels. If an object type o is attached to a channel s, i.e. $S_T(s) = o$, then s can only be marked with objects of type o.

- a set of predicates P. Predicates define conditions on the objects that can potentially be read by firing an agency. The function T_P attaches predicates to agencies. A predicate P_1 assigned to an agency t_1 means that t_1 only can fire with tokens $o_1, \ldots, o_n$ read from the input channels of t_1, if $P_1(o_1, \ldots, o_n) = True$. If no such tokens exist, then t cannot fire even though all input channels are marked. Predicates correspond to precondition of activities as used in MARVEL [KFP88], ALF [BBCD89], and Articulator [MS90].

- an initial marking M_0 that respects the typing of channels.

In order to structure software process models, agencies can be refined. Thereby, it is possible to embed a high level activity like *design* into a high level representation of a software process model, while details of the *design* are hidden in the refinement. This notion of refinement corresponds to the notion of transition substitution as discussed in [HJS89].

Agencies, channels, and edges of FUNSOFT nets have various attributes that contribute to keeping the complexity of FUNSOFT nets (measured in number of nodes) manageable. It is, for example, possible to attach an *access kind* attribute to channels. This attribute determines if a channel is accessed as a queue, as a stack, or randomly. A further attribute is the edge type, assigned to edges by the function F_T. Edges from channels to agencies can be of type IN, CO, ST, STC. IN- and CO-edges are data flow edges, the values of objects read via such edges determine the firing of the reading-agency. ST- and STC-edges are control flow edges, the values of objects read via such edges are without any importance, just the existence of objects is required to fire the reading agency. An object read via an IN- or ST-edge is removed from the channel it is stored in. CO- and STC-edges do not remove objects from channels, they just copy them. Edges from agencies to channels can be of type OU and FI. An OU-edge is a data flow edge, i.e. an object having a value is written via an OU-edge, an FI-edge indicates that just a control token is written to the connected channel. Another attribute that reduces the number of FUNSOFT net nodes is the firing behavior of jobs. In standard Petri nets, each T-element reads objects from all channels of its preset, and it puts objects into all channels of its postset. The preset of a net node n, is the set of those nodes n' for which an edge (n', n) exists, the postset is defined analogously. The preset of a net node n is denoted by $\bullet n$, the postset is denoted by $n\bullet$. In modeling software processes more sophisticated firing behaviors are needed. We distinguish the input firing behavior of a job j (denoted by $F_{IN}(j)$) and the output firing behavior of a job j (denoted by $F_{OUT}(j)$). In Figure 1 we sketch a small cut out of a software process model. This cut out describes a simple cycle of *identify_modules, edit, compile,* and *link* activities. This example helps to motivate the need for various firing behaviors.

The first agency to be fired is the *identify_modules*-agency t_1 ("*xy*-agency" is used as abbreviation of "an agency to which the job *meeting* is attached"). A result of firing t_1 is a natural number k written to channel s_6, which indicates how many modules have been identified. The names of the identified modules are written to channel s_2. Agency t_1 has a *mult* output firing behavior (indicated by the n in the right part of the box representing t_1). That means, the number written

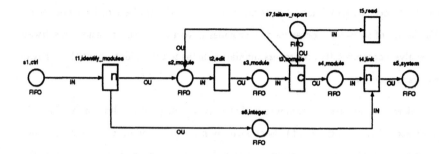

Figure 1: A cut out of a software process model

to channel s_6 indicates how many objects are written to s_2. For each job with a *mult* output firing behavior the maximal and the minimal number of objects that can be produced within one execution of that job is defined. In the given example we assume that the *identify_modules*-job produced at least one and at most 10 *modules*.

Identified modules are edited, compiled and linked. The *compile*-agency t_3 has a *complex* output firing behavior (indicated by the c in the right part of the box representing t_3) which is described in detail by the <cterm> (1 AND 2) XOR 3. This term specifies that either the first and second output channel are marked or that the third output channel is marked, i.e. a *module* can either be successfully compiled, or that it must be re-edited. In the latter case an additional *failure_report* is produced. The numbers identified in the <cterm> of the *compile*-job refer to unique numbers of edges starting from the *compile*-agency. The unique edge numbers are suppressed in Figure 1, since the meaning of the depicted FUNSOFT net is obvious. As initial marking of the shown FUNSOFT net, we assume one token in channel s_1. The *link*-agency t_4 has a *mult* input firing behavior (indicated by the n in the left part of the box representing t_4). That means, the value read from the second input channel s_6 determines how many objects are read from the first input channel s_4. In the example this ensures that the link can only take place when all *modules* are successfully compiled.

3   Validation of Software Process Models

We validate a software process model M by simulating software processes $S_1, \ldots, S_n \in SP(M)$. A simulation of a software process S corresponds to looking at one specific software process example in detail, it does not show that all software processes of $SP(M)$ have or have not certain properties. Validation of software process models provides a worthwhile contribution to software process model analysis because software process simulation helps to get an idea about the behavior of modeled software processes.

The essential weakness of validation techniques is that they do not yield results that are valid for all software processes $S_1, \ldots, S_n \in SP(M)$. Each validation result is underpinned only by experiments. One cannot be sure that each software process behaves corresponding to the validation results.

In simulating software processes we try to imitate the behavior of software processes as precisely as possible. Since we do not want to waste the resources needed in software processes, we do not manipulate actual objects, but only object names in simulating a software process. For simulating the compilation of a module, for example, we do not actually call a compiler, but we derive the name of the output objects from the name of the input object. Accordingly, we have to guess if a compilation is successful or not. This is done randomly on the basis of stochastic attributes attached to output edges of the *compile*-agency. Another attribute that is specific to software process simulation is the time-consumption. The function T_T attaches time-consumptions to agencies. The time-consumption of an agency fixes which amount of time passes between reading tokens from the input channels and writing tokens to the output channels. During software process model execution time-consumptions are meaningless.

Simulation of software processes can be exploited in two ways.

- It is possible to observe the simulation of software processes immediately, since the flow of tokens in a simulated software process is animated.
- It is possible to evaluate simulation traces. Simulation traces contain information gathered during software process simulation.

A simulation trace is produced during software process simulation by recording **basic simulation events**. These basic simulation events are start and end of agency firing, token flow via edges (including names of tokens), and occurrence of conflicts. The information gathered during software process simulation is statistically evaluated.

Below we see some results of evaluating a trace produced by simulating a software process governed by the FUNSOFT net shown in Figure 1. This trace is based on the assumption that the *identify_modules*-agency lasts 20 seconds, that the *edit*-agency lasts 20 minutes, that the *compile*-agency lasts 30 seconds, that the *read-* agencies lasts 5 minutes, that the *link*-agencies lasts 60 seconds, and that the software process model analyst decides if a simulated compilation finishes with a successfully compiled *module* or with a *failure_report* and a *module* that has to be edited again.

Derived Data:

agency	total execution time	number of executions	channel	max load	min load	mean waiting time
t1	20	1	s1	1	0	0
t2	4800	4	s2	3	0	1192.5
t3	120	4	s3	1	0	0
t4	60	1	s4	0	3	1600
t5	300	1	s5	0	1	0
			s6	1	0	4830
			s7	1	0	0

Total execution time: 4910

Some properties that can be investigated on the basis of simulation traces concern the number of objects that are dealt with in a software process, occurring and not occurring software process states (represented bt FUNSOFT net markings), idle times for software developers and tools, and bottlenecks in software processes. The simulation trace sketched above reveals that just one *edit*-agency is a bottleneck, since objects marking channel s_2 have a very high mean waiting time and that the modeled software process is human-intensive. More details about the exploitation of simulation results can be found in [DG91]. In general, the understanding of a software process model gained by simulating software processes helps to improve the model and to focus verification efforts.

4 Verification of Software Process Model Properties

Verification of a software process model means to prove that a software process model has certain properties. A software process model M is said to have a property P, if all software processes of $SP(M)$ have property P. In contrast to validation, no individual software process is investigated in software process model verification, but the software process model itself. Thus, results obtained by verifying a software process model M are valid for all $S_1, \ldots, S_n \in SP(M)$.

We consider the verification of software process model properties from a software process management point of view. Thus, we prove only such properties of software process models that are interesting for software process model analysts. A major strength of Petri nets is that there are numerous analysis facilities that are interesting for a wide range of systems modeled by Petri nets. We consider these analysis facilities from a software process management point of view.

By defining the semantics of FUNSOFT nets in terms of Pr/T nets, we are able to use analysis techniques that have proven to be useful for Pr/T nets. Additionally we use adaptations of well-known Petri net types verification techniques for directly proving FUNSOFT net properties.

We distinguish between two classes of properties. Firstly, there are properties which are independent from the execution behavior of FUNSOFT nets. These properties are called **structural properties**. Secondly, there are properties which depend on the execution behavior of FUNSOFT nets. These properties are called **dynamic properties**.

Some examples for static properties are enumerated below.

Useless object types   From a software process management point of view it is interesting to find out if object types exist for which no objects can be produced and for which no objects exist in the initial software process model. Such an object type is of no use.

Such an object type can be detected by searching source channels. A channel is called a **source channel** if its preset is empty. If an object type o_1 is attached only to source channels and if all source channels s with $S_T(s) = o_1$ are initially unmarked then o_1 is of no use. SoC(N) denotes the set of source channels of FUNSOFT N.

Definition 4.1   useless object type
Let N be a FUNSOFT net with initial marking M_0. An object type o is called useless if the

following conditions hold:

a) $\{s \in S \mid S_T(s) = o\} \subseteq SoC(N)$

b) $\forall_{\{s \in S \mid S_T(s) = o\}} : M_0(s) = \emptyset$

Infinite numbers of objects   From a software process management point of view it is interesting to find out if arbitrary many versions of an object can be produced. Such a situation
occurs potentially if an agency t_1 reads an object via a CO-edge from a channel s_1 and if
t_1 writes tokens to s_1 as well. Such situations are not necessarily faulty since there may be
other agencies which read from channel s_1 via IN-edges, but nevertheless they represent a
potential danger, such that it is worthwhile to look at such situations in detail.

Definition 4.2   statically unbounded channel:

A channel s of a FUNSOFT net N is called **statically unbounded** *if the following condition holds:*

$$\exists f_1 = (s,t), f_2 = (t,s) \in F : F_T(f_1) = CO, F_T(f_2) = OU$$

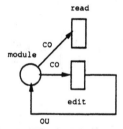

Figure 2: A statically unbounded channel

Figure 2 shows an *edit*-agency which represents the update of modules. The modules are read
via a CO-edge since it is supposed that the modules must be available for a *read*-agency all
the time. The channel storing modules is statically unbounded, since the number of modules
is only increased but never decreased.

Deadlocks   In software process models it is interesting to find out whether objects stored in a
particular channel cannot be produced if this channel is unmarked once.

A deadlock is a set of channels that, if it is token-free under one marking, remains token-free
under all successor markings. From a software process management point of view particular

deadlocks with one element are of interest, since they represent channels that must be initially marked.

The notion of deadlock is formally defined as follows.

Definition 4.3   deadlock:

Let N be a FUNSOFT net. A not empty set of channels $S = \{s_1, \ldots, s_n\}$ is called a deadlock if the following condition holds

$$\forall t \in \cup_{i \in \{1, \ldots, n\}} \bullet s_i : \{s_1, \ldots, s_n\} \cap \bullet t \neq \emptyset$$

A deadlock of a FUNSOFT net is called simple if it contains only one channel.

The algorithm for finding arbitrary deadlocks in a FUNSOFT net is of time complexity $\mathcal{O}(2^n)$ $(n = |S|)$ since it has to check all elements of $\mathcal{P}(S)$. Thus, we recommend to restrict the investigation of deadlocks to the search for simple deadlocks. For individual refinements of agencies it is possible to search for not simple deadlocks as well. It is particularly interesting to search for deadlocks of a certain size. The search for deadlocks with at most two elements, for example, can be done in

$$\mathcal{O}\left(n + \binom{n}{2}\right) = \mathcal{O}\left(\frac{n^2}{2}\right) = \mathcal{O}(n^2)$$

with $n = |S|$.

Besides the examples sketched above, other static properties are related to permanently enabled agencies, potentially permanently enabled agencies, traps, activities' conflicts, and to the question whether FUNSOFT nets are well-structured. Algorithms for checking if a FUNSOFT net has the discussed or other static properties are straightforward [Gru91b].

Other static properties are proven on the basis of Pr/T nets. For these properties we use existing tools for checking static properties of the Pr/T net representation of FUNSOFT nets. An example is the tool for calculating S-invariants of Pr/T nets developed by Genrich and improved by Kujansuu/Lindquist [KL84]. By using this tool we are able to show that the number of objects in a certain software process model part remains invariant.

Proving dynamic properties of FUNSOFT nets is more difficult. In general, it is necessary to consider all markings of a FUNSOFT net that can be reached form its initial marking. The values of most objects produced in a software process depend on human interaction (for example, the text of a program or of a documentation, or the names of software components). Thus, the values of objects of a FUNSOFT nets are unpredictable, they are fixed in the process itself. Therefore, the investigation of dynamic properties of a FUNSOFT net is based on examining quantitative markings of that net. In a quantitative marking only the number of objects stored in a channel are considered, but not their values. Correspondingly, the notion of quantitative coverability trees for FUNSOFT nets is defined. Each node of a quantitative coverability tree represents a quantitative marking. An edge of such a tree is labeled with the name of the agency whose firing transforms the quantitative marking represented by its source node into the quantitative marking represented by its destination node.

Due to the predefined firing behaviors of agencies that can be used in FUNSOFT nets, the abstraction from all object values causes some problems. If we revert to the example sketched above we recognize that the *link*-agency can only be fired, when channel s_4 contains as many tokens as specified by the value stored in channel s_6 (this corresponds to the *mult* input firing behavior of the *link*-job). In order to care for such situations we do not abstract from integer values read by agencies whose jobs have a *mult* input firing behavior.

The values of natural numbers stored in a channel that is used as second output channel of an agency t with $F_{OUT}(T_J(t)) = mult$ appear in quantitative markings. These values are needed in order to decide if an agency that reads from such a channel is enabled. Therefore, the quantitative marking of such channels consist of a natural number outlining the number of stored objects and a list of natural numbers containing the objects' values. Thus, coverability trees for FUNSOFT nets differ from coverability trees for standard Petri nets. Figure 3 shows a part of the coverability tree of the FUNSOFT net shown in Figure 1.

The example of a coverability tree shown in Figure 3 exemplifies the following features of FUNSOFT net coverability trees:

1. If an agency with a *mult* output firing behavior is quantitative enabled, then two successor markings are generated. In the sketched example the *identify_modules*-agency has a *mult* output firing behavior. This agency is quantitative enabled under the initial marking ($\odot$1 in Figure 3). In one of the two successor markings it is assumed that as few objects as possible are produced, in the other one it is assumed that as many objects as possible are produced. In

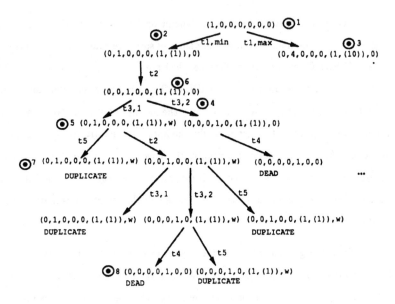

Figure 3: Example of a quantity-restricted coverability tree

the sketched example the minimal number is 1 (⊙2 in Figure 3), since no further restrictions are specified. The maximal number can be derived from the attached <mterm>. This term specifies that no more than 10 objects can be produced (⊙3 in Figure 3). The minimal and the maximal number of objects are stored in the coverability tree, since these values are needed for checking if agencies with a *mult* input firing behavior are quantitative enabled. In Figure 3 only the left branch of the coverability tree is described.

2. In the sketched example the *compile*-agency has a *complex* output firing behavior and three output channels. The <cterm> specifying the output firing behavior of the *compile*-agency ((1 AND 2) XOR (3)) consists of two <andterms>. Therefore, we pursue exactly two successor markings (⊙4 in Figure 3). In one of these successor markings, the output objects are written to the first (s_2) and second output channel (s_7), in the second one the output object is written to the third output channel (s_4).

3. The first result of firing the *compile*-agency (⊙5 in Figure 3) is derived from its successor marking by adding a token at the second position (*modules* to be edited), by deleting a token at the third position (*modules* to be compiled), and by adding a token at the last position

(*failure_reports*). The result looks as follows: $(0, 1, 0, 0, 0, (1, 1), 1)$. This marking covers the node marked with $\odot 2$. The value at the last position is actually bigger than the value at the last position of the node marked with $\odot 2$. Therefore, this value is replaced by ω ($\odot 5$ in Figure 3).

4. One possible successor marking of the node marked with $\odot 5$ is produced by firing agency t_5. This agency represents the reading of *failure_reports*. Since the channel storing *failure_reports* is covered by ω and since the arithmetic on $I\!N \cup \omega$ specifies that $\omega - 1 = \omega$, the successor marking ($\odot 7$ in Figure 3) is the same as the marking represented by the node marked with $\odot 5$. Thus, we reached a *DUPLICATE* end for which we do not figure out any further successor marking.

5. The node marked with $\odot 8$ represents a dead marking, i.e. no transition is quantitative enabled. Thus, no successor marking exists.

We use quantity restricted coverability trees for deciding about

- the deadness and liveness of agencies (corresponding to software development activities which can periodically or which cannot be activated),
- boundedness of channels (corresponding to the number of objects being in a certain state),
- the maximal number of persons that can concurrently work in a software process,
- the potential occurrence of any software process state a software process model analyst is interested in.

5 ANAMEL

The software process model analysis facilities proposed in the previous section are implemented in the analysis component **ANAMEL**. ANAMEL is embedded into the software process management environment MELMAC. Details about this embedding and the architecture of MELMAC can be found in [DG90, Gru91b, Gru91a]. The architecture of ANAMEL is displayed in Figure 4.

ANAMEL coordinates the validation and the verification component. The validation component consists of a re-animation component and of a statistical evaluation component that evaluates the information gathered during software process simulation. The verification component is sub-

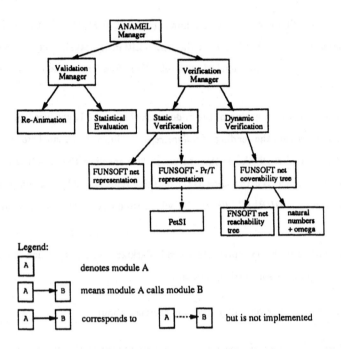

Figure 4: Architecture of ANAMEL

divided into the verification of static and verification of dynamic properties (represented by the Static Verification and Dynamic Verification components). All investigated dynamic properties are based on quantity-restricted coverability trees. These trees are encapsulated by the module labeled with FUNSOFT net coverability tree. This module is based on FUNSOFT net reachability trees (encapsulated by the module FUNSOFT net reachability tree) and a module that implements the arithmetic on $I\!N \cup \omega$. The static properties are subdivided into two groups. On the one hand there are static properties that are figured out on the basis of the FUNSOFT net representation (encapsulated by the module labeled with FUNSOFT net representation), on the other hand there are algorithms that are based on the Pr/T net representation of FUNSOFT nets (encapsulated by the module entitled FUNSOFT-Pr/T representation). The automatic transformation of a FUNSOFT net into its equivalent Pr/T net is not implemented. This is indicated by the dashed arrow from the Static Manager to the FUNSOFT-Pr/T net representation. The module labeled with FUNSOFT-Pr/T net representation restricts the functionality of the tool PetSI [KL84]. This tool is not embedded into the verification component. This is indicated by the dashed arrow from the FUNSOFT-Pr/T net representation to the box labeled with PetSI.

6   Conclusion

We introduced foundations of analyzing software process models. Analysis of software process model properties contributes to avoiding the execution of erroneous software process models. By implementing the developed analysis concepts and by embedding the analysis tool into a software process management environment, we integrate the analysis of software process models into the management of software processes. This is beyond the limits of most other software process management environments. Our current experience with the developed concepts are restricted to the analysis of academic multi-person software process models. Our future efforts will focus on the analysis of industrial software process models.

Acknowledgements:

First, I want to thank Wolfgang Deiters for his cooperation in designing MELMAC. Moreover, I want to thank the members of the MELMAC group for implementing the MELMAC environment.

The author acknowledges the contribution to this paper from all the members of the ALF consortium, who are: GIE Emeraude (France), CSC (Belgium), Computer Technologies Co. (Greece), Grupo de Mecanica del Vuelo, S.A.

(Spain), International Computers Limited (United Kingdom), University of Nancy-CRIN (France), University of Dortmund-Informatik X (Germany), Cerilor (France), Université de Catholique de Louvain (Belgium) and University of Dijon-CRID (France).

References

[BBCD89] K. Benali, N. Boudjlida, F. Charoy, and J.C. Derniame. *A Model for Assisted Software Processes*. In *Proceedings of ICCI*, Toronto, Canada, June 1989.

[BOSV89] C. Boarder, H. Obink, M. Schmidt, and A. Völker. *ATMOSPHERE, Advanced Techniques and Methods of System Production in a Heterogeneous, Extensible, and Rigorous Environment*. In *Proceedings of the 1st Conference on System Development Environments and Factories Moretonhamstead UK*, May 1989.

[DG90] W. Deiters and V. Gruhn. *Managing Software Processes in MELMAC*. In *Proceedings of the Fourth ACM SIGSOFT Symposium on Software Development Environments*, Irvine, California, USA, December 1990. Appeared as Software Engineering Notes, 15(6), December 1990.

[DG91] W. Deiters and V. Gruhn. *Software Process Model Analysis Based on FUNSOFT Nets. Mathematical Modeling and Simulation*, (8), May 1991.

[Gen87] H.J. Genrich. *Predicate/Transition Nets*. In W. Brauer, W. Reisig, and G. Rozenberg, editors, *Petri Nets: Applications and Relationships to other Models of Concurrency*, Berlin, FRG, 1987. Springer. Appeared in Lecture Notes on Computer Science 254.

[Gru91a] V. Gruhn. *Analysis of Software Process Models in the Software Process Management Environment MELMAC*. In *Proceedings of the fifth Software Engineering Environments Workshop*, Aberystwyth, Wales, UK, March 1991.

[Gru91b] V. Gruhn. *Validation and Verification of Software Process Models (to appear in 1991)*. PhD thesis, University Dortmund, June 1991.

[HJS89] P. Huber, K. Jensen, and R.M. Shapiro. *Hierarchies in Coloured Petri Nets*. In *Proc. of the 10th Int. Conf. on Application and Theory of Petri Nets*, Bonn, FRG, 1989.

[KFP88] G.E. Kaiser, P.H. Feiler, and S.S. Popovich. *Intelligent Assistance for Software Development and Maintenance. IEEE Software*, May 1988.

[KL84] R. Kujansuu and M. Lindquist. *Efficient Algorithms for computing S-Invariants for Predicate/Transition Nets*. In *Proceedings of the 5th International Conference on Application and Theory of Petri Nets*, 1984.

[MS90] P. Mi and W. Scacchi. *A Knowledge-Based Environment for Modeling and Simulating Software Engineering Processes. IEEE Transactions on Knowledge and Data Engineering*, 2(3), September 1990.

[Pet81] J.L. Peterson. *Petri Net Theory and the modeling of systems*. Prentice-Hall, 1981.

[Rei86] W. Reisig. *Petrinetze (in German)*. Springer, Berlin, FRG, 1986.

[SW88] W. Schäfer and H. Weber. *The ESF-Profile*. In *Handbook of Computer Aided Software Engineering*, New York, 1988. Van Nostrand.

[TBC+88] R.N. Taylor, F.C. Belz, L.A. Clarke, L. Osterweil, R.W. Selby, J.C. Wileden, A.L. Wolf, and M. Young. *Foundations in the ARCADIA Environment Architecture*. In *Proceedings of the ACM SIGSOFT/SIGPLAN Software Engineering Symposium on Practical Software Development Environments*, Boston, 1988. Appeared as Software Engineering Notes, 13(5), February 1989.

Lecture Notes in Computer Science

For information about Vols. 1–420
please contact your bookseller or Springer-Verlag

Vol. 464: J. Dassow, J. Kelemen (Eds.), Aspects and Prospects of Theoretical Computer Science. Proceedings, 1990. VI, 298 pages. 1990.

Vol. 465: A. Fuhrmann, M. Morreau (Eds.), The Logic of Theory Change. Proceedings, 1989. X, 334 pages. 1991. (Subseries LNAI).

Vol. 466: A. Blaser (Ed.), Database Systems of the 90s. Proceedings, 1990. VIII, 334 pages. 1990.

Vol. 467: F. Long (Ed.), Software Engineering Environments. Proceedings, 1969. VI, 313 pages. 1990.

Vol. 468: S.G. Akl, F. Fiala, W.W. Koczkodaj (Eds.), Advances in Computing and Information – ICCI '90. Proceedings, 1990. VII, 529 pages. 1990.

Vol. 469: I. Guessarian (Ed.), Semantics of Systeme of Concurrent Processes. Proceedings, 1990. V, 456 pages. 1990.

Vol. 470: S. Abiteboul, P.C. Kanellakis (Eds.), ICDT '90. Proceedings, 1990. VII, 528 pages. 1990.

Vol. 471: B.C. Ooi, Efficient Query Processing in Geographic Information Systems. VIII, 208 pages. 1990.

Vol. 472: K.V. Nori, C.E. Veni Madhavan (Eds.), Foundations of Software Technology and Theoretical Computer Science. Proceedings, 1990. X, 420 pages. 1990.

Vol. 473: I.B. Damgård (Ed.), Advances in Cryptology – EUROCRYPT '90. Proceedings, 1990. VIII, 500 pages. 1991.

Vol. 474: D. Karagiannis (Ed.), Information Syetems and Artificial Intelligence: Integration Aspects. Proceedings, 1990. X, 293 pages. 1991. (Subseries LNAI).

Vol. 475: P. Schroeder-Heister (Ed.), Extensions of Logic Programming. Proceedings, 1989. VIII, 364 pages. 1991. (Subseries LNAI).

Vol. 476: M. Filgueiras, L. Damas, N. Moreira, A.P. Tomás (Eds.), Natural Language Processing. Proceedings, 1990. VII, 253 pages. 1991. (Subseries LNAI).

Vol. 477: D. Hammer (Ed.), Compiler Compilers. Proceedings, 1990. VI, 227 pages. 1991.

Vol. 478: J. van Eijck (Ed.), Logics in AI. Proceedings, 1990. IX, 562 pages. 1991. (Subseries in LNAI).

Vol. 480: C. Choffrut, M. Jantzen (Eds.), STACS 91. Proceedings, 1991. X, 549 pages. 1991.

Vol. 481: E. Lang, K.-U. Carstensen, G. Simmons, Modelling Spatial Knowledge on a Linguistic Basis. IX, 138 pages. 1991. (Subseries LNAI).

Vol. 482: Y. Kodratoff (Ed.), Machine Learning – EWSL-91. Proceedings, 1991. XI, 537 pages. 1991. (Subseries LNAI).

Vol. 483: G. Rozenberg (Ed.), Advances In Petri Nets 1990. VI, 515 pages. 1991.

Vol. 484: R. H. Möhring (Ed.), Graph-Theoretic Concepts In Computer Science. Proceedings, 1990. IX, 360 pages. 1991.

Vol. 485: K. Furukawa, H. Tanaka, T. Fullsaki (Eds.), Logic Programming '89. Proceedings, 1989. IX, 183 pages. 1991. (Subseries LNAI)

Vol. 486: J. van Leeuwen, N. Santoro (Eds.), Distributed Algorithms. Proceedings, 1990. VI, 433 pages. 1991.

Vol. 487: A. Bode (Ed.), Distributed Memory Computing. Proceedings, 1991. XI, 506 pages. 1991

Vol. 488: R. V. Book (Ed.), Rewriting Techniques and Applications. Proceedings, 1991. VII, 458 pages. 1991.

Vol. 489: J. W. de Bakker, W. P. de Roever, G. Rozenberg (Eds.), Foundations of Object-Oriented Languages. Proceedings, 1990. VIII, 442 pages. 1991.

Vol. 490: J. A. Bergstra, L. M. G. Feljs (Eds.), Algebraic Methods 11: Theory, Tools and Applications. VI, 434 pages. 1991.

Vol. 491: A. Yonezawa, T. Ito (Eds.), Concurrency: Theory, Language, and Architecture. Proceedings, 1989. VIII, 339 pages. 1991.

Vol. 492: D. Sriram, R. Logcher, S. Fukuda (Eds.), Computer-Aided Cooperative Product Development. Proceedings, 1989 VII, 630 pages. 1991.

Vol. 493: S. Abramsky, T. S. E. Maibaum (Eds.), TAPSOFT '91. Volume 1. Proceedings, 1991. VIII, 455 pages. 1991.

Vol. 494: S. Abramsky, T. S. E. Maibaum (Eds.), TAPSOFT '91. Volume 2. Proceedings, 1991. VIII, 482 pages. 1991

Vol. 495: 9. Thalheim, J. Demetrovics, H.-D. Gerhardt (Eds.), MFDBS '91. Proceedings, 1991. VI, 395 pages. 1991.

Vol. 496: H.-P. Schwefel, R. Männer (Eds.), Parallel Problem Solving from Nature. Proceedings, 1991. XI, 485 pages. 1991.

Vol. 497: F. Dehne, F. Fiala. W.W. Koczkodaj (Eds.), Advances in Computing and Intormation - ICCI '91 Proceedings, 1991. VIII, 745 pages. 1991.

Vol. 498: R. Andersen, J. A. Bubenko jr., A. Sølvberg (Eds.), Advanced Information Systems Engineering. Proceedings, 1991. VI, 579 pages. 1991.

Vol. 499: D. Christodoulakis (Ed.), Ada: The Choice for '92. Proceedings, 1991. VI, 411 pages. 1991.

Vol. 500: M. Held, On the Computational Geometry of Pocket Machining. XII, 179 pages. 1991.

Vol. 501: M. Bidoit, H.-J. Kreowski, P. Lescanne, F. Orejas, D. Sannella (Eds.), Algebraic System Specification and Development. VIII, 98 pages. 1991.

Vol. 502: J. Bārzdiņš, D. Bjørner (Eds.), Baltic Computer Science. X, 619 pages. 1991.

Vol. 503: P. America (Ed.), Parallel Database Systems. Proceedings, 1990. VIII, 433 pages. 1991.

Vol. 504: J. W. Schmidt, A. A. Stogny (Eds.), Next Generation Information System Technology. Proceedings, 1990. IX, 450 pages. 1991.

Vol. 505: E. H. L. Aarts, J. van Leeuwen, M. Rem (Eds.), PARLE '91. Parallel Architectures and Languages Europe, Volume I. Proceedings, 1991. XV, 423 pages. 1991.

Vol. 506: E. H. L. Aarts, J. van Leeuwen, M. Rem (Eds.), PARLE '91. Parallel Architectures and Languages Europe, Volume II. Proceedings, 1991. XV, 489 pages. 1991.

Vol. 507: N. A. Sherwani, E. de Doncker, J. A. Kapenga (Eds.), Computing in the 90's. Proceedings, 1989. XIII, 441 pages. 1991.

Vol. 508: S. Sakata (Ed.), Applied Algebra, Algebraic Algorithms and Error-Correcting Codes. Proceedings, 1990. IX, 390 pages. 1991.

Vol. 509: A. Endres, H. Weber (Eds.), Software Development Environments and CASE Technology. Proceedings, 1991. VIII, 286 pages. 1991.

Vol. 510: J. Leach Albert, B. Monien, M. Rodríguez (Eds.), Automata, Languages and Programming. Proceedings, 1991. XII, 763 pages. 1991.

Vol. 511: A. C. F. Colchester, D.J. Hawkes (Eds.), Information Processing in Medical Imaging. Proceedings, 1991. XI, 512 pages. 1991.

Vol. 512: P. America (Ed.), ECOOP '91. European Conference on Object-Oriented Programming. Proceedings, 1991. X, 396 pages. 1991.